Fictions at work:
language and social practice in fiction

LANGUAGE IN SOCIAL LIFE SERIES

Series Editor: Professor Christopher N. Candlin

Fictions at work: language and social practice in fiction

Mary M. Talbot

LONGMAN
LONDON and NEW YORK

Longman Group Limited,
Longman House, Burnt Mill,
Harlow, Essex CM20 2JE, England
and Associated Companies throughout the world.

*Published in the United States of America
by Longman Publishing, New York*

First published 1995

ISBN 0 582 085225 CSD
ISBN 0 582 085233 PPR

British Library Cataloguing-in-Publication Data

A catalogue record for this book is
available from the British Library

Library of Congress Cataloging-in-Publication Data

Talbot, Mary, 1954–
    Fictions at work : language and social practice in fiction / Mary
Talbot.
        p.   cm. — (Language in social life series)
    Includes bibliographical references and index.
    ISBN 0–582–08522–5. — ISBN 0–582–08523–3 (pbk.)
    1. Fiction—Technique.   2. Fiction—History and criticism.
I. Title.   II. Series.
PN3355.T35   1995
809.3—dc20   94–5273
                                                                    CIP

Set by 8 in 10/12pt Palatino
Produced by Longman Singapore Publishers (Pte) Ltd.
Printed in Singapore

Contents

Author's Acknowledgements

My thanks are due to the following for their invaluable advice and comments on all or part of the work in progress: Leo Baxendale, Peggy Baxendale, John Coulthart, Val Gough and Colin Greenland for their help with individual chapters; Stephen Gallagher for his untiring assistance in hunting down publishing details; Karsten Schou for his responses to the first complete draft. I am grateful to the series editor, Chris Candlin, for his careful, considered comments on the manuscript at every stage and for his support and advice throughout.

The influence of contact with professional creators of fiction is incalculable – especially Iain Banks, Leo Baxendale, Ramsey Campbell, Colin Greenland, Stephen Gallagher, Gwyneth Jones, Alan Moore and above all my spouse, Bryan Talbot. Finally, I must acknowledge the inspiration from members and guest speakers at the Preston Speculative Fiction Group. All errors are of course entirely my own.

Publisher's Acknowledgements

We are grateful to the following for permission to reproduce copyright material:

Victor Gollancz Limited/St. Martin's Press Inc. New York, NY, for extracts from *White Queen* by Gwenyth Jones. Copyright © 1991 by Gwenyth Jones; Harlequin Mills & Boon Ltd, for extracts and cover from *No Gentleman* by Kate Walker, first published in Great Britain in 1992 by Mills & Boon Ltd; Hodder & Stoughton Limited/the author's agent for extracts from *Lair* by James Herbert; the author's agent/Alfred Knopf Inc. for extracts from *Woman on the Edge of Time* by Marge Piercy. Copyright © 1976 by Marge Piercy and Middlemarsh, Inc. first published in Great Britain 1979 by The Women's Press Ltd, 1979; D.C. Thomson & Co Ltd, for an extract from *Jackie* 20.9.1986 and for the use of photo material from *Jackie* No 1154 p 33, Panel 8 (February 15, 1986) (our Figure 4.2) and No 1144 pp 30, 31, 33 (December 5, 1985) (our Figure 4.3). © D.C. Thomson & Co Ltd; The Women's Press Ltd/the author's agent for extracts from *Busy About the Tree of Life* by Pamela Zoline, first published 1988 by The Women's Press Ltd, 34 Great Sutton Street, London EC1V; Bryan Talbot for the rat illustration in Chapter 5 'The tale of one bad rat' © 1994 Bryan Talbot.

Part I

Fiction as social practice

ONE

What is fiction?

Life, the aggregate of defined actions, events, or experiences, only becomes plot, story, theme, or motif once it has been refracted through the prism of the ideological environment, only once it has taken on concrete ideological flesh. Reality that is unrefracted and, as it were, raw is not able to enter into the content of literature.

(Medvedev and Bakhtin [1928] 1978)

We all tell stories – at mealtimes, in the pub, in court. We tell one another stories about what has happened, or supposed to have happened. When we chat to one another, we very often make stories about ourselves – about our excursions and exploits, about our thoughts and feelings. We create stories out of our memories – turning our lives into words and keeping our past alive. That's what stories are.

They are all around us. The news on television is full of stories. So are history books. We make narratives out of sequences of events all the time, even when involved in kinds of activity we would not associate with storytelling at all. A child writing up a science experiment in school, for instance, has to produce a report of the series of actions she has undertaken: 'I took a piece of potato, hollowed it out, and put it in a glass dish . . .', and so on. She will be told in time that the scientific discourse she is learning requires her to depersonalize by using the passive tense of the verb ('a piece of potato *was taken*'), which does not need a personal pronoun, to make her report-writing seem more objective. But she will continue to produce stories in her reports.

Narrative is a feature of a whole range of different genres with very different uses in and across cultures. These include reports, like the scientific one above giving an account of something done in the past, and procedures for how to go about doing something in

3

the future. It is possible of course to detail the characteristics distinguishing these two factual genres. In the context of language education, for example, Jim Martin (1989) examines the differences between Recounts, Procedures, Reports, and so on (in his terms, what I have called a report above is a Recount). Nevertheless, they do share a significant characteristic with one another, and with fictional narratives: they all tell stories.

Stories are an important part of how we order the world, how we make sense of it. Turning life into stories gives beginnings and endings to continuous events. Storytelling imposes patterns on to experience – and in so doing, it gives shape and coherence to the world we live in.

Of course, not all stories are true. A story is anything with forward motion; by which I mean some kind of plot, however rudimentary this may be. The forward motion of the story may end up just going round in circles, like in this little ditty (to be repeated *ad infinitum*, or more likely, *ad nauseam*):

> There was a man called Michael Finnegan,
> He grew whiskers on his chinnigen.
> The wind came out and they blew in again.
> Poor old Michael Finnegan begin again.

The story could hardly be much simpler. A man grew whiskers, but the wind blew them back in, so he had to grow them again. Stories involve time. A series of events has to occur in time. Here we have the beginnings of a definition: the recounting of a series of events. To this we can add: the establishment of some kind of connection between them. It is as well to note at this point that there is nothing 'natural' or inevitable about the connections in narrative sequences. Film is a very recent medium for narrative, and early filmgoers had difficulties with the most basic editing techniques. They did not have the film 'grammar' with which we effortlessly make sense of establishing shots, close-ups and so on.

I have started in this way – with an emphasis on the pervasiveness of stories – in order to problematize the concept of fiction, rather than taking it as something we already know all about at the outset, and agree upon. The reason I have done this is to set the discussion of fiction in a critical mode through which we can examine its crucial contribution to the constitution and reproduction of social life. In the course of the book, I hope to provide a framework for the critical study of fiction. I will combine selective, hopefully accessible, language analysis with a focus on social context, the objective being to present fiction *at work* in society. The final section of this opening chapter outlines the book's three Parts and the contents of each of the chapters.

So what is fiction? Simply stories that do not pretend to be about real events. That's the easy answer, but of course there is more to it than that. The relation between fiction and reality is not a straightforward one. The two have a peculiar way of getting mixed up together; distinguishing the two is not quite as easy as one might think, or hope. In this introductory chapter it is this peculiarity that I want to explore. To do this my discussion will cover two key areas. First, I carry on with the examination of forward motion in stories, looking at what various literary critics have had to say about how ideology gets into narrative. Secondly, I consider how any text can be examined for its multiple and intersecting 'voices'. I demonstrate that fictional characters do not only inhabit fiction and that it can be difficult to identify a clearcut cast of characters in any text, irrespective of its status as fiction or non-fiction. I also look at some studies of 'discourse-mixing'. Here I show how discourses from different institutional contexts have a way of cropping up in fiction and how, conversely, fiction enters other discourses.

FICTION AND REALITY

Underlying Fredric Jameson's writing on 'Narrative as socially symbolic act' (that being the sub-heading of his book *The political unconscious*, 1981) is an assumption that narrative, in a broad sense of the term, is implicated in all uses of language. A lyric poem, for example – supposed to be a single moment of an individual's outpouring of thought or feeling – implies a history of which that 'outpouring' is one carefully selected moment, just as much as a drama following the classical unities of time and place has been chosen as a kind of 'distillation' of a much longer series of events and set of circumstances. The impression that the lyric is not story is itself a kind of fiction.

Jameson claims, in fact, that narrative is the form in which we receive reality. It is not just that stories help us understand the world, stories are how the world is presented to us. In other words, reality comes to us in the shape of stories.

Avowedly fictional narratives, in Jameson's view, are ideological productions in which 'strategies of containment' are embodied. These strategies frequently take the form of imaginary resolutions of real contradictions/tensions. An example from the historically somewhat distant early eighteenth century should make this clear. In this period were the beginnings of market capitalism and a bourgeois cultural revolution; people were picking up modern notions like 'freedom' and 'independence'. The eponymous heroine of *Moll Flanders* (1722) is an early example of the modern bourgeois individual. The novel can be seen to invent a formal 'solution' to irresolvable contradictions in her life. In Moll's account of her life, sexual and maternal sentiments repeatedly give way to calculated self-interest, for sheer survival. Her socially approved desire for independence leads perforce to crime. Then penitence leads to prosperity. Contradictory, incompatible drives are comfortably resolved and fitted together, in fiction. As Ian Watt remarks, Daniel Defoe 'was not ashamed to make economic self-interest his major premise about human life; he did not think such a premise conflicted either with social or religious values; and nor did his age' (1972: 143).

So fictional narratives can be seen as imaginary resolutions of real contradictions. We can examine a text's 'unconscious', so to speak, like psychoanalysts. In *Moll Flanders* the incompatibility of Puritan religiosity and emergent capitalism is comfortably smoothed over.

Let's look at another eighteenth-century example, this time in more detail. Samuel Richardson's *Pamela* provided a fantasy solution to an irresolvable dilemma for women. It was first published in 1740, and became a 'bestseller'. By this period the break-up of the socio-economic system based on domestic industry was advanced. This old subsistence economy, in which women had clearly defined positions, value and usefulness, was being replaced by a market economy.

Consider what this meant, particularly for women. In place of the self-sufficient community producing its own products for its own consumption – and needing every pair of hands to spin wool and weave it into cloth, to milk the cows and bake bread – the kind of community familiar to us was developing, one in which the economic unit is the individual earning cash wages. In theory women could be equal to men, in the limited sense of the 'equality' of the marketplace (i.e. a pound coin of yours is worth the same as a pound coin of mine, so we're 'equals'). But, of course, there were severe restrictions on work for women. In brief, paid employment was simply not respectable. Incidentally, it was during this time that 'spinster' took on pejorative overtones. This was because unmarried women were becoming liabilities rather than useful community members; there was no place for single women in the new social order. 'Old maids' became economic dependants of male relatives.

Here is the dilemma. Just as an economically secure position outside marriage was becoming increasingly difficult for women, it was simultaneously becoming more difficult for them to marry. Marriage became more important for women; it necessarily became more competitive and mercenary. The situation was aggravated by an increasing tendency for men to marry later. If men were to single-handedly bear the weight of economic responsibility for a family unit, they needed to become established as earners first: to 'make their fortunes', like so many Dick Whittingtons. Marriage marts in newspapers were common. Among the poor, women could be bought and sold like livestock; this was possible because married women had no rights, and were the property of their husbands. The prevailing legal system was patriarchal. It was Roman law, according to which the head of the household holds sway over all members, and effectively owns them. In short, when *Pamela* was written the legal system was still fully patriarchal, and economic changes were putting women in an even weaker position.

Chambermaids and other female household servants formed part of the reading public. This no doubt goes some way towards explaining *Pamela*'s popularity, since it is essentially a tale about a servant girl who marries her lord and master. It is a fantasy of upward mobility through marriage, an ingredient of modern romance fiction: the Cinderella myth. The fictional Pamela's upwardly-mobile marriage 'solves' the irresolvable problem outlined above confronting her real contemporaries.

In addition, *Pamela* provides an imaginary resolution to another contradiction. It hinges on the Puritanism of the novel, its curious combination of prudishness and prurience, of denial of sexuality and overwhelming preoccupation with it.

The novel is subtitled 'Virtue rewarded'. 'Virtue' is negatively defined as the suppression of instincts, a renunciation of sexuality. Moral virtue is cast almost exclusively in terms of sexual abstinence (words like 'chaste', 'pure' take on a sexual implication which they have largely retained). Pamela was an example of a powerful new conception of femininity, notable for its total absence of sexual feeling, which became deeply unfeminine. Watt speculates, very plausibly I think, that this new notion of 'proper' femininity probably functioned as, among other things, concealment of the very attribute women were increasingly dependent on: sexual attractiveness to men.

Prolonged conflict between male sexual desire and female 'virtue' forms the basis of the plot. It is an epic of a servant girl's resistance to a fate-worse-than-death. The contradictory tendencies – Puritan censorship/prudishness and preoccupation with sexuality – are resolved in the sanctity of marriage.

Fictional resolutions become narrative formulae, narrative paradigms that transmit a message on their own and strongly influence people's expectations in and outside of fiction. The contradictions that are 'solved' are real world phenomena. Fiction and reality are not as clearly distinguishable as we might like to think.

So one way ideology enters narrative is through the provision of the satisfactory sense of closure that comes in the way the sequence of events making up the narrative is rounded off. Fictional resolution of real contradiction through closure is one of many ways in which event sequences embody ideology. Some literary critics, at least from Virginia Woolf onwards, have taken issue with the centrality of causality in realist and naturalist fiction. Novels in these two closely related genres embody assumptions about the 'proper' kind of event and connection in narrative. Narratives should be 'scientific', rational, plausible, with no one acting 'out of character'. Recent critics who have aired the problems of naturalized assumptions about causal relations in narratives include Carolyn Steedman (1986) and Anne Cranny-Francis (1990). Steedman is examining case studies by Sigmund Freud and Henry Mayhew; Cranny-Francis is exploring the difficulties for feminist writers in undermining dominant cultural perspectives. Central to the issues addressed by both of them is the narrative incoherence of stories told by marginal voices. They simply do not make sense.

Cranny-Francis's remarks on the degree to which narrative sequencing is naturalized are of particular relevance here. She observes that 'the equation of temporal sequence with material causation' (ibid.: 10) is deeply embedded in nineteenth-century and twentieth-century Western writing and is the embodiment of a world view which is completely naturalized, to the extent of seeming to be a matter of simple common sense. As a consequence, other aspects of the non-fictional world represented in the narrative will tend also to be naturalized:

If narrative represents events in temporal (linear) sequence as a causal process, then it follows that we will read that causal process, as we read temporal sequence, as 'natural'. That causal process, in turn, inevitably encodes ideological discourses and these discourses too are read as 'natural' . . . The discourses are 'natural', the causal process is 'natural', the temporal sequence is 'natural' – and the text is very easy to read.

(Cranny-Francis 1990: 11)

In other words, the 'obviousness' of linear temporality and causality can smuggle in other 'obviousnesses'.

There are many other entry points for ideology. To identify some more of them it will be helpful to distinguish different components of narrative. To do this I shall outline a three-way distinction conveniently provided by John Stephens in his 1992 contribution to this series (*Language and ideology in children's fiction*). One component is, quite simply, the *story*. The characters and what happens to them in a narrative present 'an isomorph of events in the actual world' (Stephens 1992: 2). Another intersecting component is the *discourse*, which in narrative comprises the act of narrating, involving discourse practices, addresser and addressee. The remaining component, intersecting with the other two, is what Stephens calls *significance*: the narrative's theme, the insight (into human relationships, or whatever it may be) that it provides, its moral, if it has one. Stephens places his emphasis on the third of these components, while acknowledging that all three are purveyors of ideology.

Elements of *story* and significance have been the focus of my discussion so far. I will give some attention now to the other component, *discourse*, without which there could be neither story nor significance. The ideology-bearing nature of discourse is the topic of the first book in this series by Norman Fairclough (1989, *Language and power*). I will refer to his model of discourse as social practice in some detail in the next chapter. As a detailed illustrative example of ideologically loaded discourse, I will examine the distribution of 'standard' and other varieties of English in written fiction.

Conventionally, written standard English is used for both narration and dialogue in fiction. When confronted with dialogue in a novel, we tend to assume a 'standard', non-regional pronunciation for the audience for which it was written. (In an American novel, one would assume a Standard American sounding voice; in a Scottish novel, a Scottish voice, etc.). But we do not really hear any pronunciation at all.

To indicate 'deviations' from this, such as a 'non-standard' (i.e. regional) variety or a foreign accent, writers sometimes tamper with spellings. What alterations to spelling do is draw attention to the way words are meant to sound. Written orthography can be played around with for a sort of *ad hoc*, very unsystematic phonemic script. So British people can call to mind a strong French accent by suggesting different vowel quality or h-dropping. For example, in Steve Bell's comic strip in the UK newspaper, *The Guardian*, a French character once exclaimed: 'early smirk!' The ability to read this as the exclamation (in a caricatured French accent) of 'Holy smoke!' depends on the reader having a standard British pronunciation of 'early' and 'smirk' as a frame of reference.

Some odd spellings, for example *ennything, thuh*, do not really reflect any particular variety, but are just introducing an impression of speech; e-n-n-y is closer to most pronunciations of *any* than a-n-y. It really just constitutes a reminder that the first sound in the word is some sort of /e/ and not an /a/. In the case of the spelling of *the* as t-h-u-h, the u-h is an attempt to represent the schwa /ə/.[1] But really the main thing the spellings do is suggest lack of education. The misspellings somehow rub off on the fictitious speaker. The effectiveness of this is presumably dependent on the reader. A reader familiar with the US literary tradition of representing 'real language' (as in, for example, Mark Twain's *Huckleberry Finn*) might, however, be marginally less likely to interpret orthographic oddities in this way.

Even when authentic varieties are being represented, writers generally only give a very impressionistic simulation of them. Generally, writers will include one or two key features; occasional hints at some interesting phonological difference, the odd non-standard grammatical feature, an exotic word or two. Writers can use regional dialects as a literary device to convey subtle social, economic, educational, and geographical distinctions, just as they can in spoken language in the real world. And, just as in the real world, regional dialects are marginalized. Standard dialect is used for narration and for all 'neutral' speech representation. To illustrate the restricted use of regional dialects and the way they convey social information, below are two extracts from David Storey's *Saville*, an autobiographical account of a 'scholarship boy' growing up in a Yorkshire mining community. In the first extract the protagonist's parents are speaking, in the presence of his middle-class school-friend. The father (represented as a dialect speaker) is corrected by the mother:

> 'Oh, it'll be tea, don't worry,' his father said. 'You're not coming here to sup us watter.' 'Water,' his mother said.
> 'Water. Watter,' his father said. 'Dost think when you're thirsty it makes any difference?'

(Storey [1975] 1984: 236)

This little exchange communicates both the mother's hypersensitivity to class differences and the father's increasing isolation in his own household (Mace 1987: 31). One can see from this passage how selectively Storey represents Yorkshire English. The first cues appear in the second line in the clause 'to sup us watter'. Here we have, as it happens, an example of a lexical, a syntactic and a phonological variant respectively. *To sup* is a lexical item not used in modern standard English. The absence of any distinction between pronoun and possessive article (hence *us watter*) is not found in standard, but is a common syntactic feature of many other varieties. The spelling of *watter* indicates the father's production of an open front vowel /æ/ (a more standard pronunciation of 'water' would be /wɔːtə/). The representation of this /æ/ sound may call to mind a characteristic of northern varieties distinguishing them from southern ones: namely the distinctively different distribution of æ/ɑː (as in northern and southern pronunciations of *bath*). The only other indication of Yorkshire English is the use of the second person singular form of the verb *do*, no longer used in standard but still common in many other varieties. I notice that Storey does not use it in the next clause containing the 'hypothetical *you*' (where formal standard would have *one*), showing he knows the variety he is representing. He could have drawn the reader's attention to other phonological variants in this passage; for example, he could have altered the spelling of *make* to indicate the presence of a monophthong /e/ rather than the diphthong /eɪ/ used in standard. In his selection of phonological variants to represent Yorkshire English pronunciation, Storey appears to have focused on sociolinguistic 'markers', rather than 'indicators'. Markers are stereotypical variants with social significance, often highly stigmatized.

In the second extract, the villagers are openly hostile to the protagonist's schoolfriend, who is very noticeably an outsider:

> the miners were sitting in rows outside the pub, crouching in the gutter and along the walls, calling out suddenly to Stafford as he passed, attracted by the fairness of his hair, and the strange freshness of his manner.
> 'Dost fancy yon, then, Jack?' they said. 'Wheerst tha come from, lad. Ar't'a sure he's not a lass?'
> The laughter from the crouched rows and the odd, isolated figures standing in the road followed them down towards the house.
> 'What's the matter with them?' Stafford said. 'Haven't they seen somebody dressed decently before?'
> 'They're always like that,' he said, 'with strangers. Suspicious of anything or anyone they haven't seen before.'
>
> (Storey [1975] 1984: 244)

The miners' speech is strongly differentiated from the linguistic norm of standard dialect in the narration and in the dialogue of the two educated speakers (the grammar school boys, Saville and Stafford). This passage conveys the animosity and mistrust of the inhabitants of the mining village towards all outsiders (Mace 1987: 30). This effect is partly achieved through the density of non-standard variants in their represented speech, marking them off as 'other'.

The distribution and function of standard and non-standard varieties conventionally follow this pattern. Varieties other than standard rarely appear in fiction. When they do, they appear in dialogue only, not in the narration, and are generally marked off as deviations from the norm, which is standard dialect. Moreover, it is generally only for dialects other than standard that our attention is drawn to the sound of speech at all.[2] And, as I think is clear from the examples above, characters represented as dialect speakers are thereby being represented as in some way marginal or 'deviant'.

The following is from Walter Greenwood's *Love on the dole* ([1933] 1970). In it we can see the distribution of standard and non-standard. Narration and dialogue are strikingly different. I have distinguished omniscient narration and narration which seems to be focalized through one of the characters (the dialogue has already been marked off with speech marks):

> He forced a smile: 'Oh, Hallo, Helen,' he said, adding, unnecessarily, as they walked along: 'Goin' home for y' dinner?' [F] She sensed a constraint in his demeanour instantly. [N] She looked at him, questioningly,

wondering, her smile fading, the light dying in her eyes. After a pause, she said: 'I didn't see y' over week-end, Harry. Where were y'? Y' weren't in choir, either.'
   He shrugged: 'Aw, Ah stopped in house, readin'. Didn' want t'go out.'
   [F] He could not confess that shame of his schoolboy clothes was the real cause. It occurred to him that it would be weeks, possibly, before his mother would be able to afford him a pair of long trousers for Sunday wear. That meant sitting at home over the week-ends. It would be humiliating, after wearing overalls during the week to appear in knickerbockers of a Sunday. Until now, this prospect had not occurred to him. Glum discontent stirred in his heart. Why had some such occurrence as this always to rise to spoil one's new-found pleasure? Tomorrow's prospect was robbed of half its savour.

(Greenwood [1933] 1970: 151)

N = omniscient narration; F = character focalization

   In the narration focalized through the character called Harry there is a single feature which is non-standard: the use of the preposition *of* where standard would have *on*. Other than that the contrast with the same character's speech is striking, even though we are being given a report of what is going on in his head, a kind of interior monologue of sorts. The next to last sentence seems particularly inappropriate; it leaves me with the impression that Greenwood is showing he can 'talk proper' even though his characters cannot!

   There are striking exceptions to the rules sketched out above, some of the most outstanding of which are in the work of Black American writers, including in particular Zora Neale Hurston, and more recently Toni Cade Bambara, Toni Morrison and Alice Walker. By using varieties of English which are usually marginalized for narration, these writers are challenging/undermining dominant practices in fiction. I will not examine the way the work of these novelists functions oppositionally, as this issue has already been admirably examined by Stephens with attention to an illustrated story for children by Patricia McKissack and Jerry Pinkney (Stephens 1992: 50–3).

VOICES IN THE TEXT

Any text can be examined for its multiple, intersecting 'voices', in principle at least. Characters are not only to be found in works of fiction; all texts are to some extent 'populated'. I am not just referring here to some kind of traditional notion of dramatis personae, but to a view of texts as multi-voiced or 'dialogic'. In this view, a text has an indeterminate population of which the writer and reader are part. By way of introduction to this dialogic view of texts, I will go through a magazine extract which would be designated as non-fiction, discussing the complex of voices in it, or at least some of it. It is part of a consumer feature on lipstick that appeared in September 1986 in *Jackie*, a teenagers' magazine, which ceased publication in 1993.

(1) Ask any clever advertiser how to suggest femininity with a product, and he'll probably tell you 'a kissprint'. Lipstick on a collar, a glass, his cheek – they all suggest a woman was there. When men think of make-up, they think of lipstick.

(2) It's hardly a modern invention – women have been adding artificial colour to their lips for centuries now. Before the days of lipstick as we know it, ladies used vegetable or animal dyes like cochineal – beetle's blood – to colour their lips.

(3) The reason behind it wasn't simply to make themselves more beautiful – superstition lingered that the devil could enter the body through the mouth, and since red was meant to ward off evil spirits 'lipstick' was put around the mouth to repel his evil intentions!

(4) These days there are more complicated (and ruder!) theories. Experts in human behaviour say that it's all to do with sex (what else?!)

(5) Other 'experts' claim that the shape of your lipstick can reveal a lot about your character – i.e. if you wear the end flat you're stubborn, if it's round and blunt you're fun-loving, etc. etc. – but don't seem to take into consideration the fact that each brand of lipstick is a different shape to start with and it's easiest just to use it accordingly. So much for the experts!

(6) What *is* interesting is the way that fashions in lipstick have changed over the years. When lipcolour first came into fashion at the beginning of this century, dark colours and the style of 'drawing' on little pursed lips meant that women looked cutesy and doll-like. Later on, in the forties, film stars wanting to look lovable and 'little-girl'ish continued this, while the newer breed of dominant, business-like women opted for a bolder look, colouring right over the natural 'bow' in the lips. By the sixties 'women's lib' was in style and most girls abandoned lipstick altogether, or used beige colours to blank out the natural pink of their lips,

and concentrated on over-the-top face painting instead.
(7) Now, in the eighties, there are more colours available than ever
before – right down to blue, green and black! 'Glossy' lips, popular for a
while in the seventies, are out again, and the overall trend is for natural
pink tints, with oranges and golds in summer, on big, full lips.
(8) Large cosmetic manufacturers will have upwards of 70 shades available at a time, introducing a further three or four shades each season to
complement the fashion colours of that time. And with some companies
churning out batches of lipstick at a rate of 9,000 an hour, that's an
awful lot of kisses to get through . . . !

I imagine the easiest voices to spot were the ones clearly signalled
with reporting clauses – the 'probable' utterance of 'any clever
advertiser' in the first sentence, for example. A second look at this
opening sentence reveals an imaginary exchange going on between
the reader and a hypothetical male advertiser, both of whom have
projected texts cued by clauses containing verbal process verbs:[3]

Sayer	I Verbal process	I Receiver	I I Projection
	Ask	any clever advertiser	how to suggest femininity with a product
he	'll . . . tell	you	'a kissprint'

In the second sentence of this opening paragraph there is a character who is not given 'lines' to say: a woman set up in some kind of
clichéd scenario about marital infidelities (leaving traces of lipstick
on men's collars). In this sentence it is the smudges of lipstick that
are presented as the 'speaking' characters, not the woman herself,
whose presence they 'speak' about. This is a grammatical metaphor, since lipstick marks are inanimate. These eloquent smudges
signify (presumably to everybody) not just the presence of a
woman, but some amorous relationship with a man.

In paragraphs (2) and (3), writer, reader and some early lipstick-
wearers are set up as characters. Writer and reader are assumed to
have a shared conception of what lipstick is; this is set up in an
embedded projection postmodifying 'lipstick' ('lipstick as we know
it'). Turning to the early lipstick-wearers, the writer does not quote
or report these early users supposed own words or thoughts; what
she does is present their motivations in four cause-enhancing clauses and a fact projection. These are the cause enhancements (the
element cuing this grammatical function is in italics): they used lipcolour in order 'to colour their lips', but not simply in order 'to

make themselves more beautiful'; 'since red was meant to ward off evil spirits', they used them in order 'to ward off his [the devil's] evil intentions!' In addition to these cause enhancements containing the assumed motivations of early lipstick-wearers, there is a reported belief that 'the devil could enter the body through the mouth'. This reported belief is contained in a *Headword's* postmodifier; the *Headword* 'superstition' being a 'fact' noun postmodified by a projection. The choice of 'fact' noun makes the writer's dim view of this belief clear.

In paragraphs (4) and (5) the copy-writer reports two more sets of characters:

Sayer	I Verbal process	I I Projection
Experts in human behaviour	say	that it's all to do with sex
Other 'experts'	claim	that the shape of your lipstick can reveal a lot about your character

See how the writer responds to the words of the characters she has created. Her bracketed response (namely: 'what else?!') to the first lot of experts, the unspecified psychologists, is ambiguous. Is she endorsing what they say or ridiculing it? It is impossible to say. With the second lot of experts, presumably 'folk-psychologists' of some description, she expands on their words ('i.e. . . .') and comments disparagingly ('but . . .'), then dismisses both kinds of 'expert' on the basis of this comment. Exclamation marks very often attribute to the writer some kind of friendly, enthusiastic quality; here, I think they also contribute to establishing her distance from scientific, and even pseudo-scientific, statements.

In paragraph (6) there is a whole range of other characters, lipstick-wearers in different decades. You may have noticed how the writer's voice changed as she made the transition from critic/social analyst to fashion historian. She announces the shift by dismissing all she wrote earlier as uninteresting! As with the early lipstick-wearers, the voices of characters in this section tend to be somewhat distant; they have their preferences and motivations indicated rather than being quoted or reported. The thoughts of two sets of characters are drawn in; namely 'film stars' and 'dominant women'. But the writer's fashion-historian voice is strong, almost drowning out those of her characters. She presents the changes in lipstick fashions entirely in terms of their individual whims.

In paragraph (7) the historian suddenly becomes a fashion correspondent, taking on the familiar voice of an advertiser. Look at all the attention given to commodity availability and multiple choice, at the acausal agentless processes (processes that are represented as if they just spontaneously happen):

> there are more colours available than ever before . . . the overall trend is for natural pink tints

Cosmetics manufacturers appear briefly as characters in paragraph (8), where the writer announces their motivations as mass producers of lipstick in a cause enhancement: 'to complement the fashion colours of that time'.

The writer guides the reader's attitudes towards the voices woven into the text, postulating the reader's sympathies towards the various characters they are supposed to belong to. Something I haven't given much attention to here is the way the reader is constructed as a person with certain kinds of attitudes. Mistrust of 'experts' giving scientific statements and respect for manufacturers are assumed; so are all kinds of presupposed notions about spontaneous fashion changes, and so on. The reader is put into the position of someone who assumes real lipstick is a 'modern invention' in paragraph (2) of the extract: 'It's hardly a modern invention' (negation presupposes a corresponding positive assertion, otherwise why bother to make negative statements in the first place?). Any unpleasant quality that lipstick may have (such as being made from 'beetles' blood', for instance) is safely placed in the vague and distant past associated with some primitive Ur-lipstick used by superstitious people, all of which is subsequently presupposed to be uninteresting in any case.

One can say a great deal more.[4] Writer and reader are synthesized in a friendly relationship. The two-page article from which the single column of text we have been looking at was taken synthesizes a friendly 'all girls together' relationship, based on becoming feminine consumers – on a form of sisterhood in consumption. As an older sister might do, the editorial demonstrates the application of lipstick and gossips about it (ironically, the actual producers of the 'beauty feature' may well, of course, have been men). The beauty feature presents a feminine consumption community consisting of free individuals whose identities are established in pleasurable consumption. Lipstick is presented as a natural part of female experience, set in an historical framework of fashion and the whims of individual celebrities. As the dominant cultural perspective of consumerism is foregrounded in this magazine feature, other perspectives are marginalized by the containment of marginalized voices; for example, the 'fencing off' of scientific statements.

With this view, we can examine a text's population by looking for traces of people addressing one another, traces of characters' words or thoughts and traces of different kinds of conventional 'voice' used by a character. In picking out the different voices the copy-writer uses in the article on lipstick, and in examining the struggle between incompatible discourses in the eighteenth-century fiction, I was attending to the third kind of trace. I will now go on to examine this discourse-mixing in detail in another literary example.

A work of fiction always contains non-literary varieties of language. James Joyce's *A portrait of the artist as a young man* (1916) is a conglomeration of discourses: the language and ideas of Catholicism, of Irish nationalism, of the nursery, the playground, a very self-consciously 'poetic' strain of language. In fact this novel is a complex intertextuality of literary and non-literary fragments. It is a novel about a boy whose experience of the world is increasingly mediated through literary texts. Stephen Dedalus's language is very self-consciously 'poetic' in the later chapters. I will look at a single extract from Chapter 5: part of his villanelle-writing passage. This passage is important in the construction of his new identity as 'priest of the imagination', with the self-appointed task of forging the conscience of his people, the Irish. His new function is inaugurated in the creation of a new text, a poem.

> Towards dawn he awoke. O what sweet music! His soul was all dewy wet. Over his limbs in sleep pale cool waves of light had passed. He lay still, as if his soul lay amid cool waters, conscious of faint sweet music. His mind was waking slowly to a tremulous morning knowledge, a morning inspiration. A spirit filled him, pure as the purest water, sweet as dew, moving as music. But how faintly it was inbreathed, how passionlessly, as if the seraphim themselves were breathing upon him! His soul was waking slowly, fearing to awake wholly. It was that windless hour of dawn when madness wakes and strange plants open to the light and the moth flies forth silently.
>
> An enchantment of the heart! The night had been enchanted. In a dream or vision he had known the ecstasy of seraphic life. Was it an instant of enchantment only or long hours and days and years and ages?

The instant of inspiration seemed now to be reflected from all sides at once from a multitude of cloudy circumstance of what had happened or of what might have happened. The instant flashed forth like a point of light and now from cloud on cloud of vague circumstance confused form was veiling softly its afterglow. O! In the virgin womb of the imagination the word was made flesh. Gabriel the seraph had come to the virgin's chamber. An afterglow deepened within his spirit, whence the white flame had passed, deepening to a rose and ardent light. That rose and ardent light was her strange wilful heart, strange that no man had known or would know, wilful from before the beginning of the world: and lured by that ardent roselike glow the choirs of the seraphim were falling from heaven.
Are you not weary of ardent ways,
Lure of the fallen seraphim?
Tell no more of enchanted days.
The verses passed from his mind to his lips and, murmuring them over, he felt the rhythmic movement of a villanelle pass through them. The roselike glow sent forth its rays of rhyme; ways, days, blaze, praise, raise. Its rays burned up the world, consumed the hearts of men and angels: the rays from the rose that was her wilful heart.
Your eyes have set man's heart ablaze
And you have had your will of him.
Are you not weary of ardent ways?
And then? The rhythm died away, ceased, began again to move and beat. And then? Smoke, incense ascending from the altar of the world.
Above the flame the smoke of praise
Goes up from ocean rim to rim.
Tell no more of enchanted days.
Smoke went up from the whole earth, from the vapoury oceans, smoke of her praise. The earth was like a swinging smoking swaying censer, a ball of incense, an ellipsoidal ball. The rhythm died out at once; the cry of his heart was broken. His lips began to murmur the first verses over and over; then went on stumbling through half verses, stammering and baffled; then stopped. The heart's cry was broken.

(Joyce [1916] 1968: 217–18)

Stephen's new identity as (self-appointed) 'priest of the imagination' is inaugurated in the creation of a new text. There is a rather special kind of intertextuality here. The villanelle has a regular four-stress rhythm, which is compared with the regular, rhythmic clicking sound of the censer used to sanctify religious occasions. A very regular rhythm, which can easily be read with the same four stress pattern (with some silent beats), starts in the first paragraph. This gives the impression that the poem is born out of the surrounding prose passage. As well as this intertextuality, there is the incongruous discourse mixing of the 'sacred' (religious) and the 'profane' (erotic). The object of Stephen's desire, being addressed here as the 'temptress' in this poem, is the nebulous E_C_. This mysterious E_C_ has taken over from the fictional Mercedes, the object of his desire in earlier chapters. The character is from *The Count of Monte Cristo*.

In addition to highly literary, poetic discourse and a discourse of religion, there is a peculiar romanticizing discourse which idealizes and objectifies the desired female (influenced by *The Count of Monte Cristo*). Apart from these discourses of poetry, religion and romantic bunkum, what else is there?

The words 'rose' and 'roselike' are constantly repeated. Roses are frequent in this passage and throughout the novel; for example, a little song in the novel's opening passage:

O the wild rose blossoms
On the little green place.

Adapted from an old sentimental song called 'Lily Dale' (it should be 'on the little green grave'), this little song incorporates the colour green. Green is of course strongly associated with Ireland. (Stephen links the rose and the colour green even more closely, in a noun phrase, with his infantile attempt at repetition: 'the green wothe botheth'). Roses and Ireland. There is a traditional Rose of Ireland image associated with the Countess Cathleen. This is the name of a play by William Butler Yeats, who was deeply involved in the establishment of Irish literary nationalism (reviving and reworking traditional themes; founding the national theatre). Do all these rosy glows have something to do with Ireland? Does the nebulous E_C_ represent the temptation to Irish nationalism too, then? Whether all these connections are valid ones or not, they are possible ones, bearing in mind Stephen's self-elected role as Ireland's literary high priest.

Discourse-mixing is particularly noticeable in the Joyce passage, but this kind of intertextuality is not a phenomenon that is restricted to certain kinds of text. It is a property of *all* texts. As Gunther Kress categorically states: 'no text can be the site of the realization of a single discourse' (Kress 1988: 134). One text contains multiple discourses.

Conversely, one discourse can be found in different texts. It is the presence of a single discourse type in two contrasting texts that

Kress (1988) investigates. He first pinpoints specific characteristics of medical discourse in an advertising booklet for Fluphenazine, a drug used in the treatment of schizophrenia. Having done that, he then goes on to find some of these characteristics in a doctor–nurse romance by the publishers Mills & Boon.

Kress observes in the advertising text a strong tendency to nominalize processes; that is, processes tend to appear in nouns rather than in verbs. For example, the noun phrase *repeated hospitalization* contains the processes to repeat and to put into hospital. This kind of representation has certain consequences for other grammatical choices. When processes appear in noun phrases they tend to be relationally linked with other noun phrases by means of prepositions (e.g. *fewer hospitalizations, fewer drugs IN the hospital*) and the possessive verb *have* (e.g. *the patient HAS a poor response ... HAS a history of repeated hospitalization*) (Kress 1988: 128–9). Another consequence of nominalizing processes can be the blurring of distinctions between very different kinds of process-agent relations. Examples Kress gives of nominalizations encoding processes with very different agents are *the unreliable tablet-taker, the poor absorber* and *the paranoid schizophrenic* (ibid.: 130).

Kress remarks on the consequences of this particular mode of representation of events, people and processes. As he says, the medical advertising text systematically represents a world full of objects rather than processes, with the emphasis on classifying objects rather than on action on or with people. The distinction between person and disease is blurred; patients become bundles of attributes (ibid.: 130–1). When Kress turns his attention to the Mills & Boon romance, he finds the same kind of objectification, blurring of process-agent relations. Examples of this kind of tendency in medical discourse are used in the doctor–nurse romance text to give it a sense of authenticity. So for example we are told about *a cardiac arrest ... the new anorexic girl* and *Mr Lomond, on Addison [Ward] for the control of his diabetes* (ibid.: 135).

Another contribution to the volume containing Kress's analysis of medical discourse deals with a striking illustration of how robust a discourse-type can be, across genres and through time. Terry Threadgold (1988) traces a single 'discourse of race and gender' from contemporary newspaper coverage following a series of murders committed by a half-caste aboriginal and some of his family in 1900, through a journalist's report in 1959 on racism in that coverage, to a fictionalized version in a novel in 1972. Although generically quite distinct, all three encode many of the same racist assumptions and white male perspective. The ethnocentrism and androcentrism survive unscathed.

ABOUT THIS BOOK

This book has begun by placing its subject, fiction, at the heart of human experience. It is divided into three parts. Chapters 2 and 3 develop the concepts and issues introduced in this first chapter. Together they make up Part I: the introductory part which sets up the framework used in Parts II and III. Chapter 2 deals with discourse, readers and genres. In it, I examine the following: i) a dual view of *discourse* as both action and convention; ii) subject positioning, actual and implied readers, narrative-type and the positioning of readers; iii) usages of the term *genre*, genre-evaluation and genre-marginalization. This is the most technical chapter; at the end is a short summary of the key terms, *discourse* and *genre*. Chapter 3 returns to the subject of text population. Here I do three things: i) consider text population in a more theoretical way, explaining the various uses of the concept of intertextuality from which it derives; ii) expand on the practical issue of how to identify voices, giving a detailed checklist with discussion; iii) work through two examples in detail.

Part II develops the issue of fiction's contribution to the constitution and reproduction of social life. Each of the two chapters in it concentrates on a particular genre, chosen for its wide popularity. Each contains close, detailed analyses of sample texts and draws on historical and ethnographic work, where available. In Chapter 4, I look at romantic fictions and their place in the lives of girls and women. Using women's popular fiction as an example, the chapter examines the socially reproductive potential of fiction, including an exploration of the function of romance as 'escapism'. I consider principally romance stories published by Mills & Boon, but take into account what can in a sense be described as their 'opposite': the modern 'steamy' romantic novel, which has taken on some feminist elements and consequently intensified the genre's contradictions. This chapter also gives some attention to the declining sub-genre of the photo-romance. Chapter 5 looks at the other face of gothic fiction: its darker side, horror. In addition to close focus on specific texts, this chapter considers the more general question of horror fiction's notoriety. It examines the ways that horror fiction functions as containment and asks: why is it censured, and even censored? I argue that 'moral outrage' and 'righteous indignation' contribute to the control and delimitation of fictions produced for 'the masses'.

Part III considers fiction's potential as a contributor to social change. These chapters deal with the writing and reading of fiction and their potential for empowerment. Chapter 6 examines 'empowerment' through fiction in general and deals with reading and writing 'against the grain'. It explores how readers take up critical positions, how writers creatively disrupt genre conventions to denaturalize them, and the problem of inaccessibility such disruption can create. It also examines some attempts to give marginal writers and readers access to fiction. In Chapter 7 I look in detail at an example of fiction for empowerment. For this I examine science fiction – a genre with a tradition of social criticism – in the hands of feminist writers. This genre has provided a framework for criticizing dominant patriarchal patterns of gender relations and speculating about alternatives, for estranging readers from familiar kinds of social identity and relationship. In this final chapter, I examine: i) some feminist science fiction which sets out to make the familiar strange; ii) the use of science fiction as a 'testing ground' for language reform; iii) a critical utopia which is exposing social injustices and looking for alternative social structures and relations, in particular engaged in reconstructing gender; iv) explorations of social change: feminist science fiction that deals with cultural takeover and its consequences.

TWO

Discourses, readers, genres

The function of fiction as an art form sets it apart from other uses of language, such as the lipstick article we looked at in Chapter 1. But fiction is still important as a resource for understanding the non-fictional world. Fiction texts are part of a kind of discourse which, like all discourse, takes place under specific conditions of production and consumption and both enables and constrains the people involved in it. This second chapter begins with an outline of the view of discourse as social practice to be applied to fiction. It deals with various general issues and concepts which we will need later on: discourse and subject positions in fiction; genres and the kinds of character and situation naturalized in them, constraints on change in genres, how genres are evaluated.

TEXT VS. DISCOURSE

In linguistics, the term *discourse* is sometimes used interchangeably with *text* (e.g. Stubbs 1983). More often the two are set in opposition, to make some kind of distinction between two views or aspects of language. I use *text* to mean the observable product of interaction: a cultural object; and *discourse* to mean the process of interaction itself: a cultural activity. The distinction between *text* and *discourse* I am making is an analytical one between the observable materiality of a completed product and the ongoing process of human activity (Widdowson 1979; Brown and Yule 1983; Halliday 1985). I do not use the terms to distinguish between spoken and written language, nor between dialogue and monologue. Text is the fabric in which discourse is manifested, whether spoken or written, whether produced by one or more participants.

So the distinction is between product and process, between object and activity. As I said, *text* here refers to the observable product of interaction (whether language-production or language-interpretation). A *text* may be either written or spoken, since spoken language can be tape-recorded and thereby transformed into an object of analysis. In the actual production and interpretation of a stretch of language (a simple example being a conversation) the interactants have access to historically prior texts. These are products of previous interaction, which make up the conversants' interactional history. In reporting previously uttered speech, for instance, a fragment of an earlier text is embedded in the current text. *Text*, then, is a 'frozen' observable substance, a concrete cultural object. The text-product may actually exist in a physically substantial way, as marks on paper or impulses on magnetic tape. However, it *may* only exist in the, possibly mistaken, memories of people; indeed with the texts of previous conversations this is almost always the case (since we do not, fortunately, tape or otherwise keep a record of every conversation we have!).

Discourse is not a product but a process. To analyse it we need to look at both the text itself and the interaction in which the text is embedded. A text is part of the process of discourse. It is the product of a writer/speaker and a resource for a reader/hearer. As a resource, a text consists of cues for interpretation processes; as a product, it consists of traces of production processes.

As a resource for the interpreter, a text consists of lexico-grammatical realizations. These realizations relate to the three basic language meta-functions (in systemic linguistics) which inhere in any text: the ideational, interpersonal and textual functions of language (see Table 2.1). The ideational function is perhaps the most familiar, referring as it does to the function of language to communicate ideas, and logical relations between those ideas. It refers to language as a 'contents', 'about' something. The interpersonal function refers to the function of language to establish and maintain social identities and relationships, to influence people. The textual function refers to the text-creating function of language, the strictly textual contribution to the construction of coherence between elements. The lexico-grammatical cues in a text are encodings of ideational, interpersonal and textual kinds of meaning. They are interpreted with the help of other resources beyond the text.

Discourse is produced and interpreted by specific people in specific institutional and broader societal contexts. Institutional and

Table 2.1 The three language meta-functions and principal types of lexico-grammatical realization

Ideational	(representation)	processes, participants, circumstances, transitivity
Interpersonal	(social identities and relationships)	speech roles, modality
Textual	(text-creation)	thematic organization, information cohesion structure,

societal structures always impinge upon discourse, bestowing specific social identities and power relations upon interactants and giving them different resources: different access to language, to representations of knowledge/beliefs. (It follows from this, incidentally, that these resources are not mutually accessible to all; these resources should not be confused with any notion of 'mutual knowledge'.)

In discourse interpretation, features of text and context serve as cues which activate specific resources. Interpretation is achieved in the dialectical interplay of cues and resources. It is a complex of different processes in which the resources serve as interpretive procedures (procedures which serve for the analyst of language as well as the language-user). At any given point, among the resources for interpretation are previous interpretations; for example, interpretation of 'higher level', global elements of text are dependent on interpretation of local elements, such as the 'lower level' local coherence and the meanings and surface forms of utterances. The interdependency of interpretation in different domains is not one-directional: it is 'top-down' as well as 'bottom-up' (as in the example above). Listeners will automatically select the appropriate homonym on the basis of a given context; they are unlikely to hear *seller* as *cellar* in the stockmarket, for instance.

SUBJECT POSITIONING OF READERS IN FICTION

In becoming involved with fiction texts we are engaging in the processes of discourse. Our participation in the discourse is passive in the sense that it is not 'binding'. It does not ask things of us, in the way that a summons from the courts or a request from a friend does. Reading fiction is 'time-out'. But our participation in discourse through a fiction text is active in the sense that we initiate it and can presumably bring it to a close at any point.

In the act of reading, readers are also active in the sense that they are actively interpreting. In doing so they are constructed as social subjects. I am using the term 'subject' in the double sense of one-who-does-something and one-to-whom-something-is-done. A reader, just like any language-user, is an active agent and simultaneously unknowingly constituted in the act of using language. The extent of the reading subject's autonomy as an interpreter who invests a text with meaning is diminished by focusing on the enactment of language conventions which mediate between society and individuals. As the part played by these conventions is foregrounded, the importance of the individual consciousness of subjects diminishes; or, rather more accurately, it is seen as a function of those conventions, not developed independently of them. The illusion of the subject's autonomy has been amusingly labelled the 'Münchhausen effect' by Michel Pêcheux (1982: 108); the reference is of course to the Baron's feat of holding himself up by his own pigtail as he leaps over a crevasse. As reading subjects, we have the illusion of self-determination, of being able to pull ourselves up by our own bootstraps.

Drawing on resources as interpretive procedures on any level requires of the reader a kind of complicity. When the connections between elements of a text are simply obvious, then the reader's complicity and subjection is total and unreserved. This, I had better say straightaway, is not *necessarily* a bad thing. Consider the following, the opening two paragraphs of *The shining levels*, an autobiographical novel by John Wyatt, head warden of the Lake District National Park:

> I have been a countryman all my life. I have had a straw in my mouth, a stick in my hand, and a dog at my heels almost from the day I could walk. As a child this made me a peculiar misfit because I was brought up in a Lancashire industrial town within sight of a coal tip, within sound of a cotton mill, and almost within smell of a black pudding and tripe factory.
>
> But lemon-yellow charlock grew upon the tip. The poplar hawk moths flew among the hen pens. The larks soared from the fields beyond the allotments; and within fifteen minutes walk there was a blessed wood. And I knew where the kingfisher flashed from the bank

of its stream; and where the watervole nested, and the water-shrew trailed its pearl-bubbles. Beyond that there were the Pennine moors. Within a sixpenny bus ride there was the Peak District with its escarpments, pot holes, and gritstone crags, and I lived for long light evenings and the week-ends.

(Wyatt 1976: 7)

Recognition that the second sentence is a kind of rewording of the first requires a reader who can manage to supply the 'missing link':[5] the distinctively masculine stereotype according to which straw-in-mouth, stick-in-hand and dog-at-heels are all properties of a 'countryman'. In sentence three, the noun phrase, 'a peculiar misfit' prepares the reader for some kind of disjunction in what follows: some kind of person or surroundings in opposition to 'countryman'. So that is what the reversed causal connector 'because' cues. The characterization of the mill town which follows only makes sense for a reader who can supply the stereotype (although an outsider will not be in a position to recognize it *as* a stereotype; is tripe *really* made in factories?). The coherence of the first three sentences of paragraph two again depends on specific knowledge, the ability to recognize in the second paragraph the continued opposition of countryside and Lancashire town established through the stereotypes in the first:

Country	Town
lemon-yellow charlock	tip
poplar hawk moths	hen pens
larks	allotments

The text from which the extract above was taken has an implied reader, someone who can readily supply the necessary information resources to make coherent sense of it. Every text can be said to have such an implied reader, an imaginary addressee for whom the text was written, someone with particular sets of ideas and values, notions of common sense, and so on. Actual readers have to negotiate with the subject positioning of the implied reader inscribed in the text. If an actual reader has a great deal in common with the reader 'in' the text, then she is likely to take up the positions constructed comfortably, unconsciously and uncritically. As the distance (social or temporal) increases between writer and reader, the negotiation required of the reader is likely to become more substantial and difficult, and the likelihood of actual readers fitting the writer's implied reader is correspondingly diminished. For example, Defoe seems to have had particular kinds of expectation of the sensibilities of, and conventions familiar to, his readers, in his preface to *Moll Flanders*. For a modern reader it is difficult to see the point of his reassurances and disclaimers; his denial of authorship is simply puzzling, and the claim of authenticity as autobiography in Moll's own words contradicts his assurances about the language having been 'cleaned up' and his promise to be morally uplifting. The effect for a modern reader is irony. Not so for the contemporary reader. The implied reader for whom Defoe wrote was familiar with religious tracts with a high moral and didactic tone, and with early manifestations of journalistic documentary writing (factual reporting of the kind we take for granted), but suspicious of telling tall tales about contemporary commoners for their own sake. Most of the early novelists had close connections with printing, publishing and journalism and framed their novels as factual documents, posing as merely editors.

The construction of an implied reader puts writers in a powerful position, in the sense that they can assume all kinds of shared expectations, commonsense attitudes and even experiences. Actual readers in the target audience are likely to take up the subject positions of the constructed implied reader. In the case of *The shining levels*, the reader is likely to experience a sharpening of appreciation for the natural world. There is great potential for manipulativeness in this kind of power relation. The interaction is asymmetrical and writers are in a position to place all sorts of beliefs, and so on, as givens in people's heads. Sometimes writers go to a great deal of trouble to give the impression of familiarity, even intimacy, with an audience of people who as individuals are in fact quite unknown to them (see Talbot 1990 and 1992 for detailed examination of the construction of synthetic friendship and intimacy in *Jackie* magazine). One way of doing this is through use of direct address, as if the writer is addressing a reader personally. This practice has been dubbed 'synthetic personalization' (Fairclough 1989: 62). However, actual readers do wield a kind of power too. Readers put severe constraints on writers in their demands as consumers. Writers are not free to make changes to the significant features of the genre in which they are operating. This is particularly clear in the case of romance fiction. I turn specifically to matters relating to genre in a later section of this chapter.

In considering the subject positioning of readers in works of fiction it is essential to distinguish some broad types of interpretive position. Catherine Belsey (1980), on the analogy of the grammatical distinction between declarative, imperative and interrogative forms of sentence, distinguishes between three kinds of text. The 'declarative' text imparts certain knowledge to a reader, 'whose position is thereby stabilized, through a privileged discourse which is to varying degrees invisible' (Belsey 1980: 91). This kind of text tends to establish/reinforce shared values, commonsense attitudes, by offering familiar subject positions to the reader. Whether it succeeds in this or not depends of course on the actual reader. Distinct from the 'declarative' text is the 'imperative' kind, which Belsey characterizes as propaganda, the type of text which reinforces established subject positions, but in opposition to others: 'Propaganda . . . exhorts, instructs, orders the reader, constituting the reader as a unified subject in conflict with what exists outside' (ibid.: 91). Here the discourses are not hidden. There is open, overt opposition of two or more: conflict between discourses is explicit. The 'interrogative' text, in contrast with both the others, does not reinforce established subject positions and does not offer a unified reading position. Belsey's key distinction is between the kind of interpretive position offered by realist texts (which she sees as 'declarative') and more disruptive, 'interrogative' kinds of interpretive position offered by various other types of text, including in particular those which have multiple, fragmented points of view and those which display rather than conceal their own artifice.

Perhaps the most important consideration of all with regard to readers and subject positions is the interpretive position constructed for the implied reader by the narration at a given point. There are basically three kinds of narration: omniscient, first person, focalized. The kind of interpretive position constructed by all three depends on how they are used, but it is possible to indicate tendencies. Omniscient narration, since it has a way of effacing the narrating process, *tends* to construct the reader as recipient of common knowledge. This is partly because it is very often used in texts of the 'declarative' type, in which the reader's attention is carefully turned away from the narrative process itself (and indeed from language; in 'declarative' texts, language is used as though it were a transparent medium for transmitting content). First person narration tends to push the reader into subject positions identical to those of the narrator, *unless* the narrator is particularly fallible (like Dowell from Ford Madox Ford's *The good soldier*) or unpleasant (like Alex in Anthony Burgess's *A clockwork orange*, 1961, or Frank in Iain Banks' *The wasp factory*, 1984). Focalized narration tends to be interspersed with omniscient narration (as we saw in the extract from *Love on the dole* in Chapter 1), and tends to draw the reader into complicity with the focalized character. Focalized narration tends to encourage a reader's identification with the focalized character, since she is shown the world through that character's 'eyes'. It can therefore be a powerful means for manipulating readers into subject positions. Occasionally texts make use of a combination of all three. A particularly interesting example of this is *The bluest eye* (1970), Toni Morrison's first novel, which presents a detailed picture of the social conditions and relations in which father rapes daughter. The regular shifts from omniscient narration, interspersed with narration focalized on a wide range of characters including victim and rapist, to retrospective first person narration by a friend of the victim, help Morrison to give a rounded picture of a whole community.

DISCOURSE, DISCOURSE TYPE, ORDER OF DISCOURSE

I have already introduced the term 'discourse' as it is used in linguistics to refer to the process of linguistic interaction, the production and interpretation of texts. There is a contrasting use of discourse in the work of Michel Foucault. Discourses for Foucault are historically constituted social constructions in the organization and distribution of knowledge. Medicine, for instance, is a body of knowledge, practices and social identities. Medical discourse defines health, sickness; it also determines who has the power to define, in the social identities it bestows. In contrast with the analysis of discourse in linguistics, Foucault does not analyse concrete text samples (see Fairclough 1988 or 1992 for discussion). He does however make brief observations about the notion of a concrete whole text in *The archaeology of knowledge* (1974), which are interesting. 'The materiality of a book,' he says, is only one kind of 'unity', and not the most significant. For example, a missal and an anthology of poems are both books, but it is the unity each derives from a discourse that constitutes them as 'missal' and 'anthology'. Foucault observes that the unity of a single actual text, a physical book with front and back cover, is weaker than the 'discursive unity of which it is the support' (ibid.: 23). Discourses may not be as obviously tangible as individual texts, but they are more durable. Foucault's use of the term *discourse* is rather different from the use of the term in linguistics and a little difficult to square with the linguistic sense of *discourse* as situated action between people. What he provides is a view of language as *discursive*, which avoids a false division between action and convention. This false division is embodied in the distinction between *langue* and *parole* that linguists often make. First coined by Ferdinand de Saussure (1916), this distinction separates the whole language system as an abstract set of rules (*langue*) from the act of speaking (*parole*). What Foucault does is to examine the social constitution in language of accumulated conventions related to bodies of knowledge, by investigating how power is exercised through conventions, including how they define social identities.

A recent linguistic combination of the two senses of discourse – as action and convention – is in Fairclough (1989). He remarks on the 'felicitous ambiguity' of the term *discourse*, and the more general *practice*, to refer both to an actual enactment and to a social convention governing actions:

> the individual instance always implies social conventions – any discourse or practice implies conventional types of discourse or practice
>
> (Fairclough 1989: 28)

He also plays on this ambiguity to underline the way social practices, including discourse, are both enabling and constraining, providing the social conventions within which it is possible to act. (Jacob Mey, 1985: 24, makes a similar point less formally with a distinction between 'structured use' and 'useful structure'.)

Applied to creators of works of fiction, this double view of social practice as both enabling and constraining in nature underlines the limitations of originality and creativity. Individual writers are only able to create given certain social preconditions which make the activity of creation possible. Those preconditions are the complex of social conventions that govern fiction-making. Fiction as social practice enables the creation of new texts, within constraints. As social subjects, writers are constrained to act within the social positions set up in discourse types. These constraints are what make action possible; subjects are enabled by being constrained. As I said at the outset of the discussion of readers' subject positioning above, the subject is both an active agent and passively shaped. The double use of the term *discourse* collapses the artificial division between an individual action and a conventional practice, since the one cannot exist without the other. Actions are only possible because of the conventions for enacting them. Conventions only exist insofar as they are performed.

Subject positions and relations between them are set up in discourse *types*. A single individual is placed in a wide range of subject positions. She is not an autonomous entity who exists independently of these positions and social relations, but constituted in the act of working within various discourse types. From the beginning of her entry into social life she is positioned within varied institutional and societal structures, which bestow upon her specific social 'roles'. In consequence, we can consider any individual as a constellation of subject positions bestowed by different discourse types. In the work of Foucault, these discourses are systematically organized sets of conventions forming practices. Fairclough's original contribution is to construct a model of discourse as social practice allowing detailed linguistic analysis of the interaction of individuals as realizations of these subject-shaping practices. It is an attempt to put into operation a social theoretical view of discourse as socially constitutive. His dual perspective on discourse (both linguistic and social theoretical) enables him to attend, on the one hand, to concrete texts and production and interpretation processes and, on the other, to the social conditions determining processes and their consequences for social subjects.

The major social institutions involved in the production and distribution of fiction texts are publishing, cinema and broadcasting. Each of these institutions has its own complex order of discourse structuring the discourses and genres within it. So the social institution of publishing, for example, is structured into various domains and sub-domains associated with different kinds of practice. Just one of these domains, journalism, itself involves a whole range of discourse-types which collectively make up what we know as 'journalism'. The institutional order of journalistic discourse is structured into a range of practices, each with its own historical development and characteristic elements. These include kinds of publication (the products of the industry: tabloid newspaper, women's magazine, etc.) and also discourses drawn upon in putting together these publications (knowledge from the world of medicine, or from the social sciences, perhaps) and genres used (editorial board meetings, interviews, etc.). I will deal with the distinction between discourses and genres in the next section.

It is here we can see the Foucauldian sense of discourses as conventional, as systematically organized sets of conventions forming practices. Just as a social institution determines types of practice (conventions) which in turn determine actual practices (actions), so orders of discourse determine the types of discourse that determine actual discourses. This complex of determining influences emphasizes the shaping of actual discourse production and interpretation by higher level structures beyond the immediate situation of utterance. It amounts to an expansion of the notion of context to include the social formation.

The three 'level' structuring relating orders of discourse, types of discourse and the actual activity of discourse also makes it possible to account for the presence of more than one discourse type in discourse. Discourses are not simply mechanical implementations of discourse-types but 'the creative extension-through-combination of existing resources' (Fairclough 1989: 31). Recall the small sample of journalistic discourse taken from a magazine for teenagers we examined in Chapter 1. It contained a range of practices, none of which were 'intrinsically' journalistic in nature (although some of them – advertising, in particular – do have a long-standing involvement with the particular conglomeration of discourse-types found in women's magazines).

Fiction texts cut across a range of orders of discourse. Works of fiction – products of the discourses of publishing, the cinema and broadcasting – enter into discourse elsewhere, in other institutional contexts; the family, education, the marketplace. Families time their meals around particular TV programmes. A trip to the cinema to see the latest Spielberg film can be someone's 'birthday treat' shared by a whole family. Students read set texts, selected for them by designers of syllabuses, teachers. Fiction texts also enter discourse in a another sense. As objects with exchange value, books and videos are involved in complex series of interactions in transactional commercial discourses.

GENRE

In Chapter 1, I referred to Terry Threadgold's (1988) investigation of the robustness of a 'discourse of race and gender', across different genres and through time. We saw how this single discourse could appear and re-appear in texts which were generically very different. I also referred to two texts analysed by Gunther Kress (1988), which both contained a medical discourse: an advertisement for a drug and a doctor–nurse romance story. Advertisements and romance stories are examples of two very different *genres*. It would not be difficult to think of other genres in which medical discourse might be found, although there are certainly some in which we would expect it more than others. We would be somewhat surprised if it was not present at some point in a doctor–patient consultation, for instance. But it could be drawn upon in a television documentary, or a newspaper article, in casual conversation, or even in a poem, all of which are types of genre, following current usage in critical language study (e.g. Fairclough 1992) and social semiotics (e.g. Hodge and Kress 1988). A genre is a set of discoursal conventions associated with some kind of socially ratified activity. It can be seen as a framework or schema for action. The conventions that go to make up a genre typically govern interpersonal and textual considerations, rather than content. For instance, one could write a report about practically anything, but there are constraints upon the kind of compositional structure it could have and still be a report.

To clarify and expand on the distinction between discourses and genres, let me return for a moment to Kress's two texts containing medical discourse. The advertisement (for a drug used in the treatment of schizophrenia) is both produced and interpreted within the medical institution; both writer and reader are professionals in that institution, defined as such by the discourse. It is an informative text, distributing knowledge within the medical institution (it is also constituted in commercial discourses, but that is another matter again). In the case of the doctor–nurse romance story, by contrast, the relationship between writer and reader is not institutional but generic. Without the genre, there would be no relationship at all. The story, a text generically distinct from the advertisement, is intended to entertain rather than inform. Medical discourse is present in displaced form, adding authenticity to the fiction, establishing a sense of 'community' or shared experience between writer and reader, and so on.

The linguistic usage of the term 'genre', outlined briefly above, is the one I prefer. However, the term is a familiar one elsewhere, particularly in literary criticism and publishing, and as my subject matter here is fiction it would be unhelpful to ignore these other usages. It is always employed for classification of texts into groups of some sort, but the term is variously used for classification by compositional structure, medium, content, imprint (e.g. Mills & Boon), even by creator (Alfred Hitchcock and Agatha Christie, for example). The conflation of genre with medium is a tendency which is worth some consideration. A particular medium may be strongly associated with certain story and character types and a specific readership. This is very much the case with comic books in English-speaking countries, especially in Britain, and is also true of the video medium. In Britain, the comic book contains a type of visual narrative which is held in low esteem, despite the variety of fiction now available in the medium. The only widely known comics are the children's weekly publications and, in recent decades, the 'superhero' publications from the United States. Creators on both sides of the Atlantic working in the medium find it very difficult to break this mould. The new term 'graphic novel' used for fiction in the medium is an attempt to remedy this situation, which has had partial success (see Sabin 1993). Comics could, in principle, be about anything and for anyone; there is no *necessary* link between medium and genre. A recent non-fiction publication uses the comic book medium for an intriguing exploration of the nature of the medium itself (McCloud 1993).

In institutions in which literature is studied, the term *genre* is generally used to distinguish the three major literary forms of poetry, drama and the novel. In the more traditional literature departments, courses are structured around these three textual forms: poetry in term one, drama in term two, or what have you. Generic distinctions within (and to some extent across) these forms are also made by literary scholars and critics: epic, tragedy, romance, realism and so on are different generic categories. In publishing, on the other hand, genres are marketing categories. Genre in this sense hinges on audience identification and targeting: interpersonal considerations. Publishers deal with a broader spectrum of texts than literary critics and students. Marketing category genres include 'mainstream' writing and, confusingly, 'genre fiction'. (They also include non-fiction: cookery books, books on gardening, travel, maths textbooks, autobiography, dictionaries, and so on.)

The notion of 'genre fiction' needs some examination and I will return to it later. First, we need to give some attention to the similarities between usages of the term 'genre' in different domains. There are considerable overlaps between usages in publishing, in the academic literary world and in linguistic analysis. Interpersonal and textual considerations are always important as generic variables. The formal, textual properties of specific genres are highly conventional. A simple example is the distinctive 'look' of different marketing category genres; fashions vary, but clear contrasts are maintained between romances, travel books and so on. Textual conventions within texts also vary according to genre. Novels are narratives, usually linear and plot-driven, and exceptions are considered to be 'experimental' and hard to read. Readers have strong expectations of exposition, complicating action and satisfying denouement. In Colin Greenland's *Michael Moorcock: death is no obstacle*, there is an extensive interview in which Moorcock talks about the writing process. He uses an amusing metaphor for the textual structure of his 'commercial fiction'. He had to throw it together very rapidly, with little possibility of revision, an experience he likens to 'flying a very ramshackle aeroplane':

> You got it off the ground. You got it into the sky. You kept it there by whatever tricks you could manage. And at the end of the day you landed it safely, by whatever means. The landing was always the difficult bit!
>
> (Greenland 1992: 136)

Another textual similarity linking novels together as a generic grouping is the overwhelming tendency for them to consist of a combination of narration and dialogue, varying only within the range of possible variations we considered earlier. More specific textual properties vary considerably from one kind of novel to another. The misleading cohesion linking different protagonists in Toni Morrison's *Jazz* (1993), for instance, deliberately makes characters from different time periods difficult to distinguish; this contrasts sharply with the massive redundancy in signalling of the protagonists in Mills & Boon romances.

Turning to interpersonal considerations, the kinds of relationship taken up through a text and the implied reader constructed 'in' it are genre specific. For example, an essential ingredient in horror fiction is the writer's attempt to produce fearful responses from the reader, requiring close identification with victims at specific points in the narrative (this is examined in Chapter 5). In other genres, the

matching of protagonist and implied reader is very important.
Moorcock aimed his 'sword and sorcery' fantasy novels at a predominantly male adolescent audience. In the Moorcock interview
mentioned above, they discuss his sword-wielding fantasy heroes.
These heroic figures are incarnations of the 'Eternal Champion',
who is 'really just an eternal adolescent':

> You're appealing to a fallible reader, giving them a fallible central char-
> acter to identify with. Those fallibilities may be emphasised, made
> grandiose, but most adolescents' sense of their own fallibility is grandi-
> ose anyway!

(ibid.: 5)

The relationship set up between writer and reader in novels is
generic; that is to say, it is the genre itself which creates the relationship.

So one can draw points of similarity between the different kinds
of 'grouping' of texts embodied in various usages of the term *genre*.
Texts within a particular genre tend to realize the interpersonal and
textual language functions in similar ways. Texts in highly formulaic genres (i.e. some of the so-called 'genre fiction' categories, see
below, pp. 38–41) can also be strikingly similar ideationally. Some
formulaic genres are permeated with the same discourse; a very
obvious example of this is the medical discourse in doctor–nurse
romances. Similarly, spy stories written before the demise of the
Soviet Union almost invariably draw upon Cold War discourse.

The existence of a literary 'mainstream', as defined in the discourses of education and publishing, entails the existence of
something outside it. 'Genre fiction' refers to a range of fiction identified as non-mainstream (with the strong implication of
'non-literature'), subdivided into the marketing categories of science fiction, fantasy, romance, horror, western, detective fiction,
thriller, and so on. (Literature then curiously takes on the label of
'non-genre'.) The marketing categories for so-called genre fiction
are defined in terms of particular narrative formulae, character
types and situations expected by target audiences. These conventions place quite rigid constraints on what writers can create, and
audience identification and targeting by publishers leads to excessive pigeonholing of whatever they do produce. The effect of this
pigeonholing is to exclude authors from a potentially much wider
audience, particularly from 'mainstream' fiction readers who avoid
stories with generic labels attached to them, but also readers of

other genres. Science fiction readers for instance tend to avoid fantasy, thereby missing out on Gwyneth Jones' *Divine endurance* (1985), which was published under that label. The visibility of the conventions of 'genre fiction' is usually viewed negatively by literary critics, unless they are being used as raw material by authors already established as 'mainstream'. Kingsley Amis, Margaret Atwood and Russell Hoban, for example, all three of whom are considered to be mainstream authors, drew upon a range of conventions from science fiction for *The alteration* (1978), *The handmaid's tale* (1987) and *Riddley Walker* (1980) respectively. The 'mainstream' itself is of course far from being convention-free, since discourse-production is always the enactment of existing practices (see earlier discussion, pp. 32–3). But the conventions are not so clearly mapped out, allowing considerably more leeway for individual authors and at the same time giving the impression of greater originality. Whether we decide to see the three novelists above as mainstream authors who drew on science fiction for their own purposes or authors who have 'crossed over' into the realm of science fiction depends on where we want to set the boundaries. There is no doubt where the boundaries are set in publishing, however. All three are published in the 'fiction' category and do not rub shoulders with science fiction on the shelves of libraries and shops, although science fiction readers would quite confidently identify them as such. To exist in both camps is rare and requires considerable determination on the part of individual authors. One such author is Iain Banks who, as the cover blurb of a recent novel, *The crow road* (1992) tells us, 'writes both fiction and science fiction'.

Genre categories, once established, appear to be highly robust, taking on a commonsensical quality for publishers and librarians, if not for writers. A British researcher into romance fiction (Mairead Owen, whose work I will come back to in Chapter 4) found this to be the case when she contacted librarians for her survey through public libraries of romance readers:

> The definition of 'romantic fiction' I deliberately left to the librarians who, interestingly, considered it unproblematic. Romantic fiction consisted of those books shelved under romantic fiction or sent by the publishers or the library wholesalers as romantic fiction.
>
> (Owen 1990: 42)

This commonsense perception presumably springs from the need to catalogue and organize actual books. As Owen observes, it can be curiously at odds with romance writers' own perception of their writing. Catherine Cookson does not consider herself to be a romantic writer, for example. Owen quotes the following from a letter she received from the author:

> You see, I do not consider myself to be a romantic writer in the sense in which the word is used today. It is only since Granada Television filmed *The Mallens* that this word was applied to my writing; and the paperback firm, solely for the purpose of appealing to the public, continued it from there.'
>
> (ibid.)

Some literary critics who have turned their attention to what is known as 'popular culture' have avoided facing the difficulties of genre divides by choosing 'safe' examples. Walter Nash begins *Language in popular fiction* (1990) by announcing his intention to deal with 'enjoyably bad books' (these turn out to be novels by Barbara Cartland and Ian Fleming, among others, and a range of very down-market women's magazine stories). He follows his rather back-handed compliment with an outline of the merits of 'popfiction'. Although disposable and unserious, it induces compulsive reading and an understanding of 'ordinary people'; it touches on 'common sympathies', and above all it offers 'the keen experience of danger, of anxiety, of love, of sorrow, of triumph, but all without the intruding shadow of the actual' (ibid.: 2–3). Nash follows this outline of the qualities he admires in disposable 'popfiction' by carefully reasserting his, and his implied reader's, preference for 'serious' literature. 'Our deeper allegiance', he informs us, lies elsewhere; namely with the 'classics', which have the capacity to illuminate and enlarge our 'perceptions of human nature and conduct' (ibid.: 3). He does eventually, at the end of his introductory chapter, introduce the notion of a cline of quality (with 'popfiction' at one end and 'classics' at the other), but the effect of his treatment is to reinforce with a vengeance the mainstream genre distinction and the prejudices associated with it.

Another critic, Patrick Parrinder, is rather more aware of the mainstream genre boundary as a problem. Stating a preference for the term 'paraliterature' to refer to all those texts which have been given no place in any literary canon (following Darko Suvin 1979: vii), he rejects the straightforward association of popular culture, mediocrity, unseriousness and disposability. He observes that 'literary culture' is tolerant of mediocrity within its ranks, but hostile to mediocrity outside them:

> Paraliterature . . . is not the lowest kind of literature in qualitative terms (there are many more bad sonnets written each year than bad SF novels), but, rather literature's dialectical opposite.
>
> (Parrinder 1980: 46)

This does not obviate the mainstream genre distinction, however. It is difficult to see how being 'literature's dialectical opposite' is any advance on being 'enjoyably bad'.

On a more positive note, there has been a good deal of feminist attention to genre, in both its traditional academic and its modern publishing senses. Women's special relationship with the novel form and the absence of work by women in the more public genre of drama have been issues in feminist literary theory and criticism at least since Woolf raised them in *A room of one's own* (1929). Rather more recently, publishers' marketing genres have become a focus of attention for the analysis of gender. As Helen Carr says:

> since the norms and expectations of each genre are enmeshed with the norms and expectations of society as a whole, they seem a particularly fruitful point to focus on – how gender enters into and is constructed by the form of the genre, and how and perhaps why those constructions may change.
>
> (Carr 1989: 7)

Feminist criticism has largely ignored the mainstream genre boundary, except to query it, and it is not difficult to see why this should be the case. The humanist assumptions of shared 'human nature', articulated so clearly in Nash's formulation of classic literature's qualities above, are highly problematic for feminism.

Finally, a few words about genre-mixing are needed. Genres are not rigid or fixed, and there is no such thing as a 'pure' genre. Mixed genre is normal. That no fiction text belongs purely and unequivocally to one genre is implicit in what I have said above about the constraints of marketing category genres on authors and readers. Admittedly, exceptionally formulaic publications, such as the romances from Mills & Boon, do look like relatively clear examples of a single, 'pure' genre. However, in the broader, linguistic sense of genre with which I opened this section, even a highly formulaic romance contains a combination of genres. Genre-imitation is a necessary part of novels, whether the letter- and diary-writing of epistolary novels (such as Mary Shelley's *Frankenstein* or Samuel Richardson's *Pamela*) or the simulated small talk so essential in Mills & Boon. A well-known example of genre imitation on television is the 'captain's log' which opens every episode of *Star trek*. Some rather exceptional examples are hoaxes, like Orson Wells' use of a news reporting genre in his dramatization of *The war of the worlds* for US radio.

FICTION AND SOCIAL REPRODUCTION: CENTRES AND MARGINS

When I A Richards announced that 'The arts are our storehouse of recorded values' (Richards 1924: 32), he was not referring to art forms known and loved by the majority of the population, the contemporary equivalents of *Star trek*, or Mills & Boon. The arts he had in mind were those believed to represent and preserve the values of a cultural élite. Literary criticism, practiced in academic and publishing institutions, contributed to the reproduction of dominant class interests (as indeed it still does). The élite, which Richards and his implied reader were both assumed to be members of, was middle class, white and predominantly male.

There is no need for me to elaborate at great length on the way in which the 'recorded values' of middle-class white men have been presented as universal, neutral, apolitical, timeless. This has already been done elsewhere, in the extensive critique of liberal humanism and expressive realism by Belsey (1980), for instance. Instead, I will end this chapter with some discussion of marginalization.

By assuming possession of the centre, everyone else is relegated to the margins. We have already given some attention to this process in considering the invidious distinction between mainstream and genre fiction. By a similar operation of silently claiming the centre, the fiction of other countries and ethnicities, and all women, is placed on the margins of 'high' culture. In British higher education, courses with names like Commonwealth Writing, Women's Writing, Black Writing clearly mark off the assumed deviations from the norm, however benign the intentions may be of those who offer such courses. The Commonwealth does not seem to include Britain; the centre of literary concerns does not seem to include white women or black people of either sex. Joanna Russ (1984) gives an entertaining and eye-opening account of the various strategies by which women's writing has been marginalized by critics and excluded from the 'literary canon'. These strategies include denial of agency ('she didn't write it'), the application of a double standard of content ('she wrote it, but look what she wrote about'), false categorizing ('she wrote it, but she isn't really an artist, and it isn't really art'), claims of anomalousness, isolation, and so on (Russ 1984).

A consequence of having universal, timeless values at the centre is to place the political in the margins. One way of preserving the illusion that literature is asocial and outside the domain of the political is to establish its value as principally aesthetic. Another is to establish literary language as distinct from and distant from 'ordinary' language use. Both of these views are implicit in the Kingman Report (DES 1988) on language in British primary and secondary education.

SUMMARY OF DISCOURSE AND GENRE

A major difficulty in interdisciplinary work is conflicting, or at least differing, usages of key terms. In this chapter on discourses, genres and readers, I have presented not one simple usage of each term but, in the case of discourse and genre, two or more. So what follows is a summary of the ones I will be making use of in later chapters.

Discourse:
1. Linguistic, and accompanying paralinguistic, interaction between people in a specific context (the 'situated language in use' of the branch of linguistics known as discourse analysis).
2. A collection of knowledge and practices generally associated with a particular institution or group of institutions. It is often used less specifically to refer to pervasive discourses, e.g. in the case of a racist discourse on ethnicity or a sexist discourse on gender there is no straightforward connection with specific institutions. The term is now common in literary and other kinds of cultural criticism.

Genre:
1. A specific text type characterized primarily by the kind of

relationship it sets up between its users and certain textual properties. A genre in this sense (from critical language study and social semiotics) can also be seen as a socially recognized activity type that can span over a wide range of discourses. It is perhaps most easily understood by thinking of 'typical' examples: e.g. a lesson and an essay are distinctively different genres in education.

2. A marketing category. This applies to books only, but not necessarily fiction. Put crudely, the identification on the back cover.

TAKING IT FURTHER

An alternative, reader-centred way of discriminating between different interpretive positions is offered by Stuart Hall's distinction between 'dominant', 'negotiated' and 'oppositional' readings (Hall 1980). Gillian Brown and George Yule (1983) is a good linguistics book dealing with discourse analysis. For further clarification of *order of discourse, discourse* and *genre*, chapters 3 and 4 of Fairclough (1992) are helpful, although they do not deal specifically with fiction. An alternative is the more recent Fairclough (forthcoming), which attends specifically to the mass media. Chapter 2 of Kress (1985) contains a clear contrastive analysis of three spoken genres (interview, conversation, lesson). There is a chapter surveying literary applications of the term *genre* in Palmer (1991). Mary Eagleton's reader (1986) contains a chapter on issues of gender, genre and fiction.

THREE

Intertextuality and text population

The frontiers of a book are never clear-cut: beyond the title, the first lines, and last full stop, beyond its internal configuration and its autonomous form, it is caught up in a system of references to other books, other texts, other sentences . . . it indicates itself, constructs itself, only on the basis of a complex field of discourse.

(Michel Foucault 1974)

The notion of 'text population' was introduced in Chapter 1. In this chapter, I develop the concept, both theoretically, in terms of explaining the various uses of the concept of intertextuality from which it derives, and practically, with attention to the practical matter of how to identify the 'voices' populating a text.

The term 'intertextuality' was coined by Julia Kristeva in her development of the notion of 'dialogism' in work written in the 1920s by the Soviet linguist, Mikhail Bakhtin. Basically what the term is intended to express is a sense of the fragmentation of unities or blurring of boundaries. Any text contains, is part of and is constituted by, the society which produced it and that society's history. Intertextuality expresses the rather dizzying concept of a text as a bundle of points of intersection of other texts. It makes the notion of what a 'single' text is, something of a problem. Kristeva uses the term to express the concept of a text as the intersection of a heterogeneous array of texts and semiotic practices in the process of which people's identities are constructed. Drawing on a range of conception and uses in literary semiology and linguistics, I will establish three forms.

FORMS OF INTERTEXTUALITY

One sense of intertextuality is to do with *interaction*. This sense comes from text linguistics and covers the connection between two or more people's texts in interaction. At the other extreme, the term intertextuality is used to express a sense of diversity: the way a text is made up of conventions from all over the place ('a Cultural Salvation Army outlet' of heterogeneous fragments, according to Vincent Leitch, 1983: 59!) Elsewhere (Talbot 1990) I have called this the *heterogeneity* sense. A more manageable label we can use here is *discourse type*. Midway between the two extremes, a text may inter-textually connect with external texts; that is, with texts outside the current interaction. Texts have an associated field of other texts; texts that are quoted as expert testimony, repeated as evidence, commented on favourably, hotly disputed. We can call this the *prior text* sense of intertextuality.

Interaction

In order to examine how a text is embedded intertextually in history and society, we need to consider how it comes into being in the social practice of discourse. The word 'text', Hodge and Kress inform us, 'comes from the Latin word *textus*, which means 'something woven together' (Hodge and Kress 1988: 6). Spoken interaction consists of two or more interweaving texts, each utter-ance settling into the 'intertextual' context of the utterance following it, as the interaction proceeds through time. In the *interaction* sense of intertextuality, then, face-to-face communication (whether real or imaginary) is intertextual. Each speaker produces a separate text; interactants intertextually connect their utterances. So exchanges (question-answer pairs, etc.) are intertextually connected.

In the case of a written text, since the reader is not contributing as a producing participant, the interaction between participants takes place through the writer's text alone. Writer and reader are interact-ing through exchanges initiated in every case by the writer. The various speech functions in these exchanges assign roles to interac-tants. Basic speech functions are questions, offers, commands and statements. In this focus on speech functions, we are concentrating on the interpersonal component of the grammar. In producing a statement, the writer takes on the role of giver of information and the reader takes on the corresponding role of recipient.

In addition to inspection of primary speech functions, sometimes a finer analysis of the function of an utterance will be needed. Martin Montgomery (1988) makes some useful observations about the spoken one-way discourse of a *Radio 1* disc jockey. He observes the frequency in radio talk of 'response-demanding' utterances (questions and commands) and also 'expressives', for example congratulating, apologising, commiserating, criticizing:

>   . . .what's the gossip today?
>   . . .can you see that?
>   . . .stop that it's dirty!
>   . . .poor dear with a name like that
>   . . .it's plagiarism fellas come on that's a two-day-old story

These contribute to the simulation of two-way discourse:

> To treat the audience as if they were in visual contact with the speaker, available for greeting and capable of responding to the discourse, is to construct a sense of reciprocity even in its absence.
>
> (Montgomery 1988: 94)

'Expressive' and response-demanding utterances are common in written language too. Here are two examples from *Jackie* magazine; a criticism in a horoscope and an editorial greeting:

> What a rat you've been recently. Isn't it time you stopped thinking about yourself and treated the people around you a bit better?
>
> (18 March 1989: 17)

> Hi again, you lot!
>
> (20 September 1986: 2)

They are also common in advertising, as in the simulated personal address with questions in this headline from a car advertisement in the *Radio Times* (5 March 1987):

> The best thing in your life? Is he four years old, the image of his Dad and destined to captain England? (with accompanying photograph)

Other features contributing to 'a sense of reciprocity' in radio discourse that Montgomery examines are short shifts of speech role within the speaker's statements as information-giver (which he refers to as shifts in 'speaker alignment'). These involve short interjections in spoken discourse, occurring in separate tone units, which he calls 'interpolations'. Interpolations are often response-demanding or 'expressive' utterances. They are represented in brackets in these examples:

Statement:	. . . er Lisa	Lisa Counter . . .
Interpolation:	(heh)	(poor dear with a name like that)

Statement:	Uranus in Sagittarius	
Interpolation:		(please please)
(Statement):		is urging and even compelling you to
	sever a few ties	
Interpolation:		(oo that could be painful couldn't it)

Writer and reader are not the only possible interactants in written discourse. Consider the following sample of written discourse published in *Jackie* magazine (7 March 1987: 29)). It was taken from a page full of reconstructed 'street interviews' with shoppers at Greenwich Market:

> EMMA
> *'I'm down here trying to find a denim jacket – this one isn't mine – it's only on loan! I like The Smiths and The Blow Monkeys, and I hate Howard Jones and Royalty.'* Treason! Outrage! The most exciting thing that's happened today? *'This!'*

Here there is a 'position statement' followed by an outraged exclamation and a question followed by an enthusiastic response. These are only coherent if interpreted as pairs of utterances. Such pairs of utterances are often referred to as 'adjacency pairs'. They contribute to the orderly organization of talk. Writers often use response-demanding utterances and responses in representing interaction between characters, as in the *Jackie* extract above. Here is another 'interview'; this time I have marked off the utterances:

Statement:	I'm only here by mistake – I got off the bus too early on the way to a friend's house.
	I am very pleased though, 'cos I've stumbled on a pair of ski pants which actually fit me!
Comment:	Hmmm.
Question:	A teensy bit large aren't they?
Answer:	'Course not.
Statement:	My ambitions are to travel the world and to go on an archaeological dig . . .

In mass media discourse, writers sometimes use response-demanding utterances, such as commands and questions addressed to the reader, thereby giving the impression of two-way discourse between producer and mass audience.

Prior text

Distinct from the immediate sense of intertextuality as the interaction of two people, a particular text may have explicit connections with an earlier specific text. We can say that a prior text is 'embedded' in a current one. Perhaps the most obvious manifestation of a text connecting with a prior text is in quotations and reports. Forms of speech representation involve explicit metalinguistic reference to a prior text external to the ongoing act of communication; the connection of one text to another is foregrounded.

Speech representation is a form of text allusion. The text alluded to is historically distant. Allusion involves deliberate reference to an earlier text by reusing a fragment of it. Robert de Beaugrande and Wolfgang Dressler (1980), by way of example, present allusions in later poems to a fanciful pastoral by Christopher Marlowe (1599). I shall repeat here the opening lines that de Beaugrande and Dressler quote. Marlowe's pastoral begins as follows:

> Come live with me and be my love,
> And we will all the pleasures prove
> That valleys, groves, hills, and fields,
> Woods, or steepy mountain yields.

The first of the poems de Beaugrande and Dressler present as allusions to this pastoral is Walter Raleigh's rebuttal (c. 1600) (on behalf of an untrusting nymph!):

> If all the world and love were young,
> And truth in every shepherd's tongue,
> These pretty pleasures might me move
> To live with thee and be thy love.

The second allusive poem is John Donne's pastiche (1633):

> Come live with me and be my love,
> And we will all the pleasures prove,
> Of golden sands and crystal brooks:
> With silken lines, and silver hooks.

As de Beaugrande and Dressler say, Donne parallels Marlowe's lyrical shepherd with an even more lyrical fisherman, who claims that if his lover bathes in the river the fishes will be so attracted to her that he will be able to dispense with fishing tackle. We can say that these allusive poems contain two voices, one of which is using the other 'against its will'. De Beaugrande and Dressler also quote Cecil Day-Lewis's parodic rewrite (1935) which begins:

Come, live with me and be my love,
And we will all the pleasures prove
Of peace and plenty, bed and board,
That chance employment may afford.

I'll handle dainties on the docks
And thou shalt read of summer frocks:
At evening by the sour canals
We'll hope to hear some madrigals.

de Beaugrande and Dressler contrast the last two lines quoted above with two lines of Marlowe's:

By shallow rivers to whose falls
Melodious birds sing madrigals.

The parodic rewrite undermines the view that

The lives of shepherds and other working classes are spent in ornate dalliance and merriment, with nature as a purveyor of luxurious toys and trinkets.

(de Beaugrande and Dressler 1980: 188)

All Raleigh and Donne take issue with are the shepherd's proposals. Day-Lewis mocks 'Marlowe's mode of selecting and communicating about a topic.' His parody is oppositional:

The force of this text is its opposition to the very principles and conventions underlying Marlowe's original.

(ibid.: 188)

Another way an external text is 'embedded' in another text is through presupposition. Presupposition triggers may signal the placement of some antecedent text in 'intertextual' context. By using presuppositions a writer can postulate an audience with shared interactional histories. Jonathan Culler (1981) has suggested looking at presuppositions in literary text, for which he uses a restricted notion of intertextuality. His approach is limited but nevertheless useful. A presupposition is said to refer back to a prior sentence present in a current one as an 'intertext'. It is of considerable literary importance which propositions are presupposed (that is, placed in an 'intertext') and which are asserted; the 'intertext' invoked can bring in another voice. In other words, the author presents a previous text in using a presupposition. Culler draws an example from William Blake's 'The tyger'. In asking:

What immortal hand or eye
Could frame thy fearful symmetry?

Blake presupposes an earlier discourse, which may not necessarily have existed as a specific text, where it is taken as given that an immortal hand or eye framed the tiger's fearful symmetry and so on. He uses the presupposition to presuppose the existence of a text, on which he can voice his attitude. Contained in the lines are two voices; the poet's own, and a presupposed 'voice' whose expressed belief he is questioning;

the problem of interpreting the poem becomes essentially that of deciding what attitude the poem [sic] takes to the prior discourse which it designates as presupposed.

(Culler 1981: 114)

Culler cites a stanza from Baudelaire's 'Un Voyage à Cythère':

It was not a temple with bosky shades
Where the young priestess, in love with flowers,
Passed, her body consumed by secret flames,
Her robe blowing open in the fleeting breezes

Here I assume the poet is parodying a poetic tradition. Culler picks out 'It was not a temple' and points out that while logically it only presupposes 'It was something', rhetorically it presupposes that someone expected (or, one would conventionally expect) there to be a temple. He goes on to say that this presupposition is intensified by the weight of the rest of the stanza

and makes the whole stanza the negation of an intertextual citation, the negation of something already in place as a discursive supposition, the negation of the language which poetic tradition might have applied to Cythère.

(ibid.: 116)

What he is saying therefore is that the 'rhetorical presupposition' draws into the poem a voice from outside it. This external voice is the literary tradition which Baudelaire is parodying.

Presupposition search is no more than a device for looking for likely spots for intertextual elements. In the parodic example Culler identifies a presupposition; but even without the negation cuing a presupposition, the stanza could still be parodying an existing literary convention. What I assume Culler implies, although he does not quite say it, is that the stanza is a parody; it contains two voices which constitute part of the poem as an intertextuality. These two voices are in conflict within the parodic word.

As the connection to an antecedent text becomes more attenuated, the words of that prior text become less easily attributable to a producer: a real or imaginary person. In the literary form known as parody, for instance, the target may be placed in 'intertextual' context, either as a specific historically antecedent text, as when Donne parodied Marlowe, or an imaginary one, as when Baudelaire parodied a poetic sub-genre in which poems were likely to contain 'a temple with bosky shades' and such like. Baudelaire's poem may not connect with a specific historically prior poem in 'intertextual' context, as Donne's does, but it claims to, using the device of negation. The prior text kind of intertextuality, then, relates to interactional history, real or otherwise.

Discourse type

So we have looked so far at intertextuality in the weaving together of two texts in interaction and at intertextuality in the relations between a current text and another text in the 'intertextual' context. In the production and interpretation of discourse, language users draw upon other resources. This is where the *discourse-type* sense of intertextuality comes in. A single text contains diverse conventions, for which readers draw upon resources relating to the institutional and societal dimensions of context. To interpret Baudelaire's poem, for instance, a reader draws upon a wide range of resources for interpretive procedures: knowledge of conventions of poetic genres, of the activity of poetry and, beyond the 'world' knowledge specific to literature, a heterogeneous collection of conventions.

Conventions which are brought into interpretation inevitably have an intertextual quality. For instance, schemata, frames and scripts which provide, as Fairclough says, 'stereotypical patterns against which we can match endlessly diverse texts' (Fairclough 1989: 164) are accumulations of past practices for text organization. These have developed over time in intertextual relations constructed across texts to become conventional. A convention is the accumulation of past actions; the enactment of a practice is intertextually connected to all previous enactments of that practice. Providing a common basis for these resources, the concept of inter-

textuality blurs the boundary between them. It does this by presenting texts as essentially dialogic. In this way, the boundary
between overtly dialogic interaction and the conventional is
blurred: a social convention comes about as the cumulative result
of historical events. Its continuity is created by the intertextual connection of past interactions. See, for instance, the view of 'the
classroom' as a single text in Michael Halliday and Ruqaiya Hasan
(1985), in which they take 'the classroom' as one, chronologically
very long text, built up of a great many smaller texts. The entire
school learning experience is linked by a pervading intertextuality,
to do with the way the theory and practice of education, as institu-
tionalized in a particular culture, is embodied. The way it is kept
going; in other words, tradition. There is a sense in which the classroom is one long text, that carries over from one year to the next
and from one stage of schooling to the next. Sometimes the connections will be made explicitly, by actual allusion to previous lessons,
to experience of earlier years of schooling (i.e. *prior text* intertextuality). Most of the time, though, what has gone before is
taken-as-given; not being explicitly alluded to, but part of what
everyone involved needs to know about in order to make any sense
of what is going on at all. However, against this impression of historical continuity, which gives an illusion of a single linear
progression or development of classroom discourse up to the
present day, we need to set discontinuity (consider all the different
fragments that find their way into the classroom: different kinds of
language use, conflicting objectives).

The *discourse-type* sense of intertextuality also covers a phenomenon for which 'inter*discursivity*' might be a better label: the
heterogeneity of texts which contain multiple genres, discourses
and a wide range of conventions from different sources. For an
example of such heterogeneity in fiction, recall the medical discourse in romances we looked at in Chapter 1. The heterogeneity of
literary language was central to Bakhtin's concerns, who you may
recall was Kristeva's inspiration for the notion of intertextuality in
the first place. He argued that literary texts are not discrete entities,
but contain non-literary varieties.

An article on genre by Kress and Threadgold (1988) provides
some useful illustrations of the pervasiveness of heterogeneity as a
property of discourse, with which I shall finish this section. They
discuss three texts in their article, one of which is a feminist short
story by Audrey Thomas which rearticulates patriarchal narratives

in a feminist 'voice', or counter-discourse. For example, the religious narrative of the annunciation is retold by a resistant Mary
('No, really, some other time'; 'I never accept free gifts') who is
forced to comply (like 'the servant summoned to the bedchamber
... honoured ... afraid. Or perhaps like Leda.'). A little later, the
writer comments unfavourably, but with resignation, on the patriarchal nativity narrative in which women's experience of childbirth
is absent: 'Unfair to gloss that over ... to make so little of the waiting ... the months ... the hours. They make no mention of the
hours; but of course, men wrote it down. How were they to know?'
(Thomas 1981: 7–18) The text is realized in interactive conversation-
al mode; quotation marks, questions, and so on. The conversation
genre is paradoxically what gives the 'short story' genre its generic
status (Kress and Threadgold 1988: 235).

Kress and Threadgold also observe multiple genres and discourses in a non-literary text: a transcription of recorded voices of two
children who are supposed to be having their afternoon nap. They
identify a 'let's pretend' genre, the topic of which is feeding pup-
pies; this draws on a discourse of dog-breeding which the children
(Threadgold's own) apparently participate in with their mother.
They also find an 'instructional genre', as the sister is training her
younger brother in 'let's pretend', that is, teaching him how to be a
participant in the 'let's pretend' genre. For this she uses the discourse of parental control, as used by her mother. Other genres in
this multi-genre text are a 'negotiation' genre (for possession of a
toy rabbit to take to bed with her), a 'bedtime story' genre, a 'nap
genre' and others. The sense of genre that emerges is of topics and
ways of speaking related to situation and activity types:

> There is ... dialogism at work here, not merely in the usual sense of a
> dialogue between the participants in a conversation, but dialogism in
> Bakhtin's sense whereby this text dialogues with the other 'voices' of
> the culture, by referring to them intertextually and also constructing, for
> the participants in this dialogue, positions of compliance or resistance
> with respect to those other 'voices'. It is also a text which dialogues with
> fictionality, a text which paradoxically, in constructing a fictional world,
> constructs the 'real' and constructs places for apprentice subjects within
> that 'real'.
>
> (Kress and Threadgold 1988: 234–5)

SUMMING UP

So where does this leave us? All the conceptions of intertextuality set out in some way to undermine the illusion that a text is self-contained. What intertextuality does is introduce history and heterogeneity to the text. The *interaction* and *prior text* senses of intertextuality do this by fracturing the boundaries between text and context. What counts as a single text? Does two-party interaction contain one text or two? In reportage, is the text reported part of the text reporting it, or is it a separate text? And similarly in the case of a presupposed text, is it part of the text in which it is embedded, or is it outside it? (The answer to each of these questions is that it is both.) Intertextuality in its *interaction* and *prior text* senses enables us to fracture the boundaries of text, interaction and 'intertextual' context; what counts as 'single' text is indeterminate. Intertextuality in its *discourse-type* sense enables us to view a text as a heterogeneous collection of conventions and to view these conventions enacted in discourse from a dialogic perspective as accumulations of past practices.

Using the intertextuality concept as I have outlined it to look at a work of fiction means examining it as a sort of mixed bag of voices, kinds of language. This includes attention to citations, allusions to earlier works and so on, but it goes way beyond that sort of back-referencing. It is about variety-and-dialogue, viewed simultaneously; about voices responding to other voices and different varieties of language rubbing shoulders with one another in the same text. I will provide a range of features as points to focus on for analysis shortly. Before presenting these, however, I am going to work through a sample analysis informally. For this I have chosen to look at Joseph Conrad's *Heart of darkness* (1902). I have chosen this text for two reasons. It is a novel layered, as it were, with voices, and hence particularly suitable for illustrative purposes. It is an example of 'high literature' which is held in high regard for its expression of humanist values.

Example 1: extracts from Conrad's *Heart of darkness*

Conrad presents the narrative of *Heart of darkness* through the mouth of a storytelling seaman, Marlow, on board the *Nellie* on the Thames. This character's narration is itself full of other people's voices. We are constantly being given bits of speech reported in one way or another; very often in a quite distanced way, with the narrator-Marlow's disparaging remarks thrown in. The following is an example of this quite early in the narrative. Marlow has informed his listeners of his urge to work in Africa and is giving an account of his encounter with his 'excellent aunt', who had used her influence to get him appointed as the skipper of a river steamboat there:

> I had been represented to the wife of the high dignitary, and goodness knows to how many more people besides, as an exceptional and gifted creature – a piece of good fortune for the Company – a man you don't get hold of every day. Good heavens! and I was going to take charge of a two-penny-half-penny river steamboat with a penny whistle attached! It appeared, however, I was also one of the Workers, with a capital – you know. Something like an emissary of light, something like a lower sort of apostle. There had been a lot of such rot let loose in print and talk just about that time, and the excellent woman, living right in the rush of all that humbug, got carried off her feet. She talked about weaning those ignorant millions from their horrid ways 'till, upon my word, she made me quite uncomfortable. I ventured to hint that the Company was run for profit.
>
> 'You forget, dear Charlie, that the labourer is worthy of his hire', she said, brightly.
>
> (Conrad 1989: 39)

The religious discourse of missionary zeal is clear, driven home with the inclusion of a biblical allusion. Marlow's tone in representing it is distinctly sardonic. Indeed, throughout his narration all references to religion are heavily ironic; Brussels, the location of the company employing him, is a 'whited sepulchure', his white fellow-travellers are 'pilgrims'.

Marlow is critical of other characters and other discourses. Two pages later, in relating the bizarre sight of a French warship firing shells into apparently empty forest, he says the following:

> There was a touch of insanity in the proceeding, a sense of lugubrious drollery in the sight; and it was not dissipated by somebody on board assuring me earnestly there was a camp of natives – he called them enemies! – hidden out of sight somewhere.
>
> (ibid.: 41)

What exactly is it that Marlow is so critical of here? A look at a related scene makes it clearer:

> I could see every rib, the joints of their limbs were like knots in a rope;

each had an iron collar on his neck, and all were connected together
with a chain whose bights swung between them, rhythmically clinking.
Another report from the cliff made me think suddenly of that ship of
war I had seen firing into a continent. It was the same kind of ominous
voice; but these men could by no stretch of imagination be called ene-
mies. They were called criminals, and the outraged law, like the
bursting shells, had come to them, an insoluble mystery from the sea . . .
Behind this raw matter one of the reclaimed, the product of the new
forces at work, strolled despondently, carrying a rifle by its middle. He
had a uniform jacket with one button off, and seeing a white man on the
path, hoisted his weapon to his shoulder with alacrity. This was simple
prudence, white men being so much alike at a distance that he could not
tell who I might be. He was speedily reassured, and with a large, white,
rascally grin, and a glance at his charge, seemed to take me into partnership in his exalted trust. After all, I also was a part of the great cause of
these high and just proceedings.

(ibid.. 43)

The explosion he hears is an 'ominous voice', and reminds him of
the crazy shelling of the coastline by the warship. What is this
voice, what does it 'speak' about? It is the discourse of Empire, 'an
insoluble mystery from the sea': the discourse of aggression and
exploitation, of the brute force of technological superiority. Since
we have heard Marlow mimicking the religious discourse of capital
previously, we already know how he feels about the attitude of
missionary piety taken up by the Company. So we are able to read
Marlow's account of his encounter with the guard, 'one of the
reclaimed' and a partner in 'the great cause', as heavily ironic.

In another scene, we are given a verbal glimpse of the enigmatic
character of Kurtz, through the voices of two corrupt Company
administrators. Listen to their mockery of the missionary idealism
in Kurtz's talk, their ridicule of the official, self-justifying rhetoric of
Empire that he uses. This passage is a good example of the multiple
'layers' of voices Conrad weaves into his novel, so I will quote a
fragment large enough to make it visible. There are four levels of
interaction, if we include i) author and reader; ii) Marlow-as-story-
teller and his listeners on the deck of the *Nellie*; iii) the two
administrators; iv) one of the administrators and Kurtz:

They moved off and whispered, then their voices rose again. 'The
extraordinary series of delays is not my fault. I did my best'. The fat
man sighed. 'Very sad'. 'And the pestiferous absurdity of his talk', continued the other; 'he bothered me enough when he was here. "Each

station should be like a beacon on the road towards better things, a centre for trade of course, but also for humanizing, improving, instructing".
Conceive you – that ass! And he wants to be manager! No, it's – ' Here
he got choked by excessive indigation, and I lifted my head the least bit.
I was surprised to see how near they were – right under me.

(ibid.: 65)

We know that Marlow has a dim view of these administrators.
Because of this, their words are discredited, so we don't know what
to make of their ridicule of Kurtz's words.

Marlow repeatedly criticizes official language of Empire, but not
when it comes from Kurtz later in the narrative. Why? Even the
Company men's hostility seems to have some reverence in it.
Marlow somehow identifies with him, even hero-worships him
(see, for instance, his comments at Kurtz's death, ibid.: 113.) The
white people on the boat are on a 'pilgrimage' to Kurtz. So Marlow,
and the Company men, are supporting what they criticize.

Marlow seems to be somewhat trapped. Is there any counter-discourse at all, any way of opposing the rhetoric of Empire from
outside it? A likely place to look is surely in the voices of those
being exploited. What have they got to say? How, if at all, is the
language of the oppressed and exploited being presented? What
about the voices of black people?

Most of the time African voices are totally absent.

So what kind of description of African communities and individuals do we get? A frequent device is to describe the indigenous
population as an impersonal force, inanimate object, or dumb creature: e.g. a 'thing that couldn't talk' (ibid.: 56). Not very promising.

> We could have fancied ourselves the first of men taking possession of
> an accursed inheritance, to be subdued at the cost of profound anguish
> and of excessive toil. But suddenly, as we struggled round a bend, there
> would be a glimpse of rush walls, of peaked grass-roofs, a burst of yells,
> a whirl of black limbs, a mass of hands clapping, of feet stamping, of
> bodies swaying, of eyes rolling, under the droop of heavy and motion-
> less foliage. The steamer toiled along slowly on the edge of a black and
> incomprehensible frenzy. The prehistoric man was cursing us, praying
> to us, welcoming us – who could tell?
>
> (ibid.: 68)

We have to remind ourselves, with some effort, that these are people singing and dancing, people using language. What we have
here is raging xenophobia.

There is very little African speech at all. The two occurrences, brief as they are, are strongly marked off as 'other' through use of orthographic deviations. The 'Cannibal headman', employed by Marlow for the upriver trip, says *'give 'im to us, we eat 'im'* at one point. Other than that, there is the servant who brings the news of Kurtz's death, represented like this:

> Suddenly the manager's boy put his insolent black head in the doorway and said in a tone of scathing contempt – 'Mistah Kurtz – he dead'.
>
> (ibid.: 112)

Marlow dislikes this African view, shies away from the words of contempt. They have to be opposed, by trying to salvage some moral value in Kurtz (ibid.: 113). Notice the term of reference applied to the servant, presumably an adult, and the description of his manner.

Marlow has no access to discourse other than that of Empire; he cannot think outside the rhetoric of exploitation and oppression he despises. Hence his reteat into cynicism and extreme solipsism. (The above discussion of *Heart of darkness* was inspired by an excellent study by David Murray, 1987.)

'VOICES' IN THE TEXT: A TEXT POPULATION

> Our practical everyday speech is full of the words of other people: we merge our voice completely with some of them, forgetting whose they are; others we take as authoritative, using them to support our own words; still others we people with aspirations of our own which are foreign or hostile to them.
>
> (Mikhail Bakhtin [1927] 1984)

Through intertextuality we can look at the subjectivity of language-users. From an intertextual perspective, a text is a 'textual dialogue'. It consists of a mesh of intersecting 'voices'. In looking at the interaction of texts in the form of face-to-face interaction, we necessarily attend to the interaction of speakers: literal voices here, with no need for scare quotes. Here, looking at text-intersection *is* looking at speaker-interaction, since identification of functional relations between speakers' texts requires knowledge of what the speakers are doing and who they are. That is, we need to know what speech roles are assigned to speakers in exchanges.

Intertextuality presents us with a far more complex textual dialogue than this, however, containing other 'voices' less immediate than those heard in speech itself. In written or spoken discourse, the addressee does not interpret a simple linear sequence of text produced by a single addresser. The text she encounters is a complex of 'living voices': an intertextuality. The speaker or assumed writer is just one of these 'voices'. Some of these 'voices' will be foregrounded and attributed to a real or imaginary character, others will not. For every prior text there is a presumed originator of it as an utterance: some 'speaking' character who is set up as its producer, whether or not this is made explicit. When the writer is representing the purported words of another, she may distance herself from the character. She may interfere with this 'voice' to various degrees, in terms of faithfulness to the 'original' and her alignment to it as a reporter; that is, whether she goes along with the words represented or criticizes them. As the connection to an antecedent text becomes more attenuated, as in presupposition, the words of that prior text become less easily attributable to a producer: a real or imaginary person.

A third kind of 'voice' relates to the discourse-type sense of intertextuality. A speaking subject is a 'function' of an utterance; that is, the utterance sets up subject positions. Subject positions and relations between them are set up by the diverse conventions drawn into discourse. A single individual is placed in a wide range of subject positions. She is not an autonomous entity who exists independently of these positions and social relations; she is constituted in the act of working within various discourse types, in enacting conventional kinds of activity, taking up topics. For example, in interaction people take up subject positions specific to discourse-type, 'ventriloquizing' for them. The subject positions available provide conventional 'voices' for people to use. In taking up a subject position at a particular point in discourse, a person speaks in a conventional 'voice': one may speak as a parent, as a judge, teacher, drawing upon fashions of discourse associated with family interactions, the classroom, the courts.

Any text is necessarily a tissue of voices, containing an indeterminate 'population'. It is not the product of a single author; the author herself is multiple, fragmented, and part of the 'population' of a text. It is likely to contain 'external' prior texts, but these are unlikely to be attributable to a specific, clearly defined set of characters. In summary, these 'voices' relate to the three forms of intertextuality as follows:

Interaction	–	Interactants
Prior text	–	Characters
Discourse-type	–	Subject positions

Intertextuality and 'text population'

The concept of intertextuality provides a view of the language user's relation to text in which she is multiply positioned as a social subject. A text is the product of the social activity of discourse. It provides textual cues as resources for the reader, who interprets them by drawing on other resources in interaction and the social context in which the interaction takes place. Through these resources, the act of reading places the reader in relation to the text, the text's producers and the social world. Among them are prior texts and discourse conventions. The current text is itself a resource, in providing textual cues, through which text and convention can be drawn in. In this way, reading places subjects in a 'textual dialogue'. Readers are positioned as subjects through intertextuality. With intertextuality, then, we can view the complex of intersecting 'voices' that a reader is caught up in when she reads a particular text; or to put it another way, we can look at who she has to associate with to read the text at all.

EXAMINING A TEXT POPULATION: FEATURES TO FOCUS ON

Interactants

By attending to the various speech functions in exchanges, we can assign speech roles to interactants. I gave four basic kinds above: statements, questions, offers, commands. Sometimes it may be appropriate to consider their expressive value: e.g. we may want to identify utterances as criticisms, apologies. A writer may use adjacency pairs in her representations of interaction between characters in her text. She may use response-demanding utterances in direct address to the reader, foregrounding the writer–reader relationship and setting up the expectation of reader response. Still attending to the foregrounding of writer–reader interaction, recall what we saw in chapter 2 about the construction of implied readers and synthetic personalization. The use of the pronouns *you* and *we* and modal elements is something else to look out for.

In attending to to the *Interactants* element of a text population, it can be useful to distinguish between interaction between producer and audience and representations of dialogue between characters within the narrative. Some types of fiction draw attention to the interaction of producer and audience; others studiously avoid it.

Characters

Prior text intertextuality provides a range of interesting ways of examining a text as a mesh of intersecting 'voices'. From explicit quotation to the construction of taken-for-granted ideas as presuppositions, a writer can place supposed earlier texts into the text she is producing. By looking for these we can examine all kinds of things, such as the writer's attitude towards 'voices' other than her own or her postulation of a reader with specific desires or prejudices. Here are some focusing points. The words of characters may be quoted or reported, marked off by speech marks and/or cued by a verbal or mental process verb (e.g. *saying, asking; thinking, wishing*). As well as cueing a character's words, reporting verbs may tell us something about the implied viewpoint of the reporter. For instance, if she uses the verb *claim*, she is clearly not associating herself with what she reports, but putting herself at a distance from it (e.g. 'some people claim to have seen ghosts'). The attitude she takes up is part of her identity.

Reportage conjures up characters out of nothing. The characters, whether they are imaginary or real, are the writer's creations. She may present their likes and dislikes in a very straightforward way; it is worth looking out for mental process verbs such as *like, prefer* and similar terms that indicate choice or preference. Less explicitly, certain kinds of noun may introduce prior texts: the words or thoughts of characters which may not be so noticeable. Verbal and mental process nouns (e.g. *assertion, decree; feeling, desire*) may cue traces of character's words or thoughts, as in 'the feeling was that holders of sterling were about to sell'. This kind of construction, where prior texts are embedded as postmodifiers of verbal or mental process nouns, can be highly mystificatory. It tends to de-personalize, presenting the viewpoint of one set of people as if it were universally held. Even more extreme are 'fact' nouns (e.g. the *fact* that . . ., the *superstition* that . . .). The interesting thing about 'fact' nouns is that when the prior texts that they put into texts are uncontentious ones, they tend to pass unnoticed. For example, the magazine article we looked at in Chapter 1 contains the following: 'the way *fashions have changed over the years'*.

Another point of focus for attending to prior text intertextuality is presupposition. Projections, the quoted and reported texts considered above, are meta-linguistic (with the 'borderline' case of fact projection).[1] At their most explicit they foreground the external texts as utterances in projected clauses. By contrast, external texts that are set up as presupposed tend to be backgrounded ideas and may only be detectable when they are encountered by the 'wrong' subject. For example, 'When you're trying your hardest to impress that hunk in the sixth form . . .' (*Jackie* 20 September 1986) sounds positively ridiculous! Presuppositions are a way of setting up shared assumptions and experiences as common ground. This common ground is deniable/contestable, but since it is presented as given it tends to pass unnoticed. The presupposed idea that *there are times when you are trying to impress that hunk in the sixth form* is presented as uncontentious and attributed to the targeted audience of 12- to 14-year-old schoolgirls. But it jumps out at a reader outside the targeted audience.

It is not, though, as it may seem at first glance, just that the presupposed idea is false. Presuppositions provide an interesting point of focus for identifying what is taken as given in discourse. The example below is from a photo-romance published in *Jackie* (I look at the story in Chapter 4). It is about a girl who argues with boyfriends. She worries about it, and a boy addresses her with the following:

I think your problem is you haven't met the right boy before.

This mental projection contains three presupposed ideas: two existential presuppositions ('you have a problem', 'there is a right boy') and a temporal contrastive ('you've met the right boy now'). Fairclough observes that the use of presupposition provides producers of mass media discourse with an 'effective means of manipulating audiences through attributing to their experience things which they want to get them to accept' (Fairclough 1989: 158). In advertising, one way of promoting a commodity is to establish the need for it by placing this need in intertextual context, as in the following advertisement for hair remover:

Are you doing enough for your underarms?

The producers are attributing the presupposed idea that *you are/-should be doing something for your underarms* to potential consumers.

Presuppositions can be placed in intertextual context by being contested in the negation of positive assertions, as in the following extract from another teenagers' magazine, *Blue Jeans* (24 April 1986):

> No amount of make-up and hair stuff will turn you into a glamorous chick if your gnashers aren't in good condition. It's nothing to be proud of if you haven't been to the dentist for the past five years – you're only asking for trouble . . . your dentist isn't there to give you nightmares and inflict unnecessary pain on you.

Fairclough asks what the motivation is for making all these negative assertions (since the same points could have been made positively) and observes:

> The writer is evidently using negatives as a way of implicitly taking issue with the corresponding positive assertions . . . But that would be a rather peculiar thing to do unless their assertion were somehow connected with this discourse. What the writer in fact seems to be assuming is that these assertions are to be found in antecedent texts which are within readers' experience.
>
> (Fairclough 1989: 154–5)

A similar point is made by Torben Vestergaard and Kim Schrøder (1985: 26–7) concerning negative claims made about products in advertising texts; for example, the claim that a moisturizing cream is 'not greasy or sticky'.

Presuppositions are cued by a wide variety of textual features and I will not attempt to cover them exhaustively. Here are some common ones. The definite article in *the right boy* cues the existential presupposition 'there is a right boy'. 'You have a problem' is more accurately described as an 'attributive' presupposition, as I have represented it in an attributive relational clause. The possessive article *your* cues a presupposed attribute. A 'temporal contrastive' presupposition is cued by *before*. The presupposed idea in the 'hunk' example is in a subordinate temporal clause marked by *when*. Various adverbials cue presuppositions which might be called entailments: *not often, always, all the time, enough* (e.g. *not often* 'presupposes' *sometimes*).

Subject positions

In producing discourse, an addresser always speaks from a social position; she necessarily establishes a social identity for herself and at the same time some relationship with her addressee. As I said in Chapter 2, interaction through mass media texts is asymmetrical and puts producers in the powerful position of setting up addresser and addressee. The kind of feature to look at for attention to the heterogeneity sense of intertextuality and the diverse subject positions consigned to the reader depends very much on the text under investigation. I will simply suggest the kinds of conventional element that might be worth attention. To say anything at all about the subject position element of a text population we need to consider the institutional and societal context of its production and interpretation. (The reader may like to refer to Fairclough, 1989; for example, his account of how a discourse type in a specific situation is governed by institutional and societal structures.) For the sample analysis below, I read Suzanne Graver's (1984) sociologically grounded work on George Eliot's writings as background. There may be all kinds of clues to the various conventions of genre and discourse-type drawn upon by an author: character and situation types, topics and purposes, frames and scripts, classificatory schemes, grammar and vocabulary choices may be typical of particular kinds of discourse. Significant clues may be in the contents of presupposed ideas placed in the reader's head.

Example 2: an extract from Eliot's *Middlemarch*

The rest of this chapter looks at another extract in detail. I have chosen this extract from *Middlemarch* principally on the strength of what Roger Fowler (1981: 88–91) says about it, but also because I have enjoyed the book for its feminist theme and the frequent wry remarks in it about what we would now call sexist assumptions.[6] He uses the extract below to illustrate his discussion of literature as discourse and applauds George Eliot's choice of foregrounded authorship. The prominence of the author and objectivity in narrative were already under critical debate in reviews when Eliot was writing. Fowler refers to this as a 'crisis' in the development of European prose fiction, which she was aware of. In Fowler's words,

I quote George Eliot to illustrate the explicit signals of modality, of narrative discourse, in an author who was aware of the crisis and chose not to erase her own and her reader's voices but to dramatise them in full dialogic intercourse . . . the effect is magnificent.

(Fowler 1981: 90)

But the text of *Middlemarch* is only part of the discourses in which it was written and read; and it is always read in specific times and places. Now a revered text that belongs in 'The Literary Canon' (and studied in courses on English Literature as an example of, for instance, 'all Victorian literature being a response to industrialization') *Middlemarch* was enormously popular with the reading public including reviewers right from the start. It first appeared in 1871–2, in serial form, and in a revised version in one volume in 1878. Reviewers praised her for her sense of 'community' and her 'compassion' and claimed to enjoy the way she articulated their thoughts for them. One reviewer, acknowledging the educational purpose that Eliot herself[7] professed for her literary discourse, referred to her as 'our Great Teacher'.

The prevailing social conditions at time of writing were, put in the broadest terms, those of Victorian capitalism and patriarchy. Now, readers of fiction are only held by pleasure, so that representing and criticizing patriarchal social constraints on women, as she did in *Middlemarch* and elsewhere, placed her in something of a predicament. For if people are constituted in patriarchal social order, and even in privileged social positions and actually benefiting from social practices oppressing women, how do you stimulate critical awareness or even hold them as readers at all? In fact, some reviewers did report having suspicions that she manipulated her readers; for instance, one writer in the *Saturday Review* accuses her of using her 'gifts . . . to betray him [the reader] into unconscious, and perhaps unwilling, admissions' (quoted in Graver 1984: 272). In the extract, interaction between writer and reader is set up explicitly in the text (placed in italics below). The reader is constructed as a character. Reading the extract places us in specific reader positions, which I shall go on to examine. First, the extract:

(1) *Was he not making a fool of himself?* (2) *– and at a time when he was more than ever conscious of being something better than a fool?* (3) *And for what end?*
(4) *Well, for no definite end.* (5) *True,* he had dreamy visions of possibilities: (6) there is no human being who having both passions and thoughts does not find images rising in his mind which soothe the passion with hope or sting it with dread. (7) But this, which happens to *us*

all, happens to some with a wide difference; (8) and Will was not one of those whose wit 'keeps the roadway': (9) he had his bypaths where there were little joys of his own choosing, such as gentlemen cantering on the highroad might have thought rather idiotic. (10) The way in which he made a sort of happiness for himself out of his feeling for Dorothea was an example of this. (11) It may seem strange, but it is the fact, that the ordinary vulgar vision of which Mr. Casaubon suspected him – namely, that Dorothea might become a widow, and that the inter-est he had established in her might turn into acceptance of him as a husband – had no tempting, arresting power over him; (12) he did not live in the scenery of such an event, and follow it out, as *we all* do with that imagined 'otherwise' which is our practical heaven. (13) It was not only that he was unwilling to entertain thoughts which could be accused of baseness, and was already uneasy in the sense that he had to justify himself from the charge of ingratitude – the latent consciousness of many other barriers between himself and Dorothea besides the exis-tence of her husband, had helped to turn away his imagination from speculating on what might befall Mr. Casaubon. (14) And there were yet other reasons. (15) Will, we know, could not bear the thought of any flaw appearing in his crystal: (16) he was at once exasperated and delighted by the calm freedom with which Dorothea looked at him and spoke to him, and there was something so exquisite in thinking of her just as she was, that he could not long for a change which must some-how change her. (17) *Do we not shun the street version of a fine melody? – or shrink from the news that the rarity – some bit of chiselling or engraving per-haps – which we have dwelt on even with exultation in the trouble it has cost us to snatch glimpses of it, is really not an uncommon thing, and may be obtained as an everyday possession?* (18) Our good depends on the quality and breadth of our emotion; (19) and to Will, a creature who cared little for what are called the solid things of life and greatly for its subtler influences, to have within him such a feeling as he had towards Dorothea, was like the inheritance of a fortune.

(Eliot [1871–2] 1979: 509–10)

Fowler points out the questions at the beginning of the extract (1 to 3), saying that the 'authorial persona' addresses these both i) to the reader and ii) to Will in interrogation, with the reader doing 'jury service'. He also points out that the sentence (4) following is an answer. Questions and answers are speech functions we assign to utterances. The point of perhaps labouring the obvious in this way is that actual readers are being set up as though they were tak-ing part in some kind of two-way discourse with the author. I think the simulation continues into the next sentence (5), on the strength of the connective value we need to assign to the first word in it

('True'). The writer seems to be acknowledging something an inter-locutor has just said. The two responses lead me to see the questions before them as the *reader's* supposed questions. I am not intending to rule out Fowler's identification of the passage as an interrogation of Will, but to add a supplement to it: readers may be in the position of jurors doing jury service, but they are also in the dock, as I intend to show. (A better metaphor might be the confes-sional: a genre relating to confessional discourses.) We have just been given an account of Will's close friendship with Dorothea, a married woman. Eliot, who assesses protagonists' conduct and motives throughout the novel, is voicing what she expects the read-er herself to be thinking (and wanting to ask) at this point:

Question :	Was he not making a fool of himself? [I hear you ask] – and at a time when he was more than ever conscious of being something better than a fool? And for what end?
Answer:	Well, for no definite end.
Statement:	[*Oh come on. You've told me how much they were enjoying one another's company and that she was sure to outlive her husband – he must have been aware of the possibilities . . .*]
Response:	True, he had dreamy visions of possibilities . . .

The reader appears to be in the text, along with the writer. This impression is borne out by looking at other textual features relating to interaction of writer and reader: pronouns. There are four uses of an inclusive *we/us*, two of them modified with 'all', and there are three related possessive articles. These contribute to the writer's attribution of certain beliefs or assumptions to 'you and me' or 'everybody': a shared subject position of 'common humanity'. She sets herself and the reader up as like-minded people. Some of the beliefs/assumptions themselves are placed in reports. Before turn-ing to these reports, however, here are two other points in the narrative where the writer–reader interaction is foregrounded. In (17), note the modal elements as the writer presses the reader for agreement:

> (17) Do *we* not shun the street version of a fine melody? – or shrink from the news that the rarity – some bit of chiselling or engraving *perhaps* – which *we* have dwelt on even with exultation in the trouble it has cost *us* to snatch glimpses of it, is *really* not an uncommon thing, and may be obtained as an everyday possession?

The other, in (11), precedes a foregrounded fact projection in which the writer is giving information not already known to the reader.

Here is the only other example of a modal element attached to the writer's illocution. (Most of the others attach to Will's thoughts.) I can almost hear her insert direct address (so I've put it in for her!):

> (11) It *may* seem strange, [*dear reader*], but it is the fact, the ordinary vulgar vision of which Mr. Casaubon suspected him – namely, that Dorothea might become a widow, and that the interest he had established in her might turn into acceptance of him as a husband – had no tempting, arresting power over him.
>
> (Eliot [1871–2] 1979: 509–10)

The modal verb ('may') in a pre-sequence to the fact projection makes the writer-reader interaction prominent again; the writer is preempting the reader's disbelief.

The reader's presence as an interactant goes further than this. She has an identity of sorts. By looking for some of the prior texts, we can identify a reader made responsible for certain things which are placed in 'intertextual' context. For instance, this reader is given a share of the writer's knowledge of Will's thought processes, cued by projection structure in (15), in a report of what 'we know'. (The report could extend to the rest of the lengthy sentence as well.):

> (15) Will, *we know*, could not bear the thought of any flaw appearing in his crystal . . .

There are all kinds of things we learn about Will's mental activity. We have been given a share of the writer's knowledge of him (see above, p. 68) and he is the subject attached to many of the modal and expressive elements in the passage. There are few verbal or mental process verbs cueing prior texts attributable to Will, but there are a great many nouns relating to his mental state and mental activity such as 'choosing' (9), 'thoughts', 'consciousness', 'imagination' (13), 'feeling' (19). These tend to appear in the experiential meaning of the grammar as a Possessed Attribute, like the generic human being's 'passions and thoughts' in (6). I see these as textual cues to a discourse of psychology. In the act of drawing upon this discourse type the reader is being positioned as an analyst of Will's thoughts/emotions. Presupposition triggers are grammatical cues to backgrounded prior texts placed in the reader's head. In the extract, frequent cues to this backgrounded kind of prior text are definite descriptions. Least obviously report-like, the existential presuppositions they set up sound like statements of fact. The following are definite descriptions cueing existential presupposition of something shared by us (writer and reader):

(12) our practical heaven
(18) our good
(18) our emotion

Apart from these, there are still other definite descriptions whose presuppositions are set up as fact and appear to be the reader's. These tell us more about the background knowledge the reader is expected to have. Some of this knowledge is about the story so far:

(11) the interest he had established in her
(13) the existence of her husband

At the point of reading the extract these are already givens, established in the text prior to it and part of its interactional history. Here the knowledge presented to the reader as already given, by means of presupposition, was indeed introduced to the reader earlier in the narrative. Most of the definite descriptions, however, cue presupposed cultural and psychological knowledge. The following are candidates, only those in (17) are explicitly connected to both writer and reader (with a pronoun):

(11) the ordinary vulgar vision
(13) the latent consciousness
(15) the thought of any flaw appearing in his crystal
(17) the street version of a fine melody
(17) the rarity – some bit of chiselling or engraving perhaps – which we have dwelt on
(17) the trouble it has cost us to snatch glimpses of it
(19) the solid things of life
(19) its subtler influences
(19) the inheritance of a fortune.

At the top of the list above is a definite description which cues a presupposition that 'there is an ordinary vulgar vision'. This is subsequently attributed to Casaubon, and detailed in a formulation (cued by 'namely'). But, as I have suggested, the reader has already pointed out these 'possibilities' and is therefore already implicated in the presupposed 'vulgar vision'. This suspicion of Casaubon's 'that Dorothea might become a widow, and that the interest he [Will] had established in her might turn into acceptance of him as a husband' has direct bearing on the plot. It leads Casaubon to put a codicil in his will, impoverishing Dorothea should she marry Will after his death. The reader has been caught out, caught in possession of the 'vulgar vision' shared by the gossiping community and Casaubon. In other words, in a subject position in patriarchal social order. In the next to the last paragraph of the novel, 'we' are explicitly held responsible for the oppression of all those like her:

> we insignificant people with our daily words and acts are preparing the lives of many Dorotheas, some of which may present a far sadder sacrifice than that of the Dorothea whose story we know.

(ibid.: 896)

Looking at the *Middlemarch* extract, we can look at characters other than producer–interpreter set up. There are a great many other fictional interactions in the passage, some of which are quite deeply 'embedded' in Eliot's narrative and not readily apparent. There are nevertheless there. For example, there is an imagined dialogue between Will and 'everybody' cued by verbal processes ('accused', 'justify' (13)) and a verbal process noun ('charge'). Gossip serves a social function. In the novel, it precedes characters, giving them texture/depth as social beings so that they exist in a social as well as a personal universe. It is very important in the novel and affects the action (Will feels constrained to leave the locality).

There are a number of characters whose words or thoughts are less conspicuous but nevertheless still present: what 'Gentlemen cantering on the highroad might have thought' (9) about Will, Mr Casaubon's suspicions (11) and the gossip that 'Everybody' indulges in (13). From Dorothea we have the report of an utterance only (16), with no indication of what she said. The nearest we get to Dorothea in this extract is an intimation of her 'calm freedom' of manner from Will's viewpoint when she speaks to him. I wonder what she says.

TAKING IT FURTHER

The sample analysis above may have called to mind other writing with similar foregrounding of author and reader. The features I suggested under *Interactants* in this chapter can be used to examine such foregrounding closely. The features entered under *Character* can be used to examine other aspects. For instance, does the writer claim to have access to characters' thoughts? Which ones, and what effect does this have? Another thing to try is locating presuppositions. Why are they placed in the background rather than being asserted? Which presuppositions are carried forward from earlier in the story? Which are smuggled in as common knowledge? On the basis of them, who does the writer think you are?

An insightful application of intertextuality which is a little different from the one in this chapter, but related to it, is in Fairclough (1992). His application contains a twofold distinction between manifest (easy to perceive) and constitutive (in the background) intertextuality.

Part II

Fiction and social reproduction

FOUR

Escaping into romance

Romance is a women's genre. Romance is a kind of content – repro-
ductions of dominant representations of femininity, of masculinity,
and of relations between women and men – found especially in
soap operas, in films, and in magazine and pulp fiction. Neither of
these generalizations is very satisfactory because, as is the way with
generalizations, neither is entirely true.

What do we mean by romance? It is not always produced and
consumed exclusively by women; Samuel Richardson's *Pamela*
(1740), which I touched on briefly in Chapter 1, must surely be a
member of the romance category (a 'classic' even, recalling Walter
Nash's cline of quality that I referred to in Chapter 2, with
'popfiction' at one end and 'classics' at the other). And yet there is a
romance marketing genre targeted specifically at women readers
and written exclusively by women; or at least, presented as such,
being published under women's names. In fact, there is a whole
range of types of romance, which we should perhaps view as sub-
genres: the so-called 'bodice-ripper' novels to name just one. Mills
& Boon alone have three major categories: Romance, Silhouette
Sensation and Medical Romance. Other categories include
Masquerade Historical (the 'Regency Romance' label) and Euro-
romance (a recent addition especially for the Year of European
Unity).

Why look at romance? It is apparently important for women;
Mills & Boon are part of a conglomerate of the biggest publishers of
romance fiction, which currently sells about 250 million copies a
year worldwide. (This does of course assume that sales figures are
reliable as an indication of popularity, rather than of intensiveness
of marketing strategies: advertising, direct sales.) Given this apparent importance, as feminists we must ask why. The answer to this
question, I will argue in this chapter, is that romance fiction offers

women participation in ultimately successful heterosexuality, in the service of upward social mobility, and a kind of triumph for femininity – and all without any transgression of society's expectations concerning gender identity. To put it simply, women can achieve what they want through their 'natural' (i.e. naturalized) femininity, not by subverting it.

Using romance fiction as an example, in this chapter I will examine the socially reproductive potential of fiction, including an exploration of the function of fictions as 'escapism'. I will refer to two extensive ethnographies on romance readers. One of these, carried out in the United States by Janice Radway (and published as *Reading the romance* 1987), was my source for the notion of romance as 'escapism'. The other is some unpublished British research (Owen 1990). After examining a Mills & Boon romance in some detail, I will give some attention to examples of a contrasting sub-genre of romance fiction: the 'photo-romance' produced for teenagers. In conclusion, I will consider the impact of feminism on the genre, examining the way feminism within romance is articulated in a discourse of bourgeois individualism.

'WOULD YOU REALLY MARRY ME AND LIVE IN YORKSHIRE?': MILLS & BOON'S STORIES OF GENDER AND CLASS

According to Radway's principal informant, romance reading is 'good therapy and much cheaper than tranquillizers, alcohol or addictive TV serials' ('Dot', quoted in Radway 1987: 52). Radway's informants were women living in Smithton, Ohio; all customers at a particular bookshop there, with the exception of her principal informant, Dorothy Evans, whose customers they were and through whom she contacted them. Radway knew of Evans as a non-academic specialist in romance fiction through Evans' review newsletter for bookshops and editors. She collected her information by a combination of questionnaires and long series of group discussion sessions. Their reading included the Harlequin romance, Harlequin being the equivalent of Mills & Boon in Canada and the United States (the two publishing companies merged in 1970).

Owen's sample of informants was a much larger and more representative sample of romance readership, not restricted as Radway's was to self-selecting informants, all of whom turned out to be full-time housewives. Owen contacted them initially through the public libraries in the Metropolitan Borough of Wirral, Cheshire. From well over a hundred completed survey questionnaires, she found that her informants were from a range of backgrounds and occupations; for instance, 13 per cent were students and 23 per cent retired. Only 13 per cent were full-time housewives. She followed up her initial quantitative research with in-depth interviews with individual readers (and, incidentally, she also interviewed librarians, writers and editors).

Radway discovered that her informants valued the act of romance reading itself as a means of 'escape' from their duties as housewives and mothers. Romances are used as a self-indulgence giving them time-out from family demands. This function of romance reading is quite simply a strategy for avoiding being constantly 'on call' to attend to the needs and wishes of husband and children. Reading is a solitary activity, and the reader is not available to other people. She is effectively not there, to the consternation of husbands, according to several informants. As Radway sees it,

> the men's resentment has little to do with the kinds of books their wives are reading and more to do with the simple fact of the activity itself and its capacity to absorb the participants' entire attention.
>
> (Radway 1987: 91)

For the Smithton women, held solely responsible for domestic reproduction – nurturers of their families' bodies and general well-being – reading acts as a barrier behind which they can retreat and recuperate. Of course, romance readers also value the genre. They are not simply hiding behind books, but actively deriving pleasure from reading stories. Radway's informants believe romance fiction offers them comfort and reassurance, that it helps them to relieve tension and to relax. This view of the function of romance as 'escape' may well have been strongly influenced by the Harlequin advertising campaign around the time of the discussions, or shortly before:

> the books that let you escape into the wonderful world of romance! Trips to exotic places ... interesting places ... meeting memorable people ... the excitement of love ... These are integral parts of Harlequin Romances – the heartwarming novels read by women everywhere.
>
> (ibid.: 89)

Radway also reports the Smithton readers' claim that romance is not 'just' for escaping from family demands and for relaxation, but also teaches them things. They maintain romance reading has an information-giving function for them: so they are not 'just' enjoying themselves, but reading to learn. The novels are very often set in locations which are from the readers' social position exotic and sometimes also historically distant. Having been rigorously researched by their authors, the readers say, these novels have educational value. Radway interprets this 'reading for instruction' explanation as a justification for repetitive romance consumption. She sees it as something the women say to convince skeptical husbands, and interviewers, that the novels are not 'frothy, purposeless entertainment' (ibid.: 107). Judging by the accounts of Owen's librarian informants, British romance borrowers also feel the need to justify their choice of reading material in one way or another. 'Excuses' reported by librarians included the need for relaxation in order to sleep at night and the ease of carrying home large numbers of (literally) lightweight books, even though, as Owen wryly comments, the total probably outweighs *War and peace*! (Owen 1990: 78).

What is notably absent in Radway's account is any mention of the readers deriving erotic pleasure from romances. As Owen remarks, such pleasure surely accounts, at least in part, for the husbands' hostility and contempt for romances (Owen 1990: 245–6). In Owen's interviews, pleasure in the erotic element was often openly acknowledged. One teenage reader, for example, told Owen about the stresses and strains of reading erotic scenes when sitting in the same room as her father and brothers. The librarians had anecdotes on the topic, as Owen relates:

> Several librarians were amused by old ladies enjoying 'sexy' books.
> Miss Cribbins told the story of one old lady in her eighties who had brought back a 'raunchy' book and told the librarian about it.
> Concerned in case the book had offended the borrower, Miss Cribbins asked about this, but the old lady replied that on the contrary she had enjoyed it as 'it's the only way she's going to get it at her age'!
>
> (ibid.: 78)

The Smithton readers have very definite ideas about what makes a good romance. A look at these will help us to consider how fiction can function as 'escapism', so-called, which comforts, reassures and relaxes its readers. A good romance depicts a slowly developing loving relationship between a woman and a man. The conclusion must be a happy one; marriage, or the prospect of it, being the most likely. The happy ending is something the Smithton readers are adamant about. For them it is the defining characteristic of a romance, good or bad. A novel without this essential ingredient may be a love story, but it is not a romance. For a romance to be good, in addition to the obligatory happy conclusion it must also have other qualities. The happy ending must be plausible and must be the culmination of displays of the hero's tender regard for the heroine, demonstrations of his deep, sincere appreciation and respect. Not only that, this developing perfect relationship must be presented in such a way that the reader can vicariously experience the sensation of being loved so deeply and cared for so tenderly. The Smithton women's definition of romance fits very closely the guidelines produced for aspiring writers by Mills & Boon:

> from the heroine's point of view but in the third person. . . An upbeat tone and a happy ending are essential but the story must be presented in a believable way . . . the magic of falling in love . . .
>
> (Mills & Boon (cassette) 1986)

This should come as no surprise. It simply demonstrates the degree of consensus about romance as a genre and shows the dialectical relationship between producers and consumers. The women who read romances are actively involved in determining the genre since the publishers must be responsive to them. Their participation is shaped by what the publishers have to offer.

Radway argues that romance fiction provides a kind of emotional gratification, the pleasure of being the object of another's undivided attention, for a group of women whose lives rarely offer them that luxury. These women are expected to physically and emotionally 'reproduce' their families, but there is no one charged with the responsibility of doing the same for them. So they 'reproduce' themselves, through romance fiction. Romances, their readers claim, give them the opportunity for 'a good cry' (this noun phrase is mine, not theirs, but seems to provide the gist of their discussion presented by Radway 1987: 95). As Radway observes:

> Romance fiction, as they experience it, is . . . compensatory literature. It supplies them with an important emotional release that is proscribed in daily life because the social role with which they identify themselves leaves little room for guiltless, self-interested pursuit of individual pleasure.
>
> (ibid.: 95–6)

The escape provided by romance fiction is offered by the representation of a focalizing female character who is the object of another's unwavering interest and overwhelming desire. A number of critics, Radway among them, have remarked on the 'regressiveness' of the desire for such attention: to be loved unconditionally and absolutely, like an infant. Amal Treacher expresses this desire succinctly in an article on Mills & Boon:

> Mills & Boon reverberate to the unconscious phantasies, which do not disappear even in adult life, of the adult combined parent believed in in earlier years. The wish for the total love of the mother and father becomes the longing for that total love to be located within one's partner in adult life.
>
> (Treacher 1988: 80)

Radway refers to Nancy Chodorow's feminist appropriation of Freud's theory of an infant's development of selfhood to explore the mother–daughter relationship. With Chodorow's work as theoretical underpinning, she speculates that her informants find in their favourite romances both regressive fantasies of being nurtured as an infant and fantasy workings-through of the achievement of female maturity, a maturity which does not bring autonomy but the feminine self-in-relation:

> The romance does deny the worth of complete autonomy. In doing so, however, it is not obliterating the female self completely. Rather, it is constructing a particular kind of female self, the self-in-relation demanded by patriarchal parenting arrangements.
>
> (Radway 1987: 147)

The marketing category genre of romance, then, provides an emotional outlet for readers in its targeted audience. The kernel of these romances – the achievement of a fulfilling loving relationship – is irreproachable. The obstacles to their comfortably inevitable conclusions are recognizably real and serious: miscommunication, bad faith, mistrust that is believed to be well-founded, misunderstandings of all sorts. The problems with this genre, for me at least, lie with the relatively circumstantial details: what the heroine finds attractive in the hero, how they interact (especially how the hero's overwhelming desire is expressed), what they have to look forward to, who they think they are better than. Based on my own reading of British-produced Mills & Boon titles, I sketch out the character and situation types in them below. I will draw my main illustrative examples from a recent publication (Kate Walker, *No gentleman,*

August 1992), not because it provides extreme or even typical examples – it doesn't – but because it is recent and, not least, because I enjoyed it more than some of the earlier titles I have read.

Characters and situations

Starting with the male protagonist: he is invariably tall, lean, white, and ruggedly handsome with an animal magnetism which is quite extraordinary. He turns heads wherever he goes. Always a powerful person, he is generally someone who is used to being obeyed; a bully, in fact, both professionally and personally. And, perhaps it goes without saying, he is always affluent, whether a successful architect or artist or a fully-fledged capitalist. Whatever he is, he is the best, and he knows it. Mills & Boon specify that he should be 'tall, handsome and powerful', since 'no one dreams of marrying a wimp'. They do not spell it out that he should be the epitome of the patriarchal male, but that seems to be what he amounts to. As Jon Cook puts it in 'Fictional fathers', Mills & Boon heroes embody paternal power:

> All the familiar ingredients are there: the threat of violence, the law-giving nature, the ownership of the world, a power vested in physical presence.
>
> (Cook 1988: 154)

Below is an extract from *No gentleman* containing one of many detailed descriptions of the hero. A costume ball has made possible the playfulness of a detailed visual allusion to the Regency Romance character of Darcy, verbally explicit a little later:

> She . . . drew in a sharp breath as for the first time she took in the full effect of his appearance.
>
> The epitome of the Regency dandy stood before her in a rich blue cut-away coat, white shirt and crimson waistcoat, tight-fitting breeches and highly polished riding boots, a fine cravat falling from his throat like the foam that bubbled in the fountain.
>
> Anna found that she was disturbingly aware of the way the elegant coat fitted snugly around straight, square shoulders, the way its jacket was cut short at the front, falling into tails behind, revealing a slim waistline and narrow hips around which the skin-tight breeches clung in a way that even the most close-fitting denims never could. The silk shirt and elaborate cravat, which could have looked effeminate on another man, somehow had the effect of heightening the powerful masculinity of Cassidy's rough-hewn features, making them appear darker

and more forcefully male in contrast to their delicacy. It was as if the
rake in every Regency romance novel she had ever read had suddenly
stepped off the page to appear, alive and infinitely disturbing, before
her. And, like some swooning heroine of the same novels, she felt an
almost uncontrollable urge to open her fan and wave it in front of her
face to hide her blushes and cool her burning cheeks.

(Walker 1992: 28–9)

This passage lists items of clothing, collocated with details concerning colour, fabric, texture and cut, and itemizes the hero's physique
as revealed by this clothing. In doing so, it articulates a fashion discourse, spilling into a discourse of sexuality in which sexual
difference is maximized. The details of 'feminine' clothing contribute to eroticizing the difference between masculine and feminine.
The eroticized contrast is presented as the epitome of the Regency
romance hero. (I will discuss this explicit attention to fictionality a
little later on.)

The principal character, the focalizer of the romance, is a beautiful white woman, who is as the Mills & Boon guidelines say
'young, spirited and inwardly vulnerable' (and, as we saw above, a
reader of Regency romances). These days she is an independent
working woman who may attach great importance to her work and
be highly ambitious, but she is still hoping for upward mobility.
Anna, the blushing heroine above, for example, is an enterprising
businesswoman who has established her own cosmetics business,
but she harbours secret desires for the security of marriage with her
financial backer (ibid.: 16). Another feature of the romance heroine,
very much in evidence in the above extract and in the next one
below, is that she is tormented with (almost) uncontrollable urges
of one kind or another. Her mind and body seem to be perpetually
in conflict; the basic premise seems to be that women suppress their
instincts/true feelings and are thrown into a state of confusion and
consternation by a desirable man's attentions. As the relationship
develops in the romance these confused, unruly emotions are very
often expressed as anger, so that the heroine's anger is always sub-
limated desire. Here is some more of the 'Darcy' scene:

> (1) 'No gentleman,' he murmured, the softness of his tone making
> Anna's breath catch in her throat in surprise. (2) 'Is that what you think
> of me? (3) I'm sure, given half a chance, I could easily prove otherwise.'
>   (4) Then, to Anna's astonishment and complete consternation, he per-
> formed a low, elaborate bow over her hand, pressing his lips to it
> lingeringly.

(5) Her first impulse was to snatch her hand away as quickly as possible. (6) He was just playing with her, she knew that, taking on the role of Mr Darcy that his costume suggested. (7) But at the same time a small, unwary part of her heart in which the sense of magic she had experienced earlier still lingered was touched by the image he presented with that proud, dark head bent over her hand, and the moonlight bathing him in its pale, unearthly gleam. (8) No one had ever bowed to her, or kissed her hand before, and she couldn't help thinking that no other man she knew, certainly not Marc, could perform the old-fashioned gesture of courtesy with the consummate grace and total lack of self-consciousness that Ryan Cassidy displayed. (9) Acting independently of her rational mind, her pulse-rate quickened disturbingly in response to the light pressure of his fingers on hers.

(10) But then Ryan lifted his head and smiled deep into her eyes and Anna's heart lurched suddenly as she saw the gleam of cynical amusement and challenge in their blue depths.

(11) Immediately the spell was broken. (12) She knew that look of old; Cassidy was no longer the romantic Mr Darcy but the man who had treated her so appallingly all those years ago, and she snatched her hand away from his warm grasp as swiftly as if she had been burned.

(13) 'It takes more than a few fancy gestures to make a gentleman, Mr Cassidy!'

(ibid.:32)

Two characteristics of romances that I have mentioned are very much in evidence in this passage: intensive focalization through the heroine and her struggle for self-control. We can pinpoint these characteristics by examining the distribution of process types in the verbs to which the characters, or parts thereof, are the grammatical subject (for details of these process types, see Halliday 1985: 102–29). This distribution is laid out in Table 4.1. In the passage, we are seeing the world from Anna's perspective. This is reflected in the distribution of mental process verbs. If we look at the material process verbs associated with Anna, it turns out they are functioning to represent mental phenomena too. The first one, 'catch', is being used to describe a physical symptom of a mental or emotional condition. In fact, if we go through and examine the verbs which are *not* encoding mental processes, it turns out that they are either being used in description of a symptom of a mental/emotional state or metaphorically to refer to a mental/emotional state. And they are all in response to some action or appearance of Ryan's.

Table 4.1 Distribution of process-types

	Ryan		Anna	
(1)	making	(material)	catch	(material)
(4)	performed	(material)		
	pressing	(material)		
(5)			to snatch	(material)
(6)	was ... playing	(material)	knew	(mental)
	taking on	(material)		
(7)			had experienced	(mental)
			was touched	(material)
	presented	(material)		
(8)			couldn't help thinking	(mental)
			knew	(mental)
	displayed	(material)		
(9)			Acting	(material)
			quickened	(material)
(10)	lifted	(material)		
	smiled	(behavioural)	lurched	(material)
			saw	(mental)
(12)			knew	(mental)
	has treated	(material)	snatched	(material)
			been burned	(material)

Ryan's action/appearance		Anna's emotional response
(1) softness of his tone	causes	symptom
(4) performed ... bow	causes	(5) resisted impulse
(7) image he presented	causes	grammatical metaphor
(9) pressure of fingers	causes	symptom
(10) gleam ... amusement	causes	symptom

Of particular interest is the non-finite clause in (9), 'Acting independently of her rational mind', rather superfluously preceding the information about her increased pulse-rate!

Turning to situation types in romances, in essentials these have changed little since *Pamela*. The forceful male protagonist always poses some kind of threat, so that the trembling female protagonist still lives in fear of a fate-worse-than-death in some form or other in his hands; arguments and struggles, embraces and incriminations are still the substance of the narrative; the promise of happy marriage is still the wished-for conclusion. In *No gentleman* the author uses a popular ploy of placing some unpleasant, initially rather vague, encounter between the protagonists in their past as the source of tension/suspense with which the narrative begins. The title, back cover and first page blurb all emphatically announce the hero's 'caddishness' (evidently far more of 'Heathcliff' than 'Darcy' here). The front and back cover are reproduced in Fig. 4.1. The last few lines on the back cover, 'she was about to make the same mistake of giving in to him all over again!', contain two crucial presuppositions: she gave in to him once and it was a mistake. The dangerous quality of the male protagonist in the first page blurb, reproduced below, is represented in the highly conventional simile of a 'time-bomb'. Notice that we are presented right at the outset with the names of the protagonists and the presence of a misunderstanding (it has to be a misunderstanding: since he is the hero, she must have read him wrong – so why is he a 'time-bomb'?):

Ryan's presence in London was like a time-bomb, ticking away, and the terrifying thing was that she had no idea when it might blow up right in her face.
Anna had no idea what Ryan might want from her; she only knew that she had no alternative but to wait until he let her know the price he demanded for his silence. And when he did, she vowed, if it was humanly possible, she would pay it, no matter what it cost. He had hurt her so terribly once; she couldn't let him destroy her life all over again.

(ibid.: 1)

This male is nothing if not powerful! The misunderstanding, here set in place before the action begins, is crucial, as it is the obstacle to be surmounted for the achievement of the inevitable. The worse the hero appears to be, the greater the relief in finding that he is not dangerous or wicked after all, but simply misunderstood. And, perhaps, the worse he seems the greater the triumph for femininity in 'taming' him.

In addition to the character and situation types sketched above there are other conventions of romance fiction. Some of these have perhaps been implicit in what I have dealt with already. We are always given detailed descriptions of a character's appearance, if the character is of any significance at all. Hair and eye colour seem to be particularly important, but figure and clothing are also given considerable attention. There is a high proportion of speech representation, and most of the narration involves interpersonal relations: thoughts about conversations. The heroine is virtually always the focalizer of the narrative throughout. We are given detailed descriptions of her perception and feelings, which are often out of her control; descriptions of other people are focalized

Figure 4.1 Back and front covers of *No Gentleman* by Kate Walker. Mills & Boon 1992

through her; descriptions of appearance and interaction overlap with those of emotional states in details of gestures and expressions and their mis/interpretation.

The text population in the opening of *No gentleman*

What follows is detail of the opening page and a half of *No gentleman*. I will examine the text population of the passage and show how it realizes the conventions of the genre that I have outlined. The hero and his masculinity are the topic from (1); the turmoil of the heroine's emotions is evident from (6).

(1) 'SO THAT'S what he looks like!'

(2) Sonia held the glossy magazine she had been reading out at arm's length, her head tilted slightly to one side as she considered a full-page black and white photograph, her mouth pursed in a way that expressed thoughtful interest combined with sensual appreciation.

(3)'Well, I never expected that the new golden boy of the art world would be so . . .' She paused, hunting for the right word. 'So rakish! I mean, look at him, Anna –'

(4) Turning the magazine, she thrust it under the nose of the girl sitting beside her on the huge black settee.

(5) 'Isn't he the wild Irish rover personified?'

(6) Anna didn't want to look. She thought she knew exactly what she would see if she did, and she felt as if her mind had closed up, shutting itself off from memories she had no desire to recall.

(7) But Sonia was determined, and there was no avoiding the magazine that was only inches away from her face. Reluctantly, Anna reached for it and made a pretence of studying the photograph, resting the magazine on her knee so that her shoulder-length mane of waving blonde hair fell forward over her face as she looked down at it, hiding the disturbed expression she was unable to suppress.

(8) For several long, taut moments, her eyes wouldn't focus, so that the picture was just a blur, and she was strongly tempted to leave it at that, hand back the magazine with some non-committal murmur, knowing she would feel more comfortable that way. But Sonia would expect a more definite reaction than that, and avoiding the facts was a coward's way out, she told herself reprovingly. What harm could a photograph do to her?

(9) Blinking hard to clear her vision, she forced herself to study the photograph and found that from the moment her eyes met the arrogant, disdainful stare of its subject her gaze was held transfixed as a million disjointed thoughts surfaced inside her head.

(10) So this was what Ryan Cassidy had become. Once more her vision blurred as memory superimposed another, more familiar image over the one on the page – the image of a dark, tough-looking youth with shaggy, overlong hair that fell forward over a high forehead, carved cheekbones and a long, narrow mouth.
(11) 'Not quite the David Hockney type.' Sonia's voice intruded into her disturbed thoughts.
(12) He's a portrait painter.'
(13) The sharp note in Anna's voice was too revealing, betraying her inner turmoil so that she regretted it at once and turned worried green eyes towards her friend. But to her relief Sonia simply shrugged smilingly.
(14) 'Does that make any difference? I thought all artists were airy-fairy types – or just plain weird. But then you know me – thick as a plank when it comes to cultural matters. But I do know a man when I see one, and that character is definitely male with a capital M.'

(ibid.: 5-6)

To examine the text population means going through looking for features in the three headings: interaction/interactants, prior texts/characters, discourse-type/subject positions.

Interaction/interactants

The novel opens with speech. It opens on a scene of female friendship, in the form of a gossipy chat over a magazine. I was quite taken by the effective use of this technique of opening with immediate attention to the hero, focalized through a character who turns out to be not the heroine herself but a friend (a similar technique is used very clumsily in an earlier Mills & Boon called *Lucifer's brand* (Nicola West 1982)). Here it facilitates the presentation of the heroine's tension and need for secrecy as her friend forces her attention to the photograph. She does this first with a response-demanding utterance in sentence 3 of (3). This verbal command requiring attention to the photograph as a response is reinforced by the action described in (4). Again in (5) Sonia is attempting to force Anna's attention to the photograph with a response-demanding utterance, here a request for agreement. The incompletion of these – the absence of '2nd pair parts' to complete adjacency pairs – is important in establishing the tension. Characteristically, the tension is signalled in other ways as well, as we shall see. There is also a completed adjacency pair in this passage: a statement (11) followed by a comment (12).

There is no producer–audience interaction at all. Given other evidence of the producer addressing the audience directly, the question in the last sentence of (8) ('What harm could a *photograph* do to her?') might have been interpretable as such. Here, however, it is part of Anna's thoughts: a reflexive question closely linked to the end of the previous sentence, 'avoiding the facts was a coward's way out, she told herself reprovingly.'

Prior texts/characters

A total of seven mental process verbs and nouns are crammed into one short paragraph in (6) (*want, thought, knew, felt, recall; memories, desire*). These – along with the two behavioural verbs *look* and *see* – indicate with considerable intensity the onset of character focalization through the heroine. From this point on their occurrence is regular as important contributors to the consistent focalization through Anna. Examples are *was . . . tempted, knowing* and *feel* in (8).

Other points of focus I have suggested are presupposition cues. Many of the presuppositions in the passage, especially in the early paragraphs, are simply circumstantial details giving the illusion of specificity of location and physical reality. These are cued by definite descriptions (*the glossy magazine, her head*) and would make a very boring list (*there is a glossy magazine, she has a head*, etc.). A couple of definite descriptions cue assumed shared cultural knowledge: *the art world has people called 'golden boys' in it* (3), *there is a character stereotype called 'a wild Irish rover'*. The point of examining these is that they are taken to be uncontentious, but worthy of mention in a backgrounded way. There are several presuppositions which are worth noting in particular because they uncover issues or aspects the importance of which is taken for granted. Two are of the entailment type:

'So that's what he looks like!'
>>   he [Ryan Cassidy] looks like something (1)
'So this was what Ryan Cassidy had become.'
>>   Ryan Cassidy has become something (10)

The presupposition in (1) is retrieved with the help of pronominal reference. On the face of it this is cataphoric; the first appearance of the name Ryan Cassidy in the opening passage is in (10). But of course it refers back anaphorically to the name in the two lots of blurb. Somehow it lacks the cataphoric tension of Graham Greene's

'Hale knew they meant to murder him before he had been in Brighton three hours', the opening sentence of *Brighton rock* (1938). The importance of this man's looks is another signal that he is the hero. The line in (10) contains another presupposition, cued by a change of state verb *become*:

>> (Anna is in a position to know that) Ryan Cassidy was something else before

Another presupposition is produced by emphasis:

'What harm could a *photograph* do to her?'
>> *Ryan himself (rather than the photograph) has the capacity to harm her* (8)

Together these repeat and reinforce the information we have already received from the blurbs: she knows him from the past; he is dangerous.

So there are two distinct uses of presupposition, summarized below:

Physical/cultural background		Narrative tension
There is a magazine.		Ryan looks like something
There are character types:	golden boys	Ryan has become something
	Irish rovers	(Anna is in a position to know that) Ryan was something else before
		Ryan himself, rather than the photograph can harm Anna

Discourse types/subject positions

The third aspect of the text's population deals with the fragmented and multiple discoursal and generic elements in the extract. For this we need to consider the following questions. What generic conventions are enacted in the opening passage of *No gentleman*? What discourses are being drawn upon and what subject positions do they set up?

Attending to the genre question first, the features already examined under *Interaction/Interactants* are cues to the genre of conversation which is clearly being imitated here. The narration surrounding the dialogue also contains simulated features of spoken language (e.g. the pause in (3)). Such features contribute to the enactment of the conversation genre in the written text of the novel. Representations of paralinguistic features – gestures, facial expressions – also contribute to this (e.g. 'Sonia simply shrugged smilingly' (13)).

The conventions of the marketing category genre of romance that I outlined above are pervasive, as one would expect. I have already remarked on the high profile of speech representation and the pervasiveness of focalization through the heroine. Another convention I referred to was the presence of detailed descriptions of appearance. In the extract – the two opening pages of the novel – we are told about Anna's hair colour and length, and about the colour of her eyes. Ryan is described in more detail. We are given information about the features of his face. Hair and eye colour are not divulged here, but we don't have to wait long for the information which the black and white photograph cannot supply, as a few pages further on Anna drifts off into reminiscences about 'his eyes, those amazing, clear, vivid blue eyes fringed with heavy black lashes, their intensity of colour almost shocking against the harsh lines of his face and the raven's wing colour of his hair' (ibid.: 9). The secondary character of Sonia is clearly established as such because she is not described at all until later in the chapter, and then only in a comparison with Anna, providing more opportunity for detail as Anna muses about their differences in skin tone, figure and taste in clothes (ibid.: 14–15). The protagonists are repeatedly and redundantly being pointed out (we have been given their names in both blurbs already).

Other characteristics of the romance genre in evidence in this opening passage are consequences of the intensive focus on verbal interaction and having the heroine as focalizer: the detailed descriptions of her difficulties in perception and her troubled feelings, for instance. These also illustrate the heroine's lack of control, which is another common feature of these romances ('the disturbed expression she was unable to suppress', etc.). Some attention to vocabulary and grammar here will make the point more clearly. As I have already observed, there are a great many words dealing with faculties, mental processes, physical features, gestures and expressions. When the faculties and physical features mentioned are Anna's, it is they rather than Anna herself which are the agents bringing about actions or states. Sometimes Anna is the beneficiary. In (7) for example, she is unable to conceal her feelings, but her hair comes to the rescue: 'her shoulder length mane of waving blonde hair fell forward over her face . . . hiding the disturbed expression *she* was unable to suppress' (7) (emphasis mine). More often, however, her faculties simply take over and play tricks on her:

(8) her eyes wouldn't focus
(9) her eyes met the arrogant, disdainful stare
(10) her vision blurred
(10) memory superimposed another, more familiar image
(13) The sharp note in Anna's voice was too revealing

However, the 'arrogant, disdainful stare' in the photograph of the powerful male is too much even for these unruly faculties: 'her gaze was held transfixed as a million disjointed thoughts surfaced inside her head.' (9) The heroine is clearly going to have problems when she confronts the hero face to face!

What discourses are being drawn upon in the opening passage of *No gentleman*? Curiously, I initially had great difficulty identifying any. This was probably because virtually everything is in the sphere of the commonplace and the personal: sensations and appearances, things which defy any easy connection with historically constituted bodies of knowledge embedded in social practices. We can, however, begin to get round this difficulty by focusing on kinds of identity established in classificatory schemes. There is a classificatory scheme for a range of artistic types of person:

the new golden boy of the art world
the David Hockney type
a portrait painter
all artists
airy-fairy types
just plain weird

This classificatory scheme, along with presupposition-cued cultural knowledge concerning 'artistic types', establishes a certain 'glamorous' sophistication of background. This background-establishing material may be making some contribution to an information-giving function for some readers.

A single type of masculinity is also clearly established:

rakish . . . the wild Irish rover
arrogant, disdainful
dark, tough-looking youth with shaggy overlong hair
male with a capital M

Some kind of body of knowledge is certainly being drawn upon here. Ryan is represented as a dangerous, independent, yet desirable male; 'the wild Irish rover' refers I suppose to a culturally dominant conception of male sexuality as rampant and uncontrollable. His masculine gaze is penetrative and to be feared, having the power even in a photograph to 'transfix' Anna. Artists are assumed to be male, but at the same time there is some sort of problem with having an artist as hero. There is a shadow of doubt cast on the gender identity of artists. Being artistic is not masculine. The two identities sit uneasily together; there is a suspicion of homosexuality or, less serious but still quite unsuitable, being 'weird'. He is made 'whole' by the label Anna attaches to him: 'He's a *portrait painter*'. The hero, as artist (we know this already from the brushes he is holding in the cover illustration: see Fig. 4.1), is established as artist but reassuringly masculine, meaning heterosexual.

No gentleman as a 'declarative' text

On the basis of the above attention to the text population of the opening passage, *No gentleman* seems to be a 'declarative' text, in Belsey's sense (see Chapter 2). From (6) onwards, the narration is intensively focalized, encouraging our close identification with the focalized character, Anna. Various aspects of the text population analysis show up the implicit view of language as instrumental and transparent typically embodied in declarative texts.

To say that writers and readers of declarative texts view language as transparent means that they treat it unproblematically as though it were a transparent, neutral medium, as though it simply stood for the real world (i.e. you can see straight through language to the real world it represents). In the passage we have just examined, there is no reflexivity in the language used: no producer-audience interaction and, after (6), no shift in focalization. Such meta-discoursal elements are absent from the narrative. Our attention as readers is never directed towards the act of narration itself. The massive redundancy in the repeated signposting of the principal characters ensures easy readability, so it is unlikely that there will be any need to focus on the reading process itself; in order to know who the heroine is, for instance. There are no self-consciously poetic 'literary' devices in the passage, elements which might focus our attention on to the language *qua* language, rather than its content. (There are a few elaborated metaphors elsewhere, the time-bomb simile in the page 1 blurb being the first. Later on they appear notably in the erotic passages: being shot into orbit, etc.

These tend to be very clumsy and possibly indicate that writers are experiencing difficulty in finding something to replace the representations of male acts of violence – in its mildest form, the bruising of lips and upper arms – which formerly passed for erotic within the genre.)

So the language of romance fiction is treated as a transparent medium for representing content. The Smithton readers insist on the diversity of romance fiction on the basis of differences in content, in terms of character and situation. Romances, moreover, contain representations of the social world familiar to readers. The gossipy interaction over a magazine, with which *No gentleman* opens, is a familiar experience for many women: a genre they have been involved in in their own lives. (Later in the narrative, another bit of cultural background familiar to the point of 'naturalness' for readers in the targeted audience is the preoccupation with clothes, fashion, furnishings: familiar discourses.) The sustained, intensive focalization through a single character is likely to reinforce any tendency to assume that fictional representations of the social world correspond directly to the real social world. There is a certain playfulness in the intertextual reference to Regency romances in the 'Darcy' episode of *No gentleman*, which seems on the face of it to be undermining any assumption of congruence between the real and the fictional, since it foregrounds romance as a genre. It is worth noting here that this episode is intertextual in two ways. It alludes to an actual prior text, Jane Austen's *Pride and prejudice* ([1818] 1894), probably assumed to be known by the reader (Radway's readers were familiar with it). Through the literary allusion, it intertextually connects the current romance with thousands of others as well. *Pride and prejudice* is well known as the source of many of the generic conventions of romance fiction, not least the conventions governing the heroine's taste in property-owning men. Elizabeth Bennet falls for Darcy after seeing 'his beautiful grounds at Pemberley' (Austen [1818] 1894: 459). The passage is exceptional, however, and it is in any case very limited as an acknowledgement of fictionality. Indeed, it may even have the effect of reinforcing a romance reader's impression of continuity between romance and reality. An assumption of congruence and continuity between real and fictional worlds underlies the Smithton readers' claims about the educational value of romances. The view of language as a transparent, neutral medium is accompanied by the related notion that language functions purely instrumentally, i.e. language is for something other than itself. Conceiving of fiction solely in terms of its content implies an instrumental view of language.

The 'time bomb'

In the pages following the passage we examined in detail above, the enigma with which the story starts – the meaning of the 'time-bomb' image – begins to be revealed. As the two friends continue their talk over the magazine article, Anna's troubled thoughts are slowly revealed to us. She has a 'past', something about her past life that she is ashamed of. We already know it is some kind of intimate involvement with the Ryan Cassidy character in the magazine article; that much was presupposed in the blurb on the back cover. As we read on, more is revealed. They grew up in the same city . . . :

'He's an interesting character by all accounts,' she murmured, her eyes fixed on the print. 'No formal training – he's just built his reputa-tion by word of mouth, and – hey, Anna – he's from your part of the country – up north.'

As usual, Sonia gave the last two words an exaggeratedly accented intonation that was her idea of Yorkshire pronunciation, turning the 'up' into 'oop'.

'He grew up in the Churtown district of Forgeley.'

She glanced up, her eyes bright with curiosity.

'What's that like?'

'Rough,' Anna declared succinctly, giving the description a forceful, disparaging emphasis, and saw Sonia's eyebrows fly up in response so that for a moment she was gripped with a sense of panic at the thought that perhaps she had gone too far, made too much of her disapproval.

'So he's dragged himself up by his bootstraps, then.' Once more that note of sensuality touched Sonia's voice. 'A real rough diamond. Did you ever know of him when – ?'

Anna decided that that particular line of questioning was best broken off as quickly – and as non-committally as possible.

'Yorkshire's a huge county, Anna [sic] – and Forgeley a large city in it.'

'Yes, I suppose it is,' Sonia, whose knowledge of the geography of the United Kingdom ended north of Watford, agreed thoughtfully. 'And of course you and Cassidy will have moved in very different circles. You know, perhaps one day we should all go on an expedition to Yorkshire – back to your roots.'

She made it sound like a trek to the outback, Anna reflected, which, to Sonia, it probably was. The sudden quiver of fear in the pit of her

stomach unnerved her. It was over two years since she had felt this
threatened by the mention of her past – with both her parents dead and
no other family, she had thought that the carefully edited version of her
story which she had given her friends would never be challenged.

. . .Ryan Cassidy was the past; Marc was the most important part of
her present – and hopefully, if Sonia's none too subtle hints were to be
believed, of her future too.

Was it possible that he was planning on extending their new business
partnership in her natural cosmetics company into another, much more
personal form of commitment? Mrs Marc Denton. In the privacy of her
thoughts she let herself try out the sound of the name that might one
day be hers, letting it linger delightfully in her mind. Would she be fool-
ish to allow herself to hope? Ever since she had left Empire Street to
build a new life for herself she had dreamed of just such a moment, and
for months now she had known that Marc was the man with whom she
wanted to spend that future.

But her determination to leave her past behind her meant that she
had never told Marc, or anyone she had met since, the truth about her
earlier life. For the first time since she had taken it, Anna was forced to
consider the wisdom of the decision she had made years before.

(Walker 1992: 9–12)

Anna brings class in as the agenda in response to Sonia's open-
ended question, 'What's that like?' Through the focalized narration
we learn that Anna's class and regional origins are the cause of her
shame. We also learn the cause of her deep anxiety: the knowledge
that these origins constitute a threat to her desired social mobility
through marriage to her financial backer, Marc. The wished-for
marriage with Marc is represented in a discourse more appropriate
to venture capitalism than loving relationships. She is passively
waiting for a takeover bid, living in hope that his expansionist
plans will bring about her restructuring as a new being – 'Mrs Marc
Denton' – containing no element of her previous name whatsoever.
This new identity she secretly aspires to is defined exclusively in
terms of the desired capital-owning male and the relationship she
would take up with him.

Let's take a look at how the north of England is represented in
this passage, starting with Sonia's, apparently customary, mimicry
of Yorkshire English: 'oop north'. It demonstrates just how dependent on shared terms of reference such attempts to represent
particular spoken varieties are. To users of southern varieties of
English it apparently indicates the use of the phoneme /ʊ/ in contexts where /ʌ/ is expected. As a northerner myself, I do not have
the ʊ/ʌ contrast to draw upon. I first read the 'oo' as the writer's

attempt to represent a stereotypical northern variant (the long high back vowel /u:/), and assumed that the writer was using it to demonstrate the character Sonia's unfamiliarity with the variety by using the variant inappropriately. Like many real world people who have grown up in the south of England, I pondered, Sonia seems to be unaware that this phoneme is one she would use herself, in some contexts (e.g. in the words *room, fool* and *Luke*). Like them, she sees nothing wrong in mimicking the variety of English from her friend's region of origin.

In the passage that follows, there seems to be a conflation of the working class and the north into simply an undistinguishable 'otherness'. The place names play a part in this. A city called Forgeley can be nothing other than a northern centre for heavy industry – like Dickens' Coketown in *Hard times* (1854) – so most of its inhabitants will presumably be industrial workers. The 'rough' Churtown district in it certainly sounds inelegant (as if it might have churlish people inhabiting it, perhaps?). It does not take a great leap of the imagination to make a connection between Empire Street and that better known fictional location of the northern working class, *Coronation Street* . In the fancy dress scene in the second chapter, Anna's beloved Marc disparagingly refers to another guest, a young model, as 'Miss Coronation Street' and then proceeds to display at great length his contempt for her background. Given this open disparagement, it is scarcely surprising that Anna is feeling anxious.

Apart from the place names, Anna's own disparagement of and reflection on her place of origin contributes to the representation of the rough, working-class north in the extract above. The seeds of the eventual narrative resolution are sown by Sonia in her observation, articulating the discourse of bourgeois individualism, that Ryan has 'dragged himself up by his bootstraps'. Later in the novel we find out about Anna's late father, a middle-class southerner fallen on hard times, and his snobbish attitude towards their Empire Street neighbours. Her father's influence turns out to be one reason for her 'misreading' of Ryan. Anna learns, with Ryan's help, to accept her own regional origins and to be tolerant of the working-class people with whom she grew up; Ryan, in particular. Through her developing relationship with Ryan, she 'finds herself':

> 'Ryan?' His name came chokingly. 'Ryan – who am I?'
> . . .'You're a very beautiful woman, Anna, and an intelligent, creative person. You're someone who cares about others. . . You're an astute

businesswoman – the creator of Nature's Secrets – but most of all you're
you. You can be anything you want to be. If you want to leave Empire
Street behind you, then that's fine. I might have gone back to Yorkshire,
but I sure as hell wasn't going to live in Churtown for the rest of my life.
You have to face your past squarely before you can move on from it;
don't run away from it, accept it, then put it behind you. You mustn't
carry it with you like some burden that will always weigh you down.'
   Anna felt as if that burden had suddenly been lifted from her shoulders. She was on the brink of a new beginning and it felt wonderful,
with a whole new sense of freedom.
   'I'm me!' It was a sigh of release, of happiness, and Anna turned
glowing green eyes on Ryan's face. 'Thank you!'

(ibid.: 148–9)

Anna is duly grateful. Because she and Ryan are self-made entre-
preneurs, who have dragged themselves up by their own
bootstraps, we can enjoy the satisfactory narrative conclusion with
the heroine agreeing to marry one of her (socially uplifted) own
kind:

   'Did you mean what you said?' Ryan asked when at last their lips
parted reluctantly. 'Would you really marry me and live in Yorkshire?'
   'I'd live anywhere in the world with you,' Anna assured him.
   'But your company – your job – '
   'I was already thinking of ways to expand. Yorkshire – starting with
the wool hall – seems to be the perfect place. I can employ a manager to
deal with the shops here while I set up the northern end of things. You
said yourself that you sometimes have to be in London, so I can keep
an eye on everything down here too – we can combine the two bases
easily.'
   'I can't believe it – it's all too good to be true, Anna, if you only knew
how much I love you – I want to love you for the rest of your life.'

(ibid.: 188)

All that remains is the final merger in the bedroom . . .

Escaping into acceptance

The happy narrative resolution demonstrates conclusively that
existing gendered subject positions *work*. The essential preliminar-
ies to this happy ending were the heroine's discovery of her own
errors and her reinterpretation of the hero as a consequence of her
enlightenment (the disarming of the time-bomb, if you like).

Another important element is the gift of her identity from the hero (in the extract from pages 148–9 above). Anna is not complete in herself, despite her supposed economic independence and despite Ryan's assurances; her 'wholeness' is only achieved in interaction with him. She achieves not full autonomy but the self-in-relation, the only acceptable kind of feminine subject position in patriarchal cultures. The protagonists, together, achieve wholeness. It is, however, the female focalizer who needs a male partner to resolve her split identity; Ryan, if you recall, is 'whole' already.

Assuming, then, that a particular reader derives a satisfactory sense of closure from the narrative resolution of *No gentleman*, she does so only by accepting a feminine subject position congruent with that of the focalized character. This acceptance may be fleeting. It may, however, correspond with her subjectivity as female in her own life to a high degree. If it does, then the fictional resolution will have the effect of reinforcing her sense that her gendered identity is 'natural'. Her dependency, emotional and probably also economic, is presented as a natural and even desirable element of femininity.

The real problems facing women in relationships with men are 'solved' in fiction, and erased as problems. If a woman is intimidated by men, she needs to learn not to live without them or to try to change them but to interpret their behaviour in a more positive light. She needs to learn, in short, to accept things as they are.

'I HOPE THIS HAS BEEN A LESSON TO YOU': MALE AUTHORITY IN PHOTO-STORIES FOR TEENAGERS

In British magazines for teenage girls, the photo-stories (stories presented in comic strip form but using photographs) frequently deal with loving relationships between teenagers. For this reason, we can view them as a sub-genre of romance. They are, however, strikingly different from romances aimed at an adult audience, such as the Mills & Boon fiction we were concentrating on in the previous section. For one thing, the happy ending – *the* defining characteristic of a romance as far as the Smithton readers are concerned – is not always supplied. For another thing, the use of fiction for moral guidance of non-adults is apparent, and sometimes very heavy-handed.

These stories deal with the gaining or losing of boyfriends. The tensions carrying the narrative forward always relate to one or the other, if not both. The principal character, almost without exception, is a girl in her mid to late teens with boyfriend trouble of some kind. Assessment and guidance by male participants of similar age is very common. Male characters are very often there to provide moral and intellectual leadership for the female protagonist. This function seems to overlap with their function as boyfriend material. Figure 4.2 below contains an illustrative example of such moral guidance. The single panel is from a photo-story in a Valentine's Day issue of *Jackie*. It serves to make explicit the story's significance: in this case a simple moral. In it the girl is being chastized by her boyfriend and offers an apology. The unequal relation of power between them is clear in the body language in the photograph. Notice his authoritarian wagging finger and her submissive 'head cant'.[8]

Figure 4.2   'Don't Let Me Down', *Jackie* 15 February 1986

Given the didacticism of many of these photo-stories (I will look at one in detail in a moment), it is hard to see how they can be called '-escapist' in content at all. However, teenagers apparently use magazines like *Blue Jeans, My Guy* and *Jackie* (no longer published) oppositionally in the classroom. According to Angela McRobbie, all kinds of elements of non-school culture – fashion, dating, the mass media – provide strategies of resistance for many low-achievers in school. Like the Smithton readers, reading for many teenagers in school is part of a deliberate cutting off from obligations imposed on them; unlike the Smithton wives, however, they are presumably not in a position to do so openly. *Jackie* (as I recall) is read under the desk.

From its earliest years, Jackie had a combination of characteristics of adult women's magazines and girls' romance comics. Hollings (1985) reports that when it first came out in 1963 it contained fewer romance strips than existing romance comics such as *Marty*, *Boyfriend* and *Valentine* and gave space to articles on fashion and cosmetics, a regular problem page. Julie Hollings remarks that:

> Jackie proclaimed itself to be the comic for 'go-ahead teens', and was concerned primarily with being fashionable and exciting, unlike comics such as Valentine, which appeared to be still rooted in the 1950s.
>
> (Hollings 1985: 28–9)

Like other magazines it contained elements of diverse discourses, the most pervasive of which was advertising. Others included medical discourse in articles and the problem page, on puberty and occasionally pregnancy in the later years, legal discourse in the 'small print' and counselling on emotional development. Advice on social relations even found its way into advertisements, after a fashion (in this piece of advice in an advertisement: 'Don't let spots spoil your social life!').

Jackie frequently contained features about 'ordinary' people. The editorial staff apparently had real contact with teenagers (not just readers). D C Thomson claim that their communication with actual teenagers is one of the reasons why Jackie was so successful (Hollings 1985). There were frequently features consisting of or containing street interviews with people, fleamarket shopping, and so on: their likes and dislikes. These interviewees tended to be slightly above the magazine's targeted age range of 12 to 14.

The editorial also had contact with actual readers through various channels. These included the letters page, the problem page, 'make-overs', occasional 'dreams come true' (e.g. being a primary teacher for a day in one issue (18 March 1989)), 'giveaways'. All these involved the reader in becoming a writer, an action initiated by the magazine but making the reader an active participant. The editorial staff was dominant, in control of the interaction, its terms and outcome. They were gatekeepers; restricted numbers make writing-in a competitive bid for goods ('make-over', 'wish-fulfilment', 'free gift') or for access to the problem page and letters page. Space puts a restriction on the number of letters appearing in print with a response.

The photo-story I am going to focus on is from *Jackie* and is entitled 'It's my nasty mind'. The protagonist argues with boyfriends

Figure 4.3   'It's My Nasty Mind', *Jackie*,   5 December 1985

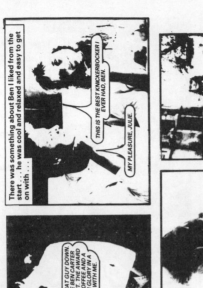

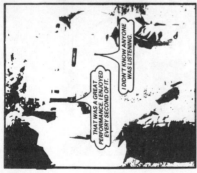

HELLO, BEN.

DON'T TALK TO ME. JULIE. YOU'RE SUPPOSED TO PRETEND I'M NOT HERE.

NOT NOW. I MEAN TONIGHT AT SEVEN O'CLOCK.

SORRY, NOT TONIGHT. I'M ALL BOOKED UP. HOW ABOUT PRETENDING YOU'RE GOING OUT WITH A BOY WHO'S INVISIBLE!

Well, that was that. There was nothing I could do but turn up alone that evening and play it by ear. So I did . . .

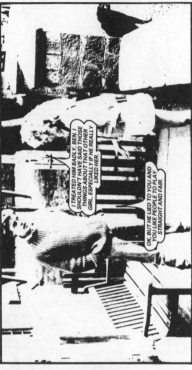

I TREATED HIM BADLY, BEN. I SHOULDN'T HAVE SAID THOSE THINGS ABOUT THAT OTHER GIRL, ESPECIALLY IF HE REALLY LIKED HER.

OK, BUT HE LIED TO YOU AND YOU LIKE PEOPLE TO PLAY STRAIGHT AND FAIR.

Finally I thought of someone — our school practical joker, Dave. He'd do anything for a laugh.

WILL YOU DO ME AN ENORMOUS FAVOUR, DAVE? PRETEND YOU'RE MY BOYFRIEND AND LET ME BAWL YOU OUT?

WELL, IF YOU LIKE. START SHOUTING, THEN.

REMEMBER MIKE?

OH, YES. "I WON'T CALL YOU A LIAR, MIKE, BUT YOU'RE SO FAR FROM THE TRUTH YOU COULDN'T SEE IT THROUGH A TELESCOPE." THAT WAS A GREAT LINE — I LOVED IT!

and loses them. It is reproduced in its entirety in Figure 4.3. Who are we associating with in reading this short story? What kind of text is it and what values does it embody? We can begin to find out by examining its 'population'.

The text population in 'It's my nasty mind'

Examining how the photo-story is 'populated' means returning to some of the cues I suggested in Chapter 3 under the headings *Interaction/interactants*, *Prior texts/characters* and *Discourse types/subject positions*.

Interaction/interactants

To consider producer–audience interaction in this story we need a distinction between author and narrator. The implied author is the anonymous source of the title and one or two of the directions for 'reading' the sequence of photographs ('To be continued', etc.). This anonymous producer is very backgrounded and does not address the audience directly. The narrator, and the main bearer of responsibility for the story, is Julie. She addresses the audience once, in panel 11 of the second page: 'I couldn't tell him I was getting fat waiting for him to show up, could I?' Here, using direct informal address with a tag question, the narrator is pressing the reader for agreement. This narrator's status is ambiguous. She is a fictional teenage girl, but photographed. She appears to be creating the text, rather than being created by it. She is both narrator and character, which raises her to the level of a historical authority about the past event she is reconstructing. She knows what she's talking about because it happened to her. The effect is the impression that the implied reader is being told a true story by another teenage girl. In fact, most of the narrative sequencing is carried by the ordering of the panels, not the first person narration.

The story consists almost entirely of pictures and dialogue. Most of the dialogue is between two sets of interlocutors: Julie and Mike, Julie and Ben. I will not go through examining every exchange, but just concentrate on those in which differential rights assigned to speakers are particularly evident. On the first page, Julie criticizes Mike, but she is indirect. In panels 3 and 4, her comments in response to Mike's statements contain the implied meaning of (that is, have the pragmatic force of) an accusation and a denial respectively. Mike appears to be under no such constraints. He comes straight out with direct evaluations, freely interpreting her behaviour for her ('you're jealous and that means . . .'). When Ben appears on the scene, at the top of the second page, his first act is to congratulate Julie on the (presumably private) argument she has just concluded. In real world interaction it would surely have been none of his business. His second act, in the following panel, is similar, as he jokingly (and highly improbably) poses as a donator of 'the Ben Carter award for effort'. Like Mike, Ben freely evaluates Julie. In the last dialogue on the third page this assessment intensifies, reaching a peak in panels 8 and 9. I will say no more about those here, as I intend to come back to them in considering discourse types a little later.

Prior texts/characters

In the detailed attention to the text population of the opening passage of *No gentleman*, we saw the contribution of mental and verbal process verbs and nouns to the intense character focalization through the heroine. In this photo-story a single character is similarly in close focus throughout. This story, however, is in pictures. The intense character focalization is still there, but it is carried by the photographs: Julie is in every single panel. There is still a large proportion of vocabulary dealing with talking, thinking, feeling, and indeed listening, discussing, shouting and arguing; it is after all a story about a girl who argues with boyfriends. Most of these mental and verbal processes involve only the characters present. The only exceptions are the girl Mike has been observed talking to and the unspecified earlier boyfriends subjected to the same treatment by Julie. A very small world, this.

Turning to presuppositions, another point of focus I suggested under this heading: as in the Mills & Boon romance, many of them are circumstantial details. However, they are not so much building up the illusion of physical reality (no need, the photographs do that very effectively) as contributing to building a sense of social reality. There are a few commonsense notions that are assumed to be shared by the implied reader that are introduced through presupposition. Panel 6 on the second page contains a presupposition that 'people fantasise about the boy they're going to meet some day'. This kind of presupposed commonsense knowledge illustrates rather clearly, I think, just how much depends on the reader. Such a presupposition would not pass unnoticed or unchallenged by the 'wrong' reader. To the reader implied in the text, on the other hand, it might seem like rather a good idea! Other presuppositions of interest are not so much commonsensical (i.e. shared as 'obvious' by anybody with any sense, in the terms of the story) as originating from an authoritative source, namely Ben. These appear in his key self-promoting utterance in panel 9 on the third page:

> I think your problem is you haven't met the right boy before.
> >> you have a problem
> >> there is a right boy for you
> >> you have now met him

Discourse-types/subject positions

This is where we turn our attention to genres and discourses. The photo-story follows some of the conventions of the romance genre that we have observed in the Mills & Boon. They are realized slightly differently, however. This is at least in part because of the difference in the age of the target audience, and the visual medium. As in the Mills & Boon extract, the genre of conversation is being imitated. I pointed to some of the features of simulated dialogue under interaction/interactants. Others are the vocabulary of 'teenagers' vernacular' – the writer's idea of how teenagers speak – occurring throughout the story ('chatting up', 'drooling', 'slide off'), including in particular a whole range of terms and expressions for talking about arguments and discontinuing relationships ('get it in the neck', 'the big heave', 'carved up', etc.). Paralinguistic features contributing to the simulation of conversation genre are of course abundantly supplied by the photographs.

The conventions of the marketing category genre of romance are realised slightly differently in this picture story. We have already seen the pervasiveness of speech representation and character focalization through the heroine. One other convention I referred to in the Mills & Boon sample was the importance of detailed descriptions of characters' appearance. In the photo-story, all the necessary information about hair, eyes, figure and clothing are provided by the photographs (with obvious limitations when printed in black and white). Another characteristic of romances I pointed to earlier was the heroine's lack of control of herself or her situation. In the photo-story there is very little written narration in which this could be represented, but nevertheless a kind of female passivity seems to be built in to the narrative. In panel 8 on the second page, she hangs around in a café on the off-chance he will return. It is true that Julie's sitting-and-waiting strategy could be interpreted as uncommon resolution and perseverance in the pursuit of her objective, and in spite of the uncertain circumstances in which she is operating. It is perfectly possible for a reader to surmise this, but it is not what is conveyed visually in panel 8, for me, and it is not backed up by her presupposed lack of sense in the following narrative box (in panel 9). Her dismissal of Mike in the last panel on the first page is certainly active; but this earlier activeness is presented as a major difficulty, something not under control, which needs dealing with.

The last point brings me to the discourse type most pervasively present in the picture story. This is a discourse of 'folk psychology', a kind of discourse frequent in the problem pages of magazines and used by agony aunts and the people who write in to them for advice. It can be seen in a number of utterances (the figures in brackets denote page number: panel number respectively):

(1: 4) You're jealous and that means you really care for me
(3: 8) Do you think I'm dreadful?
(3: 8) a bit insecure . . . a strong sense of justice
(3: 9) you're too self-critical . . . safe and secure
(3: 9) I think your problem is you haven't met the right boy

The last noun phrase, 'the right boy', is a member of an open set of expressions concerning romantic matters ('love at first sight', 'marriage', 'romance' itself). The presupposed ideas attributed to the authoritative figure of Ben belong in this category. The assumption that there are people who are 'made for one another', and that it is just a matter of these individuals meeting up, is pure folk psychology. Julie is placed in a subject position like that of the problem page letter-writer; Ben plays the part of advice-giver. Fortunately for him, one cannot help thinking!

Other conventions of the sub-genre, on the basis of this sample, are the particular narrative expectations and type of narrative resolution. The narrative tension is produced by loss of boyfriend; equilibrium is restored at the end with the acquisition of another. This implies that being a single, unattached girl is an undesirable state, and that being attached to a boyfriend is a desirable one. The narrative resolution places the heroine in the safe, secure presence of a protective male. (I may be imagining it, but the final panel looks remarkably like a wedding photograph.) It does not end with more arguing, nor with any criticism whatsoever of boys' behaviour.

Learning to live

The pedagogic function of writing for young people was never more overt than in these magazines. Writers for non-adults usually harbour some kind of intention to foster socio-cultural values of some description. As Stephens (1992) says:

> Since a culture's future is, to put it crudely, invested in its children, children's writers often take upon themselves the task of trying to mould audience attitudes into 'desirable' forms, which can mean either an attempt to perpetuate certain values or to resist socially dominant values which particular writers oppose.
>
> (Stephens 1992: 3)

In the case of teenage girls' magazine fiction, the values being transmitted are overwhelmingly conservative and patriarchal. The discourse of folk psychology seems to play a significant part in inculcating these values, not least because encountered in so many different locations. It is a discourse type that is drawn into the ongoing discourse of a range of publications in journalism (women's magazines and the tabloids in particular), in other domains of publishing, as well as presumably outside the mass media altogether.

Photo-stories in magazines for teenagers do not always have happy resolutions. Sometimes the heroine does *not* get the boy, because of some fault of her own. The social world in these stories is full of lonely, isolated individuals. Only couples count (heterosexual, of course). Radway's observation that 'longing, born of relational poverty, is implicit in all romantic fiction' (Radway 1987: 151) has particular poignancy in the light of these stories for British teenagers.

Stephens observes that fiction for children almost invariably deals with subjectivity in some way, very often charting a character's progression from an extreme of infantile solipsism to some degree of social awareness and maturity (Stephens 1992: 3). The photo-stories in teenagers' magazines are certainly about selfhood. But, like the Mills & Boon romances, they do not offer or

recommend autonomy (and I mean here simply a degree of emotional independence and economic self-sufficiency) but the
self-in-relation.

It may be that the stories I have happened to concentrate on,
mostly from *Jackie* in late 1985 and the whole of 1986, were exceptionally heavy-handed in their didacticism. A quick look at more
recent examples of fiction in the same sub-genre suggests that they
can be a little lighter. They tend to deal with basically the same
issue of how to get on with boyfriends, however. For example, 'Too
Shy' (*Jackie*, 5 August 1989) is basically a rehearsal of a courting
script for young teenage readers. There has been some decline in
the popularity of romance strips, probably as result of the severe
constraints that photography places on visual narrative. This was
certainly the editorial view in the late 1980s (see Martin Barker
(1989); also see McRobbie (1991) for some discussion of the limita-
tion of visual narrative using photographs). Before it folded, *Jackie*
had dropped the photo-story altogether. Other types of story par-
tially replaced the photo-romances. For a while in the 1980s, *Jackie*
ran a continued strip called *The grat pack*, which was set in a com-
prehensive school. This was presumably inspired by the children's
TV serial, *Grange Hill*, which was immensely popular in Britain in
the 1980s. Following a wide range of characters, the photo-story
imitated the televisual realism of the TV series, dealing with issues
of 'social realism' such as stealing and bullying.

CONCLUSION

In this chapter, I have looked at a recent Mills & Boon and at a
couple of examples of the declining sub-genre of photo-romance.
Romance is a many-faceted and changing genre, which in recent
years has begun to articulate a feminist discourse. Female dependency, in fiction for adults at least, has been toned down. In the
Mills & Boon I examined, there was some distinction being drawn
between economic and emotional autonomy. The female protagonist has some degree of economic independence, but she quite
explicitly needs a man in order to 'find herself' emotionally, and by
implication sexually. In contrast, the 'blockbuster' novels of the
1980s depict active female sexuality and economic independence
(e.g. Shirley Conran's *Lace*, 1982; Jackie Collins' *Hollywood wives*,

1983). As Helen Taylor (1989) has observed, both the heroines of these novels and their creators have been set up as feminist ideals in the press:

> celebrated in their publicity hand-outs and interviews as ideals of contemporary career feminism – Thatcherite models who demonstrate the fact that you too can get a multi-million advance if you work fourteen hours a day, regard yourself as a serious novelist, but accept the necessity for your novel to be packaged and marketed as a commodity.
>
> (Taylor 1989: 61)

Within the institution of publishing, romance has accommodated feminism, rearticulating it in terms of capitalist individualism. Indeed the blockbuster novels have a strong element of propaganda in them; in the words of Jackie Collins' dedication to her novel, *Lady boss*: 'Girls can do anything!' The female protagonists of these books are active, dynamic, forceful and economically independent, to say the least (their first million or so will have been inherited from a Greek or Italian patriarch, though). These novels contain romantic elements, but they are soap opera too, having a broad social canvas in which the heroine moves, and an enormous cast of characters, and multiple points of view in addition to the female protagonist's. A far cry from the narrow, stifling worlds containing basically one couple, that one finds in Mills & Boon. The blockbuster novels are, in places, 'imperative' texts rather than 'declarative', setting out to be deliberately combative. *Lady boss*, for example, contains frequent criticism of the way women are treated, in the workplace and in Hollywood cinema. The word 'sexism' occurs frequently. Criticisms of sexist attitudes and behaviour abound. The eponymous character, for instance, knows she needs to be on her guard with her male employees. She is sensitive to their frequent patronizing treatment of her and always makes a point of either returning or rejecting terms of endearment:

> Cooper Turner was better-looking than on the screen, with his boyishly handsome face, rumpled hair, and penetrating ice-blue eyes. He had a devastating smile, which he put into immediate action. 'So you're my new boss, huh?'
>   'Yes,' she said, going for a handshake.
>   He took her hand and gave it an extra squeeze. Behind his horn-rimmed glasses he favored her with a penetrating look. 'You're a surprise,' he said. 'I was expecting a dragon lady.'
>   'Looks don't matter,' she said.
>   'Sure they do,' he said casually, removing his glasses. 'Beautiful

women always get more attention. Not that I'm saying you're not smart,
but looks help. And honey – you've got 'em.'
   She threw it right back at him. 'And, honey, so have you.'
   He laughed. 'Touché, Miz Santangelo.'

(Collins 1990: 543–4)

In order to make any sense of the exchanges in this passage at all,
we need to draw upon frames providing cultural knowledge of i)
the importance of a woman's appearance, ii) expectations concerning women in positions of power, iii) the incompatibility of beauty
and intelligence. We need the first two of these frames to fill in
what a 'dragon lady' is, what this has to do with the 'looks' that she
says 'don't matter'.[9] Through Lucky Santangelo, the 'Lady boss' of
the title, the passage is challenging some familiar patriarchal practices: the patronising use of terms of address in the workplace, the
weight of importance placed on women's appearance, relative to
men's.

At the same time the passage is perpetuating the second of these
practices. It is perhaps inevitable that the kind of career feminism
articulated within a discourse of bourgeois individualism – that is,
the feminism that appears in these 'blockbuster' novels – should do
so. Within institutions producing visual texts for mass consumption – the cinema, tabloid journalism – looks *do* matter. They are of
paramount importance. Appearance is certainly important in the
Hollywood film industry, which is the setting for *Lady boss*.

In what sense then is romantic fiction 'escapism'? Finding fantasy
solutions to real problems is a form of 'escape'. As Radway has
argued, using romance reading to provide in fantasy an alternative
to a real, nurturant relationship temporarily 'solves' the real-world
problem. The so-called 'regressive' pleasure that romance (at least,
the 'proper' kind that Mills & Boon produce) offers is dependent on
the reader's ability to identify closely with the focalizer. A
'declarative' kind of text no doubt makes this easier, but the essential thing is close contact between writers, publishers and the
readership, in order to maintain a reasonable match between the
reader inscribed in the text and actual readers.

Such fictional, and fleeting, resolution of real dilemmas is surely
a potential of all fiction, not only, or even especially, romance. It
would not be difficult to supply examples of fiction which allows
men to experience vicariously a sense of competence and virility
beyond any person's reasonable real-world expectations (how
closely men identify with characters like Indiana Jones or Crocodile

Dundee I can only guess). Similarly, utopian fiction, whatever else it may do, primarily produces satisfaction, in solving an intractable problem; if the implied and real readers are well matched, the pleasure of 'escape' will be strong.

Radway also reports that romance readers use their reading time as a means of 'escape' from the demands of their families. My own informal enquiries among romance-reading relatives and friends suggest that they use their leisure reading in much the same way as anyone else: to relax before going to sleep, to pass the time when travelling, simply as a source of enjoyment in free time. Again, it is not at all clear to me that doing any of these things with romance fiction is any more or less escapist than doing them with other genres.

In conclusion, the notion of reading as 'mere escapism' (i.e. assuming that escape is a bad thing) is tied up with people's negative evaluation of other people's choice of reading material. This leads me to the subject matter of the next chapter: horror.

TAKING IT FURTHER

I will just mention work on romance fiction which I have not already referred to in this chapter. An important early study is Tania Modleski (1982). Anne Cranny-Francis (1990) devotes a chapter to romance, examining the difficulties involved in feminist appropriations of the genre. Walter Nash (1990) is full of interesting observations of a stylistic nature. Peter Mann (1969) is a readership survey, updated in Mann (1974); both are Mills & Boon publications. Barker (1989) is essential reading for its scrutiny of the critics of *Jackie* romances, although the focus is on drawn picture stories of the 1960s and 1970s.

FIVE

Confronting horror

Horror fantasies have been viewed by various critics as an index of the fears troubling the cultures in and for which they were produced. Joseph Grixti (1989), for instance, catalogues a range of anxieties which seem to be expressed in American horror, particularly in films. He cites *Frenzy* (1972), *Halloween* (1978) and *Looking for Mr Goodbar* (1977), among others, as films in which non-domesticated women are 'punished' (brutally murdered) for transgression of their society's expectations. Horror films crossing into the genre of science fiction such as *Invasion of the body snatchers* (1956) and *I married a monster from outer space* (1958) can be viewed as expressions of 'reds-under-the-bed' anxiety during the Cold War. Fear of the mentally ill also seems to be prominent; perhaps most famously in Hitchcock's film version of *Psycho* (1960). Mental illness is represented as evil, primitive and dangerous, necessitating firm control by the forces of law and order. As Grixti says:

> a culturally based fear of a stigmatized sector of the population is invoked and reinforced, while reassurance is provided about the efficiency and (sane) toughness of the guardians of the status quo . . . a fascination with the wild and threateningly unorthodox has been transformed into an exercise in ideological reassurance.
>
> (Grixti 1989: 25)

The customary attributes of mad people in horror fiction are the desire to murder, immense strength (usually coupled with cunning) and unstoppability. Two recent examples are Hannibal the Cannibal and Buffalo Bill in *Silence of the lambs* (1991).[10] Maniacs in horror fiction are generally male, but there are exceptions; for example, in Stephen King's *Misery* (1987) and James Herbert's novel, *Moon* (1985): both, for some reason, nurses. An earlier, decidedly unsophisticated mad male aggressor is Michael Myers from

117

the *Halloween* films. Unlike the powerful males in the romance genre, these men really *are* bad to the core. Some writers have produced subtler, and more plausible, human monsters than these; e.g. Stephen Gallagher's insanely vindictive policeman in *Down river* (1989).

A whole range of novels and films about demonic pregnancies and child monsters – including *The exorcist* (1973), *The omen* (1976) and its sequels, and *Rosemary's baby* – seem to give expression to fears about reproductive control and/or fear of rebellious youth. We can add to this catalogue of fears the rather less historically and culturally specific fear of death itself, and particularly fear of violent death. This fear is prominent in horror fiction in the United States where, as Stephen King remarks, 'the funeral parlor is taboo' (King 1982: 158). In a culture which valorizes youth, beauty and vigour, decrepitude and decay are horrifying.

This chapter is about horror in fiction. So it will not deal with the truly horrific, or even with records of it (such as, for example, the exhibition of photographs, 'Genocide against the Serbs', organized by Bojana Isakovic and banned in Britain in early 1993). Nor will I be dealing with horrific fictionalizations of real past events (e.g. *Requiem*, 1985, Shizuko Go's semi-autobiographical account of life in the Japanese city of Yokohama in the last months of the Second World War). I will not even be dealing with fictionalizations of the horrific and all-too-probable future (e.g. the semi-documentary, *The war game*, 1967, and the more recent *Threads*, 1984).

Definitions of the genre vary according to the areas of interest and agenda of the person producing it. The scope of the texts included in the genre is determined accordingly. For one critic, horror is 'a genre which proposes the contemplation and evaluation of areas of shared uncertainty' (Grixti 1989: xii). Another critic, James Twitchell, wants to focus his attention on three specific, particularly robust mythic figures (vampire, monster and transforming beast) whose popularity with the young he attributes to their function in 'fables of sexual identity' (Twitchell 1985: 7). In his view, horror fiction consists of:

> formulaic rituals coded with precise information needed by the adolescent audience. Like fairy tales that prepare the child for the anxieties of separation, modern horror myths prepare the teenager for the anxieties of reproduction.
>
> (ibid.)

For my own purposes here, I have decided to simply accept the marketing category as it stands. I include then whatever is marketed as horror, rather than trying to undermine the genre boundaries established by the publishing industry. Like the mass market romances we considered in the last chapter, horror is immensely popular. My interest in it stems in part from the fact that it is a major growth industry. Later in this chapter, I will examine in some detail extracts from sample texts by leading authors in the genre. (For the most detailed analysis, I have chosen *Lair*, written by the London-based writer, James Herbert.) I am also interested in how horror fiction functions as containment both within narratives and within and across orders of discourse. Before we can begin to address these issues however, we need to consider the social phenomenon of horror fiction's notoriety.

THE NOTORIETY OF HORROR FICTION

The romance genre incites scorn and ridicule; horror is more likely to stir up feelings of moral outrage and righteous indignation. Horror texts produced in the non-valued media of comics and video have been the objects of campaigns, ending in some cases in censorship. In Britain in the 1950s, for example, the American EC horror comics stood on trial and were subsequently banned by Act of Parliament, after campaigns by the Communist Party of Great Britain and the National Union of Teachers (among other groups; see Martin Barker's *A haunt of fears*, (1984) for a detailed examination of the British horror comics campaign). The first paragraph of the 1955 Children and Young Persons (Harmful Publications) Act reads as follows:

> 1. This Act applies to any book, magazine or other like work which consists wholly or mainly of stories told in pictures (with or without the addition of written matter), being stories portraying –
> (a) the commission of crimes; or
> (b) acts of violence or cruelty; or
> (c) incidents of a repulsive or horrible nature;
> in such a way that the work as a whole would tend to corrupt a child or young person into whose hands it might fall (whether by inciting or encouraging him to commit crimes or acts of violence or cruelty or in any other way whatsoever).
>
> (Reproduced in Barker 1984: 16)

This bill is still in operation. It iterates a popular view about the effects of visual representations of 'violence or cruelty'. It is a view frequently aired in the tabloids, but with far wider currency. Put simply, what makes people commit aggressive (violent or criminal) acts is viewing such acts performed in fiction. The claim that such representations 'incite' imitation is derived from outmoded academic/scientific views about human nature and, more particularly, about human motivation and behaviour (Grixti 1989). This is a 'conceptual hybrid' of elements from distinct discourses, an odd combination of a 'Beast Within' and a 'tabula rasa'. The first of these is a Christian concept. In Cartesian/Christian discourses on human nature, a person is made up of conflicting opposites and constant exertions are necessary to keep in check the 'Beast Within'. The conflicting opposites can be represented like this:

mind	body
civilized	primitive
spiritual	carnal
virtue	sin
angel	ape

In the behaviourist/positivist view, by contrast, a human being is not the angel-ape guilty of original sin. It is a bundle of conditioned responses etched onto a blank plate, beyond freedom, dignity and accountability.[11] A hybrid of these two conceptions produces a peculiar notion of human being as clockwork beast, a notion that can then be used to account for worrying social phenomena:

> This is a merger which can be argued to betray a widespread desire to believe in the power of extraneous forces on to which can be attributed . . . the locus of control responsible for the undeniable existence of human destructiveness and for frequently unnerving 'negative emotions'. Conflicting theoretical models thus return to points of intersection in popular discourse, and in the customary habit of reappropriating legitimized views and systematized speculative instruments (even when these are in methodological conflict with each other) in order to reaffirm established values, or else derive reassurance in the face of disturbing phenomena.
>
> (ibid.: 110)

A 'commonsensical' view deriving from this model of human nature is the copy-cat phenomenon. This is a view about the pernicious effect of certain types of fiction (usually involving pictorial representation) that has been aired in Britain in recent years by,

among others, ex-prime minister Margaret Thatcher and Mary
Whitehouse, president of the Viewers and Listeners Association (a
supposed 'moral majority' group). Complaints about falling moral
standards resulting from the pernicious influence of media texts (as
opposed to, let's say, the current government, or one's neighbours)
go back at least as far as the 1750s (Pearson 1984).

One consequence of this high profile in the mass media has been
polarization. Repression of the genre has lead to a highly aggressive sense of 'martyrdom' among some of its fans. The following is
a parody of horror – fiction, fans and writers at their absolute
worst – from a horror novel by Ramsey Campbell. It will serve to
illustrate the polarizing effect of censorship, the aggressive hostility of horror fans towards its adverse critics, and it will give some
indication of their defensive position. Campbell is a Liverpudlian
author, who is also a fan of the horror genre and film critic. The
novel is *Ancient images* (1989). The protagonist, Sandy, is a film
archivist in search of a legendary, long-lost horror movie. She has
contacted the editor of an amateur fan magazine and is making
enquiries. A horror film playing in the background, which three
men are watching with avid interest as she arrives, is simply a
spectacle of dismemberment (of a woman), accompanied by
screams and a disco beat:

> As Sandy sat down he dropped himself beside her, seesawing the
> couch. 'They write for my magazine,' he said, his voice even higher
> with pride. 'That's John in the T-shirt that writes our video reviews, and
> this is Andrew Minihin. You must have heard of him.'
>
> When she shook her head and smiled Minihin grunted, Trantom
> sniggered incredulously, John's thighs began to vibrate as if he were
> preparing to run laps of the cluttered room. 'You must've. A paper
> wanted all his books banned,' John insisted, and listed them:' *The
> Flaying. The Slobbering. It Crawls Up You. It Crawls Back Up You. Entrails*
> that they wouldn't let him call *Puke and Die*, that was the best yet.'
>
> 'I've seen them around.'
>
> 'Wondered how anyone could buy such crap, did you?' Minihin said.
>
> The three men grinned at her as if they were watching a trap. She
> imagined them as three witches with Halloween hats, and felt more in
> control. 'Not that I remember.'
>
> 'I used to, because crap is what it is,' Minihin said with a klaxon
> laugh. 'It's what you have to write to compete with films like this one
> here. If millions of silly bastards want to read it I'd be even stupider
> than they are if I didn't give it to them. Maybe some of them will grow
> out of it. I'm getting fan mail from ten-year-old kids.'

'Watch out, you'll have her wanting to cut your books,' John said.

(Campbell 1989: 74–5)

This extract presents the cynicism of an author who despises his own readership (and himself?), as well as the hack's mercenary and amoral view that whatever is popular has to be provided. This fictitious author positively relishes disapproval. In this next extract we can hear the horror fans' belligerent reaction to censorship – a combination of 'liberalism' and the perverse use of censorship as a standard of excellence:

> 'If your film was banned it must be good,' Trantom said. 'If it's horror, we're interested. We can never get enough.'
> 'No fucker tells us what to do.'
> Sandy wasn't sure if Minihin was talking about censorship or her. She found their enthusiasm more disturbing than their suspicion of her had been. It made the room seem smaller and hotter, and raw as the silenced carnage on the screen. 'So you can't tell me anything about the film itself.'
> 'It must've upset someone,' John suggested.
> 'Told them something they didn't want to know,' Minihin said.
> It was clear they were only speculating.
>
> (ibid.: 76)

Sandy leaves their flat to the accompaniment of the screams of the woman being dismembered on the video. The comment of a woman living in the flat, that 'If it wasn't her it might be us', is not very reassuring. Campbell's dim view of these fans, the video and their magazine is clear. In the chapter following, he uses his two archivist characters to air his misgivings/dismay at this bottom-line of horror fiction and its effect on film-making:

> Trantom's misspelled editorial was addressed to 'all the psychos and sickos like us'. An article by John the Maniac described weeks of wandering around seedy video libraries in search of under-the-counter horrors. Andrew Minihin's page concluded: 'They're only special effects, and if you can't tell the difference you must be sick in the head, so fuck off to a nuthouse and let the rest of us enjoy them.'. . .
> 'It isn't how squalid it is I mind so much as how meaningless.'
> 'Sure, the cinema disappearing up itself, or reverting to a kind of magic show. If you have to spend your time reminding yourself it's fake and that's the point, what is the point? Maybe it's a rite of passage for people who never grow up.
>
> (ibid.: 82)

I will return to the matter of notoriety in the concluding section of this chapter. We now need to look at some examples of horror fiction. Compared with the kind of fiction favoured by 'John the Maniac' and his friends, the extracts from the novel I am going to examine below will seem positively bland.

'IT FELT GOOD TO KILL': SCHOOLBOY DREAMS IN THE NOVELS OF JAMES HERBERT

I have chosen to attend to samples of Herbert's novels because of their popularity. His first novel to appear in print was *The rats* (1974). Since then he has had fourteen full-length novels published. These novels have remained in print since their first publication. In my local public library, there are multiple copies of each novel which are constantly on loan. They rarely find their way back to the main shelves, since they are picked up from the returned books shelf as soon as they are returned by a borrower. As they fall apart from constant borrowings, they are replaced. A large proportion of the borrowers are young teenage boys. (The above information is on the basis of informal inquiries at my own local municipal library. Sales of Herbert's books suggest that his popularity is not a local phenomenon, however.)

Herbert's stories always deal with some manifestation of evil. Something totally malevolent is always behind the action, producing the narrative tension which drives the story along. The novels generally open with something especially grisly. *Lair* (1979), the text I have chosen for detailed study, is however a sequel of sorts to *The rats* and we can consider that first novel as its grisly opening. At the end of *The rats*, we learn that the original mutant rat was brought to London by a 'professor' (mad, presumably – certainly irresponsible) who had found it at the site of nuclear testing near comfortably distant New Guinea.

The protagonists in Herbert's novels are men, in some sort of privileged position in terms of the story: the sole survivor of a Jumbo jet crash in *The survivor* (1976); a reluctant psychic who 'picks up' gruesome murders and ghoulish grave desecrations as they happen in *Moon* (1985); in *The rats*, a schoolteacher in the area of an outbreak of out-sized, people-eating rats who, improbably, becomes a key figure in the emergency operations; in *Lair*, an entomologist turned official 'ratcatcher'. The protagonist generally acquires a girlfriend as the story progresses (in *The survivor*, his girlfriend was on the ill-fated aeroplane). Character focalization is often through the protagonist, but not always. There are frequent shifts. Even the malevolence – the manifestation of absolute and uncompromising evil itself – is the focalizer in places. Such passages are sometimes marked off by italization, as in *Moon* and *Lair*. In *Moon*, the evil presence is given separate chapters to itself. In *Lair*, the evil mutant rodents (two foot long rats who like eating people) are given prologues to each of the three major sections, 'Signs', 'Onslaught' and 'Lair'. (The first one, which opens the novel, is in fact the 'epilogue' from *The rats*.)

The manifestation of evil aside, the focalizing character tends to be male and women are always presented from a man's viewpoint. Details of appearance and desirability predominate, as in this extract from early in the opening chapter of *Lair*:

> The man crawled on his stomach through the damp grass towards the prone woman. She lay unaware of his stealthy approach, her face turned towards the sun, surprised and happy to receive its warmth so late in the year. She flexed her shoulders against the rough blanket, its thickness protecting her from the wetness of the grass which even the sun could not draw out.
>
> The creeping man smiled and a gleam came into his eyes. A sound behind him made him turn his head sharply and he frowned at his two companions, silently urging them to remain quiet.
>
> The woman sighed and raised a knee provocatively; the smoothness of her legs caught the man's attention. His smile widened and he felt the pressure of the earth against his loins. He was close now, close enough to reach out and touch that wonderfully soft body. He tried to control his breathing so that she wouldn't hear.
>
> Bringing his arm forward, he snapped off a long blade of grass, then pointed its quivering tip towards the woman's face. She twitched as the fine point ran down the side of her nose, then twitched again as the tickling sensation persisted. She suddenly sat upright, vigorously rubbing at her skin as though to dislodge an errant insect.
>
> 'Terry,' she shouted when she saw his shaking body, and grabbed a handful of grass and threw it into his face.
>
> The two children behind the man laughed excitedly
>
> (Herbert 1979: 13–14)

The apparent menace in this early scene is of course a false alarm; it is not men who are the threat to people's safety in this novel, but rodents. But the apparent threat is there, before it is defused and made playful. The woman is 'prone' and she raises her knee 'provocatively' – a choice of adverb indicating the point of view of someone who feels 'provoked' (since 'provocation' does not appear to be the woman's intention). The man perceives particular, quintessentially feminine physical qualities of smoothness and softness.

When a woman is presented as the focalizing character it almost invariably indicates her violent death is imminent. The woman in the extract is luckier than she knows: we are given brief access to her enjoyment of the sun's warmth (we also glimpse her disapproval of her husband's trade union activity for a moment or two on the next page), and yet she is the victim of nothing worse than the mock-threat posed by the playful stalking we saw above. These narratives are dealing with fear. They demand emotional involvement. Close association with a character in a fearful state is essential if a reader is to share some of that sensation. Focalization through the victim is an effective way of achieving it. As Twitchell says, 'No horror exists unless we have taken the victim to heart' (Twitchell 1985: 44). When reading Herbert's novels, one soon learns to fear for the safety of any minor character brought into close focus. The wife in the extract above is fortunate enough to appear near the beginning of *Lair*. In the first section, 'Signs', the rats are biding their time. In the next section, 'Onslaught', a furtive couple whose thoughts we are given access to are not so fortunate: they are the first to be eaten alive by the rats. Later in the section, a minor character's disparaging self-contemplation, in a large plate glass window made reflective by the darkness outside, presages an attack (*'Silly, but it was almost as though the creatures were out there watching her'*); the rats burst through the glass and set upon her. Similarly in Herbert's *Moon*, we are drawn into the worried thoughts of a headmistress, and given access to her abject fear of the evil character, just before it sets fire to her school and she burns to death.

The furtive lovers are eaten by rats immediately after they have enjoyed two pages of detailed sexual activity. Scenes dealing with sex often lead directly into scenes of violent death. And the close narrative connection between sex and death goes further than this. In *The survivor*, a man just thinking about his marital infidelities while fishing on the Thames goes to a nasty watery grave within a few pages.

Another generalization we can make about Herbert's novels is his use of gender stereotypes. A short example from *The survivor* will illustrate this point. After the air disaster, there has been a series of bizarre and mysterious deaths in the locality of the field where the aeroplane crashed. The extract below precedes a recap in which all the grisly deaths are listed one after another. Notice the occupational stereotyping:

> The women met in shops and in the High Street, infecting each other with their own personal fear; the men discussed the peculiar happenings at their desks or work benches, many scornful of the suggestion that some evil was afoot in the town, but admittedly perplexed by the sequence of events.
>
> (Herbert 1976: 110)

Women go shopping, while men work. The way women's and men's talk is represented is worth noting, too. The men discuss, respond to suggestions, are scornful or perplexed; in other words, in their interaction among themselves they are intellectually active. The women are simply 'infecting each other with their own personal fear'; that is, responding emotionally and personally, not intellectually and publicly, and simply causing trouble. Herbert also perpetuates sexist naming practices, with asymmetrical usage of both terms of reference and terms of address, and sexist practices of chivalric decorum, such as giving women totally unnecessary physical assistance; for example 'He took Jenny's arm and guided her into the welcoming warmth of the pub' (1979: 69). Perhaps I should explain that in this particular scene *she* has just suggested the pub and driven him there.

One other general observation applies to various novels which I have not mentioned so far, *The fog, The Jonah* and *The dark*, in particular. These three novels were Grixti's focus of (highly negative) critical attention. He saw reflected in them the popular view of human motivation and behaviour that we looked at earlier. 'Civilization', we are to believe, is a thin veneer barely keeping in check humanity's capacity for 'naked animal behaviour': *'you're in the Force'*, the hero's girlfriend reminds him in *The Jonah, 'you know just how thin that barrier between civilisation and naked animal behaviour is'* (Herbert 1981: 68). The 'animal behaviour' Herbert has in mind here has little to do with real animals. What he is actually referring to are grisly acts of extreme barbarity among human beings.

The text population in an extract from *Lair*

What follows is detail of a passage from *Lair*, in which I will examine how the extract is 'populated'. This will mean returning once again to some of the cues that I suggested in Chapter 3 under the headings of interaction/interactants, prior text/characters and discourse types/subject positions. The extract needs little introduction. It is the end of the penultimate chapter in the section appropriately entitled 'Onslaught'. A minor character, Jan, has been badly mauled (she is the character we saw gazing at her own reflection in the glass earlier). The hero, Luke Pender, has just bumped his head, having hurled himself through a doorway in his escape from the invading rats:

(1) 'Shut it!' he screamed, and Will lost no time in doing so.

(2) The door rattled in its frame as the vermin threw themselves against it. They could hear the scratching sounds, the splintering as the creatures gnawed at the wood.

(3) Pender shook his head to clear his senses.

(4) 'Are you okay?' the tutor asked anxiously, holding on to the door-handle as if to keep it closed.

(5) 'Yes. I knocked my head, that's all.' He got to one knee and crouched beside Jan and felt her pulse. It was weak. 'We've got to get her to a hospital. I don't think she'll make it, otherwise.' He looked up at Will. 'You can let go of the door – I don't think they're that clever.'

(6) Will sheepishly dropped his hand. 'My God, listen to them. It won't take them long to gnaw their way through.'

(7) 'No, and we'd better be out of here before they do.'

(8) 'Luke, I've called the police.' It was Jenny, standing at the end of the darkened corridor, by the reception area. 'I've also called the warden, on the internal phone and warned him to keep everybody inside the living quarters until the police get here.'

(9) 'Good girl. Stay where you are, we'll bring Jan . . .' His voice broke off when he noticed something dark moving along the corridor, something low, crouched close to the wall. It was making towards Jenny.

(10) 'Jenny, run! Get away from there!' He was on his feet, running down the corridor. Jenny stood transfixed, her eyes wide with terror.

(11) The rat moved with incredible speed, Pender's footsteps galvanising it into action. It broke free from the shadows. Jenny could only step back as it sped past her, its stiffened fur actually brushing her legs. It scuttled madly around in the wider reception area, looking

for an opening, a crazed look in its eyes. Jenny leaned back against the far wall and watched in fascinated horror. Pender reached her and shielded her body when he saw the rat's frantic actions.

(12) A full-length window stood by the glass door, giving half the reception area a glass wall appearance. The rat ran at the lower pane and bounced off its rigid surface. It tried again, throwing itself at the glass with desperate strength. Pender was conscious of a police siren in the distance, the unmistakable wail growing louder with each second.

(13) The rat scrambled away from the glass and made towards them. Pender got ready to kick out at it, but the creature turned before it reached them and hurtled itself at the window once more. This time, the glass shattered and it was through, disappearing into the shadows outside, leaving scraped-off hair and blood on the remaining window fragments.

(14) 'Oh, God, Luke. It's vile. It's so vile.' Jenny leaned against Pender's back; he was too afraid to take his eyes off the broken pane in case the rats came swarming through.

(15) 'Luke. Come here, quickly.' It was Will calling from the gloomy end of the corridor.

(16) Pender grabbed Jenny's arm and took her with him.

(17) 'What is it?' he asked when he reached the crouched figure.

(18) 'Listen!'

(19) Pender heard nothing. Then he realised what the young tutor was getting at. 'The rats,' he said. 'They're gone.'

(Herbert 1979: 145–6)

Prior texts/characters

There are four human characters in this corridor scene. We can examine the intersecting texts three of them produce under *Interaction* below. (One of the characters is unconscious and in no condition to contribute actively, although her critical condition does influence the action.) There is also a horde of rats, on the other side of the door, and an individual one menacing the humans in the corridor. The distant 'voice' of a police siren indicates the imminent arrival of more characters of the human variety.

As in the written romance text sample we examined in Chapter 4, presuppositions set up throughout this passage are contributing to the deadpan realism and to the narrative tension. They are triggered in a number of ways; I will just give a few examples. Definite descriptions cue existential presuppositions; these contribute crucially to the construction of setting; for example *'the darkened corridor'* in (8) establishes that there was a darkened corridor. Temporal clause linkage (*before-* and *when-* clauses) cues presuppositions contributing to the narrative progression and tension; for example '*the creature turned before it reached them'* in (13) establishes that it nearly did so. Another temporal clause that contributes to the tension is 'It won't take them long to gnaw their way through', which presupposes, of course, that they will. One other type of presupposition is cued by contrastive stress and reiterates information about the sinister mutants that the reader has been given earlier; namely that the rats are clever. It occurs in a piece of speech representation, so we'll return to it below, when we look at the interaction.

The narrative voice from (1) to (7) seems to be omniscient narration, but could be seen as focalisation through the eyes of both male characters (on the basis of sentence 2 in (2): '*They could hear . . .'*). What is clear, however, is the shift to focalization through the protagonist, Luke Pender. This shift takes place in (8), but it is not apparent until (9), where the first mental process verb occurs with him as the grammatical subject ('noticed' in sentence 2 of (9)). What brings about the shift in focalization is an existential statement doubling as reporting clause, after a vocative: '"*Luke, I've called the police." It was Jenny, standing at the end of the darkened corridor.'* This is a construction Herbert uses frequently. There is another in the passage, in (15): '"*Luke. Come here, quickly." It was Will calling from the gloomy end of the corridor.'* This kind of construction looks deceptively like omniscient narration and seems to occlude the character focalization through the hero. The character of Jenny is arguably the focalizer for fleeting moments of terror in sentence 3 of (10) and sentence 4 of (11).

Still on the topic of prior texts/characters, it is possible to make connections between the extract and actual prior texts in the genre. It enacts scenes recognizably similar to scenes in antecedent horror texts. The menace of being mobbed in a confined space was presented by Daphne du Maurier in her short story, 'The birds' (1952), and later by Hitchcock in his film version. The second paragraph in the extract is reminiscent of a scene in the film in which an enraged flock of birds attempt to batter through a door (behind which Tippi Hedren is cowering). The menace of infestation and mobbing by rats is the theme of a lesser film, *Willard* (1971). There is another kind of linkage operating here, too. The situation type, and indeed the character types as well, might have come straight out of a text from another genre, namely the western. This kind of observation takes us to the boundary between the prior text and discourse-type senses of intertextuality. If we consider the connection to be with a specific western (say, *Wagon train*) then we are focusing on prior text. If we are concentrating on a connection with the Western genre as a whole, then we are focusing on discourse type. I will take the latter option, and return to the extract's enactment of western genre elements under *Discourse types/subject positions* below.

Interaction/interactants

In order to see the interaction represented more clearly, we can strip the narration away from the passage, turning it into a script with paralanguage directions. We can label paired actions, whether verbal or non-verbal, as adjacency pairs; for example Luke's command in (1) elicits a compliant non-verbal '2nd pair part' from Will. We can also include discernible non-responses; for example Jenny's non-compliance with Luke's command in (10). Actions with no discernible response of any kind are placed in brackets:

(1) *Command*	Luke:	'Shut it!'
Non-verbal response		Will lost no time in doing so.
(4) *Question*	Will:	'Are you okay?'
(5) *Answer*	Luke:	'Yes. I knocked my head, that's all.'
(Statement)		'We've got to get her to a hospital. I don't think she'll make it, otherwise.'
Suggestion		'You can let go of the door – I don't think they're that clever.'
(6) *Non-verbal response*		Will sheepishly dropped his hand.
Statement	Will:	'My God, listen to them. It won't take them long to gnaw their way through.'
(7) *Comment*	Luke:	'No, and we'd better be out of here before they do.'
(8) *Statement*	Jenny:	'Luke, I've called the police.' 'I've also called the warden, on the internal phone and warned him to keep everybody inside the living quarters until the police get here.'
(9) *Comment*	Luke:	'Good girl.
(Command)		Stay where you are,
(Statement)		we'll bring Jan . . .'

(10) *Command*		'Jenny, run! Get away from there!'
Non-compliance		Jenny stood transfixed
(14) *Request for comfort?*	Jenny:	'Oh, God, Luke. It's vile. It's so vile.'
		Jenny leaned against Pender's back;
Non-compliance		he was too afraid to take his eyes off
		the broken pane
(15) *Command*	Will:	'Luke. Come here, quickly.'
(16) *Non-verbal response*		Pender grabbed Jenny's arm and
		took her with him.
(17) *Question -*	Luke:	'What is it?'
(18) *Command*	Will:	'Listen!'
(19) *Non-verbal response*		Pender heard nothing.
- Answer	Luke:	'The rats,' 'They're gone.'

What is immediately apparent in the dialogue is that Luke is in charge of the situation, making all the constructive statements relating to their predicament and giving most of the orders. Will, by contrast, is ineffectual, as Luke implies with his mocking suggestion in (5). At the end of the extract, Will's perception of the rats' departure is presented not by Will but by Luke, by means of an insertion sequence enabling Luke to answer his own question.

Notice Luke's patronizing response to Jenny in (9). He had to bully her into going to the phone in the first place, a few pages earlier ('"Get help, Jenny,". . . She stood there, mesmerized by the awful scene, and he had to shove her hard. "Move!" he shouted.' ibid.: 140). She managed it, eventually. Notice also that Jenny's non-compliance in (10) is a result of her craven fear and inability to cope with the situation; Luke's in (14), on the other hand, is because he is so vigilant and has no time to spare for physical reassurances.

Discourse types/subject positions

This aspect of the text's population deals with fragmented and heterogeneous discoursal and generic elements. To attend to these we need to ask: what generic conventions are being enacted, what discourses are being drawn upon, what subject positions do they set up?

Herbert's novels are horror stories that involve confrontations with some manifestation of absolute and uncompromising evil. In *Lair*, of course, the malevolence takes the form of hostile mutant rats out to get people. So the classificatory scheme for rats in the passage seems like a good place to start:

vermin   stiffened fur
creature/s   a crazed look
rat   vile
something dark
something low

Three other frequently used terms, which do not appear in the extract, are 'mutant', 'monster' and 'Black rat'. They are once referred to as 'the Black breed' (ibid.: 102); we are told that they have been bred from black rats (the genus *rattus rattus*), rather than the commoner brown rat (*rattus norvegicus*). Attributes assigned to them elsewhere in *Lair* are 'slimy' tails (ibid.: 44), 'slanted eyes' (ibid.: 167) and 'bristle-haired fur' (ibid.: 243). (In *The rats* they are also given 'evil slanted eyes, yellow and malevolent', 1974: 177, and 'fetid breath', ibid.: 178.)

Herbert is accurate in the information provided in an early chapter by the ratcatcher hero, information about rat habitats, their two-year life span, size of litter. However, in terms of appearance or behaviour the rats in *Lair* bear no relation to real rats at all. See Fig. 5.1 for what a rat looks like. Its tail may not be attractive (to non-rats, that is!) but slimy it is certainly not. Its eyes are black and round, rather like beads. If a rat's eyes look narrower than this, then it's probably asleep. Notice its sleek fur. A rat, like any other furry animal, has to spend a large proportion of its short life in grooming activity. The only kind of rat likely to have 'stiffened fur' is one too sick to look after itself. The animal in Fig. 5.1 is a 'fancy' rat, a variety bred in captivity from the brown rat and found in pet shops and laboratories. The black rat is smaller, both in size and numbers, but otherwise very similar. Neither variety eats people, needless to say. They are scavengers, not hunters. The manifestation of evil in *Lair* has nothing whatever to do with real rats in either behaviour or appearance. But of course, they are mutants, which has to account for everything. The fear Herbert addresses in his rat stories is little more than fear of 'creepy-crawlies'; and ill-informed at that.

The passage is a fine example of masculine heroics, depicting as it does a battle between our hero and an evil mutant rat. The other two conscious characters are mere onlookers. The women, conscious or unconscious, are simply liabilities. Despite being the one who telephoned for assistance, Jenny is more like a piece of baggage than an active participant:

(15) 'Luke. Come here, quickly.' It was Will calling from the gloomy end of the corridor.
(16) Pender grabbed Jenny's arm and took her with him.
(17) 'What is it?' he asked when he reached the crouched figure.

We can infer that Jenny must have 'reached the crouched figure' simultaneously, whether intentionally or otherwise. But it is Luke who is in charge: 'Men act; women are acted upon. This is patriarchy' (Gamman and Marshment 1988: 1). There is more on gender stereotyping below, pp. 133–5.

We can focus on the representation of the protagonist's heroic actions in the passage by examining transitivity and material processes in it. The distribution of material processes and, in particular, actions represented transitively will give an indication of each character's degree of active involvement and control. By including mental processes at the same time, we can also examine character focalization. With these aims, Table 5.1 presents two things. It shows us how the transitive and intransitive verbs are distributed between the characters. It also shows us how material and mental processes are distributed (for clarity, the latter are placed in italics). As I am attending to transitivity, most of the items are verbs, but I have included a few nouns and adjectives, where relevant to the representation of material or mental processes. The English is idiomatic so, to make things clearer, I have also included some longer constructions. These are mostly *Verb Phrase – Prepositional Phrase*; for example *VP (was) PP (on his feet); VP (was making) PP (towards Jenny)*.[12] I have also included elliptical reference to a material process verb ('doing so'; thereby increasing Will's quota from two to three).

In the representation of the rat's actions, five transitive verbs are used. Two of these are reflexive ('throwing itself'; 'hurtled itself'). One of them ('brushing') has the rat's 'stiffened fur' as its grammatical subject. Luke by contrast is the grammatical subject of 14 transitive verbs, either as 'Pender' or pronominalized for all but one of them. The exception is in the non-finite clause: 'Pender's

Table 5.1 Distribution of: i) transitive and intransitive verbs, ii) material and mental processes.

Luke		The rat	
trans.	intrans.	trans.	intrans.
shook	got (to one knee)	brushing	moving
to clear	crouched	ran at	crouched
knocked	*looked*	throwing	was making (towards Jenny)
felt	was (on his feet)	hurtled	moved
noticed	running	leaving	broke (free)
galvanising	to kick out		sped
reached			scuttled
shielded			*looking*
saw			scrambled
grabbed			bounced
took			made (towards them)
reached			turned
heard			was (through)
realised			disappearing
	senses	*action*	
	footsteps	actions	
	concious		
	afraid		

Jenny		Will	
trans.	intrans.	trans.	intrans.
	standing	doing so	holding on
	stood	dropped	
	could . . . step back		
	leaned back		
	watched		
	leaned		
	terror		
	horror		

footsteps galvanising it into action.' At this point, Luke's control of the situation even seems to extend to the rat's behaviour.

Herbert's use of gender stereotypes in the sample passage is clear. We can see the sexism in his naming practices. The patronizing term of address in Luke's congratulatory comment in (9) hardly needed pointing out. Perhaps slightly less obvious is the asymmetrical use of terms of reference in the narration. The protagonist is referred to by his surname; the minor character is referred to either by his first name or by profession ('tutor'); the hero's girlfriend is referred to by her first name but not by profession. She is also a 'tutor', but we are rarely reminded of it and have been reassured early on that she doesn't *look* like one: *'Pender looked at the girl* [sic] *and . . . realised she was very attractive, not at all "tutorish"'* (1979: 51).

As I suggested earlier, the extract might have been a scene from a western. The principal elements are there in the character and situation types enacted: the tough heroism of the lone hero, his positive action in rescuing an injured party (and the code of honour underlying such an act) the ineffectual 'side-kick' and the dependent females, including one plucky one who is destined to be the hero's reward. There is even a suggestion, brought in by the approaching police siren, of the cavalry coming to the rescue in the nick of time. The passage needs only a cornered 'Red Indian' (or, more properly, 'Injun') in place of the mutant rat to be complete, and perhaps a covered wagon as a backdrop.

What discourses are being drawn in to this passage? The heroics in the confrontation of an evil presence demonstrate the protagonist's potency. Like the hero of the Mills & Boon we looked at in Chapter 4, Luke Pender is 'male with a capital M' (to quote one of the Mills & Boon characters). It seems that the same body of knowledge is being drawn upon: a discourse of gender. Luke is presented as a masculine type; tough, capable and, above all, in control. He is an authority figure; the other people are his charges.

But what about the rats? I have indicated above how little, in terms of their behaviour or appearance, they resemble real animals. The rat in the corridor is more like a cornered 'Injun'. The rat horde, like the aggressive but cowardly Injun horde, appears to flee at the approach of the cavalry, in the tradition of the western genre. It is possible to infer that the sound of the police siren drives away the horde outside. Indeed, Herbert deems it necessary to refute this implication explicitly a little later: 'The mutants left not because their acute hearing could pick up the sirens approaching in the distance, but because their hunger was satiated, their bellies glutted' (ibid.: 152). In fact, this is storytelling nonsense, since the rats have to be in two places at once: trying to get at the people in the corridor, and eating their fill of other people at a nearby 'mobile home site'. But the point is Herbert seems to expect the reader to have drawn in some kind of knowledge frame connecting police siren and breaking and entering. Why would rats, even mutant ones, attach any significance to a distant sound of police sirens? The rat in the corridor, the villain of the piece in the extract, is the enemy of law and order. From this perspective, it is presented more as hooligan than wild animal, running around frenziedly and damaging property.

'It's regrettable, but that's how it is'

The rats are represented as the ultimate evil. They are the 'otherness', which has to be confronted and destroyed – rather than studied and understood, cherished and integrated. Any potentially attractive characteristics (they are small furry animals, after all!) are misrepresented. As not only vermin but mutant vermin, they do not have the right to live. They are represented as a threat to social order and as such they must be destroyed, by whatever means necessary. In the final third of the novel the military arrive on the scene, complete with Chieftain tanks, Gazelle helicopters and 'killer gas'. From this point on, the masculine heroics reach fever pitch: 'He had never handled a gun before, but pulling a trigger seemed an uncomplicated operation' (ibid.: 169). Luke needs no instruction in the use of firearms; it seems to come naturally to him as he and the soldiers wage war on rodents in Epping Forest:

> In a rage the soldiers began firing into them, regardless of the human body, knowing the man was dead.
> 'Leave them!' Captain Mather ordered dispassionately. 'We can't help the poor sod now, and at least his body is keeping them occupied!' He kicked at the side of the truck and it drove on.
> Pender was horrified at the officer's cold logic, but he knew Mather was right. The living had to be their main concern . . .
> 'Mather!' he yelled. 'They're trying to get through the roof.'
> Mather glanced up. 'Shit,' he said. Then, 'Forget them. If we shoot through the canvas we'll only make holes that the others can use to their advantage. We'll keep an eye on them and shoot only when it's necessary.' With that, he turned his attention back to the action below.
> Pender raised the automatic rifle to his shoulder, spotted a rat wriggling its way into the vehicle at one corner, kicked out with venom, sending it toppling back, then began firing at random. It felt good to kill.

(ibid.: 172–3)

The term 'action' is being used in the sense specific to military discourse, a usage frequently imitated in fiction-producing industries.

Apart from that, the militarism owes more to *Boy's own paper* adventure stories, or their playground equivalent, than real military discourses. It is this connection which makes it difficult to suppress the imperialist and racist undertones of 'evil slanted eyes' and 'the Black breed'.

SUBTLER HORRORS

According to some critics, the implied reader of horror fiction may occupy the subject position of both aggressor and victim simultaneously. Various critics, including Carole Clover below, have likened the process involved to dreamwork:

> Just as attacker and attacked are expressions of the same self in nightmares, so they are expressions of the same viewer in horror film. We are both Red Riding Hood and the Wolf; the force of the experience, in horror, comes from 'knowing' both sides of the story.
>
> (Clover 1992: 12)

King attributes the lasting popularity of the *Frankenstein* films to the splitting of the viewer between sympathy for the beleaguered monster and the angry vengeful mob (King 1982: 75). We have already seen the necessity for close identification with a victim for the horror to work. This closeness is achieved by intensive character focalization. The splitting of the implied reader between aggressor and victim involves an additional identification with the aggressor. Herbert's novels do not seem to work this way, however. He offers either one or the other. We could see aggressor-identification in operation in the 'stalking' passage from *Lair*, in which the narration is focalized through the 'stalking' husband; more often, the focalization is through a character under threat, whether hero or minor character (and hence, almost inevitably, doomed). It is worth considering at this point some attempts to formalize the differences between kinds of horror fiction. There is a distinction often made between 'terror' and 'horror' that goes back at least as far as Ann Radcliffe:

> Terror and horror are so far opposite, that the first expands the soul, and wakens the faculties to a higher degree of life; the other contracts, freezes and nearly annihilates them.
>
> (Radcliffe; quoted in Dalby 1990: ix–x)

The terror/horror distinction is frequently reiterated one way or another by critics and practitioners of horror fiction (Stephen King uses it without any acknowledgements, presenting it as his own – King 1982: 36–40). H P Lovecraft seems to have a similar contrast in mind when he distinguishes between grisly horror stories and the 'literature of cosmic fear':

> This type of fear-literature must not be confounded with a type exter-
> nally similar but psychologically widely different; the literature of mere
> physical fear and the mundanely gruesome. . . The true weird tale has
> something more than secret murder, bloody bones, or a sheeted form
> clanking chains according to rule.
>
> (Lovecraft 1969: 143–4)

The 'sheeted form clanking chains' is rather passé, but it does have modern correlates. Conspicuous among them are creepy-crawlies like Herbert's killer rats, and also the slimier kind we saw parodied in Campbell's *Ancient images* (1989) earlier. In Lovecraft's category of the 'true weird tale', he includes some literary 'classics' – *Frankenstein* (Shelley 1818), *Wuthering Heights* (Brontë 1847) and 'The yellow wallpaper' (Gilman 1892) among them – and, perhaps more expectedly, Radcliffe's gothic novels and most of Edgar Allan Poe's output. While the terror/horror distinction is difficult to maintain, it serves as a reminder that horror practitioners them-selves are aware of the inadequacies of the bottom-line of horror as 'the mundanely gruesome'.

Modern horror fiction relies heavily upon intensively focalized visual and sensory experiences for its effect. It may be that these have to be presented in a 'declarative' kind of text, recalling Belsey's term mentioned in Chapter 2. The sample text of Herbert's we examined in detail is certainly a text of the 'declarative' type, reinforcing dominant, 'commonsensical' values and offering what are assumed to be familiar subject positions. But this is not always so, at least not quite so straightforwardly. Consider the following passage from Campbell's *The influence* (1988). The young protago-nist doesn't yet realize it, but she is dead, or at least bodiless, having been ousted by her adversary. The character focalization is intensive, but the faculties through which the narrative is presented to us are not to be trusted:

> The wall felt chill and gritty, yet it made her think of softened flesh.
> She recoiled before she had time to gasp, but the sensations clung to
> her, swarmed through her . . .

The street seemed to close around her, the long white street whose doors she had suddenly become more aware of. They appeared to be composed of the same substance as the cottages – the same as the pavement into which she hadn't noticed her feet were sinking.

(Campbell 1988: 173–4)

Here Campbell is describing the familiar made strange. Categories are confused and boundaries transgressed. Animate and inanimate are not clearly distinguishable; objects with hard texture are registered as soft; the immobile appears to move . . . This sample, in contrast with the exaggerated grisliness of Herbert's horror fiction, illustrates a subtler aspect of the horror genre as the fiction of nightmares.

The main horrors in Campbell's novel, *The influence*, are the identity loss and relational loss of the young protagonist, as her entire existence – her identity and social position as much-loved daughter in a family – is usurped by a reincarnated relative. In two of Campbell's other novels, *Ancient images* (touched on earlier in this chapter) and *Midnight sun* (1991), family problems stemming from male lineage seem to be the central dilemma being addressed. In *Midnight sun*, the protagonist inherits his father's and grandfather's ultimately deadly fascination with the elemental force of Jack Frost. Other writers have also updated traditional folklore figures. Gallagher for example, in *The boat house* (1991), centres the narrative on the unpleasant exploits of a rusalka (a European elemental, of the malign woodland variety).

There is one specific device used in horror writing, linking the genre with its gothic origins, which I have not yet mentioned. The following short extract from *Ancient images* is from a scene following the death, in suspicious circumstances, of a pierhead entertainer the protagonist has been looking for. The entertainer has seen something which terrified him and run off the end of the pier. As a consequence, everyone is feeling jumpy; there is an unknown *something* outside. This fragment of narrative description contributes to the feeling of unease:

A wind tried the window and then blundered away into the night. On the beach a piece of the dark stirred and settled itself.

(Campbell 1989: 126)

'A wind' and 'the dark' are both represented as agents of processes requiring sentience and active agency. This anthropomorphism, of the weather in this case, is a device which is effective in small doses, as here.

CONCLUSION: HORROR FICTION AND CONTAINMENT

Horror fiction can be said to function as containment, insofar as it fictionally addresses and resolves perceived problems. In addition to the fictional resolutions within individual horror narratives, the genre of horror can also be said to function as containment within and across orders of discourse. This section examines in turn each of these forms of containment.

Within horror texts, something fearful is identified, confronted and ultimately overcome. The kind of narrative resolution needed depends upon the culture in and for which it is produced. In a lot of American horror and horror-related films, 'overcoming' appears to be synonymous with punishing: punishment of those who transgress by madness or some other form of deviance. Fundamentalist Christian tendencies seem to underlie the need for retribution in such films, recent examples of which might include *Lawnmower man* (1992) and the 'Freddy' films (the series of *Nightmare on Elm Street* movies). In Herbert's fiction, as we have seen, the 'something fearful' is absolute evil in some manifestation or other and it is always overcome by the macho hero. The rats in *Lair* are an uncomplicated, ruthless adversary against which equally ruthless military might is essential for the restoration of order.

Fortunately, subtler fears and fictional treatments are not hard to find. The last section considered some of them. It is perhaps true that horror writers are, generally speaking, 'agents of the norm' (King 1982: 64); the label certainly fits Herbert, whose confrontations with horror are highly normative. But it is not always quite so straightforwardly the case. Horror is a genre addressing excess or, at Campbell puts it, 'the branch of literature most often concerned with going too far' (Campbell 1988: 3). Sometimes this means grisly people-eating rodents, but not always.

Since the 1970s, horror writing has proliferated. The marketing category genre of horror has been highly lucrative for publishers and a small number of bestselling authors. Nevertheless, as a consequence of the operation of the genre-mainstream distinction (see Chapter 2 for discussion), the horror genre still has a marginal position in both literary-academic discourses and discourses of publishing. As a kind of 'genre fiction', horror is ghettoized (or perhaps I should say 'demonized', considering the content!). Within the marginalised literary form, which as it has developed as a marketing category has been largely defined by bestselling male writers, women writers have been marginalized to the point of exclusion, as Tuttle observes in her introduction to an anthology of horror stories by women:

> Women writers tend to be seen either as rare exceptions, or redefined as something else – not horror but gothic; not horror but suspense; not horror but romance, or fantasy, or something unclassifiable but different. It has almost become a circular, self-fulfilling argument: horror is written by men, so if it's written by women, it isn't horror.
>
> (Tuttle 1990: 3)

In extreme circumstances, as we have already observed, a text in one of the lesser valued visual media may be used as a scapegoat to take the blame for a society's ills. Stanley Kubrick's film of *A clockwork orange* (1971) achieved 'demonic' status in Britain in the early 1970s.[13] The press reported copy-cat acts of 'ultra-violence' purportedly committed by groups of skinheads dressed like and named after the 'droogs' in the film. It was not actually banned (although the 'martyrs' of horror fandom like to think so), but Kubrick did eventually ask for the film to be withdrawn. What was wrong with this film? There is no reason to disbelieve the newspaper reports about violent attacks, but neither is there any reason to assume that they would not have been committed if the self-styled 'droogies' had not watched the film. Skinhead activity was common in Britain at the time. Another extremely violent film released in the same year was Francis Ford Coppola's *The godfather*. This was a family saga/gangster film (it was about the mafia: it was all kept in the family). Both films are artistically of very high quality; both have had critical praise heaped on them (according to one enthusiastic film critic *A clockwork orange* is 'like a ruby in a field of gravel' – Hogan 1986: 135). *A clockwork orange* achieved notoriety; *The godfather* was followed by one sequel, then another. There are major differences between the two, which may go some way to accounting for the divergence. Put bluntly, *A clockwork orange* shows the wrong people committing acts of violence. It also draws too much attention to its artifice and does not fit easily enough into a recognized fiction category, so that it is difficult to dismiss as 'just a gangster film', for example. It is easy to blame horrific depictions of violent acts by youths with no respect for authority, especially when so much artistic ability and effort has gone into their aesthetic representation: far easier than confronting the real social problem. It will be interesting to see whether the harrowing Australian skin-

head film, *Romper stomper* (1992), achieves similar demonic status
This brings us back to the conservatism of *Lair*, in which, clearly,
the acts of violence are being committed by the *right* people. In this
novel, the people who not only can but *must* commit acts of violence are the agents of law and order: the police, the army, the male
authority-figure of the protagonist, Luke Pender.

In concluding the last chapter, 'Escaping into romance', I said
that romance is not necessarily any more escapist than any other
kind of fiction. Fiction-reading *per se* is an escapist activity. I will
conclude this chapter on 'Confronting horror' with the observation
that horror fiction is not necessarily any more confrontational than
other genres. There is not much *real* confrontation in *Lair*, for example. None of Herbert's horror novels referred to in this chapter
diverges from the reactionary belief in the need to preserve the status quo by whatever means necessary, or the proto-fundamentalism
of belief in 'absolute evil' in some manifestation or other. What real
confrontation in fiction might be is a theme that I will take up in the
next chapter.

TAKING IT FURTHER

There are whole areas of horror fiction meriting chapters to themselves which, for reasons of space, I have not touched on at all;
forbidden eroticism and vampirism, for example. For criticism of
this theme in horror fiction, see Richard Dyer's 'Children of the
night: vampirism as homosexuality, homosexuality as vampirism'
(1988). For a challenge to it in fiction, see Jody Scott's *I vampire*: a
celebration of homosexuality, with a vampire's first person narrative. Still on the subject of vampires, interesting studies include
Anne Cranny-Francis's investigations of conservative and subversive novels: 'Sexual politics and political repression in Bram
Stoker's *Dracula*' (1988) and 'De-fanging the vampire: S M
Charnas's *The vampire tapestry* as subversive horror fiction' (1990).

The genre has received very little attention within language studies. Roland Barthes' examination of Edgar Allan Poe's 'Valdemar'
(a short story on the boundary between life and death) is an interesting application of the approach used in *S/Z*. Grixti's chapters on
Herbert and King contain some close linguistic analysis. For a psycho-
analytic approach to horror – as the almost-repressed on the borders
of the unconscious – see Julia Kristeva's *Powers of horror* (1982).

Part III

Fiction and social change

SIX

Fiction and empowerment

Poet
let the people know
that dreams can become
reality

(A N C Kumalo 1972)

Some kinds of fiction deliberately set out to denaturalize, contest or in some way put up a resistance to dominant discourses, the subject positions they offer, and the ideologies embodied in them. Cultural production, including the production of works of fiction, is crucial in the generation of versions of historical events from non-dominant perspectives, what Edward Said has called 'repressed or resistant history' (Said 1985: 94). It is also essential as part of a dominated people's awareness of their condition. Ngugi wa Thiong'o, a Kenyan writer in exile in London, makes a distinction between two kinds of literature which is close to the distinction between socially reproductive and empowering fiction which informs this book. Ngugi's concern is the literature syllabus in Kenyan schools: literature either oppresses, by shoring up dominant imperialist discourses, or contributes to the struggle for liberation from them (Ngugi 1981). This view of literature places a value on politically motivated fiction which runs counter to the dominant literary-academic notions of what makes fine literature: liberal humanist notions of universality, timelessness.

This chapter deals with both reading and writing 'against the grain'. By considering the possibilities of critical reading and writing I will examine fiction as a vehicle for empowerment. My concerns are denaturalization in both interpretation and production: resistant readings of fiction and the history of fiction, the subversion of conventional writing practices and production processes.

OLD BOOKS, NEW READINGS

One way of using fiction to empower readers is to hijack well-known texts and produce challenging new readings of them. Ngugi's rereadings of colonial literature as racist are a good example. His short but incisive critical readings counter the familiar (for many of us) racist literature about the colonies by Rudyard Kipling, Rider Haggard and Karen Blixen (Ngugi 1981: 16–18). Another example is my own critical analysis in Chapter 3 of the 'voices' permitted entry into the narrative in *Heart of darkness*.

Another non-dominant, oppositional discourse producing new readings is Anglo-American feminism. Feminism is a kind of politics. When feminists engage in literary criticism, it is perceived as part of a larger cultural analysis, not as an end in itself. As Toril Moi says:

> Feminist criticism . . . is a specific kind of political discourse: a critical and theoretical practice committed to the struggle against patriarchy and sexism, not simply a concern for gender in literature, at least not if the latter is presented as no more than another interesting critical approach on a line with a concern for sea-imagery or metaphors of war in medieval poetry.
>
> (Moi 1982: 204)

There is a (now enormous) body of work to which Elaine Showalter has given the label 'feminist critique' (1979: 25). To put it simply, this refers to the reinterpretation and assessment of the content of novels: attention to images of women and men, representations of relations between them, representations of the institutions impinging on them, of the way society shapes them. In other words, feminist critique involves critical analysis of the vision of the world and the people populating it, the kind of reality depicted. Broadly speaking, themes examined concern the reality of male control of female bodies (marriage, seduction) and male control of women's economic status (hence women's poverty, or fear of it, access to work, to educational and other resources).

Early examples of feminist critique are Kate Millett's iconoclastic readings of novels by men. Her book, *Sexual politics*, which must be the only PhD thesis to become a best-seller, presented startlingly different interpretations of the novels of D H Lawrence, Henry Miller, Norman Mailer, Thomas Hardy. The early images-of-women criticism in the 1970s, sparked off by Millett's book, focused on men's writing, whether or not the women depicted were 'true to life'. Early images-of-women criticism had some rather shaky assumptions about works of fiction mirroring reality, assumptions which clashed with the demand for positive role models for women. A little simplistic perhaps, but they were politically motivated and committed to critical, oppositional reading. (For a survey, which is not my objective here, see Moi 1988.)

As a detailed example of the kind of approach to critical reading I will investigate representations of women's talent in the patriarchal discourse of two nineteenth-century novels. For this I focus on two 'classics': George Eliot's *Daniel Deronda* (1876) and Henry James' *The Bostonians* (1886). We can start by contrasting two singers with talent in *Daniel Deronda*: the gentle, feminine Mirah Cohen and the diva, Leonora Halm-Eberstein, known professionally as the Alcharisi. (I am not looking here at another would-be singer in the novel, Gwendolen, who has been trained for gentility and dependency, not for professional singing. Gwendolen's problem is she wants the independence that a singing profession might bring, but has not cultivated the talent that might just make it possible for her.)

Mirah and Leonora: they are both Jewish, they both sing, they both ran away from their fathers. That's where the similarity ends. Mirah is the ideal 'feminine' heroine. Her voice is not strong enough for *public* performances; it is too 'delicate', and suited only for select performances in *private*. In any case she has, we are told, a deep aversion to the stage and everything associated with it. Stage people are 'wicked' and 'coarse', part of the vulgar world of work outside the home. Her tyrannical father forces her into a singing career against her will. She is not cut out for it at all, and eventually runs away. Somehow, I find it hard to imagine Mirah having the backbone. It is an extreme act of defiance of parental authority, and seems remarkably out of character, until you consider that her father is about to sell her into a fate-worse-than-death (sexual relations outside marriage), so that it is appropriate for this angelic character to resist even her father's authority.

Leonora, the Alcharisi, is a much more interesting character altogether. She is, in a sense, the exact opposite of Mirah. She does not run *away* from a career as a professional singer, but *towards* it; she leaves home to become a performer. 'Every woman', she complains, 'is supposed to have the same set of motives, or else to be a monster'. She flatly refuses to be maternal, to lead a traditional, 'proper' woman's life. She openly defies patriarchal law and taboo:

I was to be what he called 'Jewish woman' under pain of his curse. I
was to feel everything I did not feel, and believe everything I did not
believe . . . I was to care for ever about what Israel had been; and I did
not care at all. I cared for the wide world, and all that I could represent
in it. I hated living under the shadow of my father's strictness. Teaching,
teaching for everlasting – 'this you must be,' 'that you must not be' –
pressed on me like a frame that got tighter and tighter as I grew. I wanted to live a large life, with freedom to do what every one else did, and
be carried along in a great current, not obliged to care.

(Eliot [1871–2] 1979: 692–3)

No Angel of the House here. Leonora is a remarkable character for
the period. She manages to say the unmentionable; to challenge, for
example, the assumption that all women are cut out for domesticity
and motherhood. She asks, 'Had I not a rightful claim to be something more than a mere daughter and mother?' She insists that she
had a right to be ambitious, to carve out a dazzling career in the
public world of stage performance. She also makes the point that
being a loving mother is itself a talent, one that she lacked when her
son (the eponymous Daniel Deronda) was a baby. Perhaps that
makes Leonora something of a monster; but if she is, she's a monster who pleads her own case, and does so very eloquently. It is
interesting that she, almost incidentally, married a prince and had
five children: a feminine dream-come-true if ever there was one!
But she looks back on her marriage as a mistake, a bad move she
made when she thought she had lost her talent, that put an end to
her career permanently. Her title, the Princess Leonora Halm-
Eberstein, is certainly most impressive, but one cannot help
wondering why Eliot chose to have this splendidly independent
female character marry. Would she perhaps have lacked dignity as
an old unmarried woman, especially since she had given birth to
Daniel out of wedlock? Or would she have been beyond the pale
without any compensatory signs of responsible motherhood?

The stately Leonora is a minor character; she appears in just two
chapters. It is the gentle Mirah who is rewarded with happiness at
the end: in the form of marriage to our hero. Leonora, on the other
hand, suffers: for her sins, maybe.

There is evidently something distinctly 'unfeminine' about pos-
sessing talent. It goes against all the 'proper' qualities of a woman
to pursue fame actively, to seek out ambitiously distinction as a
great artist. Harriet Hawkins, in a study of themes spanning across
so-called high literature and popular culture, maintains that this is
equally true in contemporary fiction:

Ever since Lileth, the desire to play the star part rather than a support-ing role has been deemed anathema – an accursed thing – in woman. And it still is. There are very rare violations of this taboo . . . , but gener-ally speaking, a woman who aspires to and achieves great artistic distinction and fame and glory independently of any mentor cannot be officially extolled as the most admirable and sympathetic female charac-ter in any novel, film or soap-opera designed for a mass-market audience.

(Hawkins 1990: 54)

She goes on to observe that professional fame for a woman is equat-ed with personal suffering and domestic tragedy, and has a way of leading to drink, drugs and death. The alternative seems to be vil-lainy, to be the super-bitch, the *femme fatale*. Clearly women have to chose between public fame and personal happiness; between a life as an artist and the love of a man. Talent and femininity just do not go together. Leonora considers her talent, the 'force of genius' in her, to be a masculine quality. She says to Daniel, 'you can never imagine what it is to have a man's force of genius in you, and yet to suffer the slavery of being a girl'.

Before continuing our examination (of a woman's talent and what she should do with it) in *The Bostonians*, I want to draw atten-tion to a particular kind of relationship found in fiction (and examined in some detail by Hawkins): namely, that of a powerful figure, usually male, in control of a beautiful young woman, moulding her talent. Consider the following fictitious performing couple (from George du Maurier's *Trilby* 1894). A young woman named Trilby is a gifted singer when under hypnosis. When she is in control of her own body she is completely tone-deaf and talent-less: she can't sing a note. When mesmerized by the sinister Svengali, she becomes a gifted singer. One way of getting round the problem of a woman's possession of talent, and the damaging effect this has on her femininity, is to make that talent dependent on a man. Dependence keeps her femininity intact.

Verena Tarrant in *The Bostonians* has a talent for public speaking, but only when her father switches it on. She speaks on feminist issues and the narration informs us that she has the power to affect her audience deeply. Like Svengali, her father has complete control over her, a control subsequently taken over by other characters: Olive Chancellor, and finally Basil Ransom. In this novel, the con-flict between public acclaim and personal happiness is quite explicit and skilfully dramatized. We have a battle going on – with Verena as the battleground – between the Bostonian feminist, Olive

Chancellor and Basil Ransom, the patriarchal southern gentleman. Civil War in microcosm. There is no possibility of either of them making any compromises; it is a kind of Faustian conflict between absolute opposites. Verena's total shift in values and allegiances is only possible because she has been depicted as a totally spineless creature in the first place; or rather, totally dependent and lacking in internal motivation, like Svengali's Trilby.

So, she has to choose between life as an artist and life with the man she loves. Public acclaim and personal happiness are incompatible – for a woman. Conventional social relations are reassuringly restored at the end; patriarchal normality prevails. To be fair to James, he makes it quite clear that Verena is *not* going to be happy.

The above analyses demonstrate the powerful denaturalizing potential of an images-of-women type of criticism. I was able to take up a critical position because I had access to the oppositional discourse of feminism. Images-of-women criticism concentrates on the levels of *story* and *significance*. The critical interrogation is directed at characters, situations and events, which are elements of story, and at themes, an element of significance. Additional attention to the *discourse* in which the story is narrated can add insights into the way the author is manipulating the reader into certain attitudes: a fruitful addition to the images-of-women type of criticism. For example, Eliot presents the Alchirisi's defiance of patriarchal law in direct speech. She is a strong woman who, as it were, speaks for herself; she argues her case point by point, so that she is likely to win the reader's respect, if not wholehearted approval. In *The Bostonians*, by contrast, James gives the reader a very fuzzy idea of the nature of Verena Tarrant's ability as a charismatic public speaker, keeping us distant from anything she might 'actually' say. Her public appearances are presented in narration which is focalized through unsympathetic characters, so the reader is in no danger of being swept along by her rhetoric.

In my readings of the romance and horror novels in Chapters 4 and 5, I was refusing complicity, refusing to be subjected by them. Nevertheless, in reading them I was recognizing the knowledge frames, the gender stereotypes in them. Or rather, to be more accurate, not *in* them – I had to be able to bring a great deal *to* the texts in order to make any sense of them.[14] Every text has built into it an implied reader, an imaginary addressee for whom the text was written, someone who can easily supply the necessary information

resources to make coherent sense of it. If the subject position built
in for the implied reader is close to one's own, critical reading is
going to be particularly difficult. Real readers have to negotiate for
themselves with the subject positioning of the implied reader. If we
have a great deal in common with the reader inscribed, then we are
probably going to take up the positions constructed without even
being aware of doing so. As readers, we invest texts with our own
preconceptions and prejudices, or try to. If these preconceptions
and prejudices are echoed in the inscribed reader, they will be pow-
erfully reinforced; the subjection is complete.

A critical approach to language analysis is a way of denaturalizing the things we are usually unaware of bringing to texts when we
read. My approach in this book has close connections with critical
language study (CLS), a body of collaborative, synthesizing work
with the explicitly emancipatory objective of consciousness-raising
(e.g. Clark et al. 1987, Ivanic 1988, Fairclough 1989, Talbot 1990,
Fairclough 1992). Most of the work in this field has been in direct
response to the Language Awareness movement in British schooling, which has flourished in the climate of the Kingman Report
(DES 1988). In analyses of fiction with the objective of empowerment, CLS greatly augments existing approaches to critical reading.

ARCHAEOLOGY

One of the concerns of feminist literary scholarship is the rediscovery of women's writing: either simply to redress the balance or to
unearth a female tradition. This archaeological endeavour involves
finding out what, if anything, is different or special about the writing of women and, not least, why rediscovery is necessary in the
first place. Attention to what has aided or constrained women's
writing, and what critical responses to it have been, constitutes a
reinterpretation of the historical context in which fiction has been
produced and of the consequences for its evaluation. The early
development of the novel genre, women's central place in it and
how they have been elbowed out by men have been explored in
detail by various scholars, Jane Spencer (1986) and Dale Spender
(1986) being prominent among them. In reading their work, it
comes as something of a shock to discover that some of the basic
'facts' of literary history are not so rock-solid as we might like to

suppose; such as who wrote the first 'proper' novel, for instance. Apart from just setting the record straight, 'gynocritics' have established the existence of a veritable female tradition unnoticed or even suppressed by the male literary establishment. Elaine Showalter's *A literature of their own* (1977) was the study which started this off (the distinction between 'feminist critique' and 'gynocritics' is from Showalter 1979).

What happened to women's writing? Why has it been lost or undervalued? What social-interpersonal aspects of novel writing presented problems for women? Spencer has plenty to say about these matters. Before the novel had become a highly valued genre, the high proportion of women novelists was acknowledged. Writing became accepted as a feminine occupation in the eighteenth century. I should really say *more* accepted, since a woman publicly selling anything, including writing, was in some danger of condemnation. This was part of the whole process of pushing women out of the public sphere of commerce. Fame has been an outrageous thing for a woman to want, as the examination of *Daniel Deronda* and *The Bostonians* has shown, and equated with infamy. There were some very successful professional women writers in the period when women's condition in general was deteriorating (see Chapter 1). Samuel Richardson was very outspoken about the proper conduct of women, and not just in *Pamela*. These views extended to the proper conduct of women as writers: they had to be moral and modest, and above all not pushy. The achievement of renown as a writer was considered acceptable, as long as it was not accompanied by ambition. This paradox is expressed very elegantly in a couplet from a poem entitled 'Female conduct':

> True female Merit strives, to be conceal'd
> And only by its blushes is reveal'd.
>
> (Thomas Marriott 1759; quoted in Spencer 1986)

As Spencer says, 'Modest blushes were required of eighteenth-century women writers. Above all else, they were accepted on condition that they did not want to push themselves forward.' The need for morality and modesty applied equally to women's novels and the women themselves. The two seem to have been confused. The possession of talent for a woman seems to have posed problems, to sit uneasily with her femininity and place her in contradictory subject positions. Being talented and creative simply wasn't *feminine*. Women should preferably write for women about women's things; which of course is a condemnation to triviality. A constraint on women as writers was that, to avoid scandal, they were expected to remain outside the political arena.

Jumping forward to the nineteenth century, Mary Ann Evans presumably wrote under the name of George Eliot because, like other women using male pseudonyms, she wanted to be taken seriously, to be judged as a novelist and not as a woman. There were widespread practices of excluding women from active participation in the orders of discourse in which 'serious' literature was produced and limiting their access to particular discourse-types and genres. Similar invidious restrictions have been placed on women's participation in other domains. For example, women have been excluded from education; then women's ignorance as a consequence of this exclusion has been used as proof of mental inferiority and as justification for continued exclusion. Women's participation in fiction production was restricted to modes considered appropriate and feminine; this in turn led to accusations of triviality and marginality. Male critics still play at this game of 'heads I win, tails you lose'. In a fine example of what Mary Ellman (1979) calls 'phallic criticism', Anthony Burgess criticized Jane Austen for lacking 'masculine thrust and intellect', then accused George Eliot of having it: 'The male impersonation is wholly successful', this being intended as a slight (quoted in Russ 1984: 33).

Early British women novelists are of course just one marginalized group of producers of fiction who can be brought in from the margins of Anglophone literary studies by a critical re-reading of literary history. Archaeological work is also involved in finding fiction about the early colonial period from the perspectives of colonized peoples, and in finding fiction which does not marginalize the cultures and histories of 'the colonies' themselves. Ngugi's observations about literature in education serve as a reminder of the part fiction plays in colonization:

A Russian child grows under the influence of his [sic] native imaginative literature: a Chinese, a Frenchman, a German or an Englishman first imbibes his national literature before attempting to take in other worlds. That the central taproot of his cultural nourishment should lie deep in his native soil is taken for granted. This ABC of education is followed in most societies because it is demanded by the practice and the experience of living and growing.

Not so in Africa, the West Indies and the colonized world as a whole,

despite the crucial role of the twin fields of literature and culture in
making a child aware of, and rediscover his environment.

(Ngugi 1981: 3–4)

Ngugi goes on to relate an anecdote about his son laboriously
memorizing Wordsworth's 'I wander'd lonely as a cloud', without
having the faintest idea of what a daffodil might be. Daffodils do
not grow in Kenya, after all.

The perspectives of dominated peoples can be very difficult to
unearth; such silenced voices can be hard to find. One striking
exception is some of the work of Nigerian novelist, Chinua Achebe.
Achebe's three novels, *Things fall apart* (1958), *No longer at ease*
(1960) and *Arrow of God* (1964), present an African perspective on
colonialism for the Anglophone reading public; they have also been
translated into forty or so other languages, and have been repub-
lished in one volume in English, as *The African trilogy* (1988). Their
original publication was facilitated by various Scottish scholars and
reviewers, as Achebe recounts in his introduction to the trilogy.
This was fortunate but, as Ngugi says of Kenyan fiction, dependent
on 'the grace and mercy of foreigners' (Ngugi 1981: 43). Indeed
Ngugi stresses that the work of Achebe, among others, is not
African but Afro-European, since it is written in English and draws
on a European literary tradition. As the novel form and its narrative conventions are European in origin this is undoubtedly true.
Nevertheless, Achebe's work does impress on a non-African reader
the existence of an alternative literary history in Africa. African oral
literature is drawn into his work; his Igbo characters constantly
produce fables, parables, proverbs.

Ngugi highlighted the European influence on African writers
such as Achebe in the context of an ongoing debate about a Pan-
African language (Josef Schmied 1991: 121). His case is that
literature in English is inaccessible to the majority of Africans:
African literature should be in African languages. Since literacy in
African languages is as low as in English (ibid.: 120), Ngugi's case
is more relevant to drama than written forms of literature.

FICTION-PRODUCTION

In Chapter 3, I examined an extract from Eliot's *Middlemarch* in
which she artfully puts the reader on trial. She implicates her con-

temporary reader in the prejudiced views of her characters, so that she can point to their, and her own, share of responsibility for social injustices of the period. This appears to have won Eliot an appreciative audience (if sometimes grudgingly so) and the title of 'Our Great Teacher'. But, while the strategy was a clever one for its time and may have made a considerable contribution to raising the consciousness of Victorian readers, I doubt it would be well received by a modern readership.

One way of writing 'against the grain' is through the creative disruption of the conventions of the genre/s in which you are operating. Taking liberties with generic conventions has the effect of exposing them. In the next chapter I examine the genre of science fiction in the hands of feminists who do this, and who also engage in prolonged contestation of dominant discourses. Of course, there are many ways of disrupting and exposing fiction-production which, inasmuch as they produce denaturalizing effects, have the potential to empower a reader. Exposure of the fiction-creating process by displays of artifice, reflexive examination of history or story production, disruption of text structure, the fragmentation of narrative viewpoint and reading position: these are all ways of making the 'seams' show. They serve as reminders to the reader that she is engaging in discourse that is mediated generically, and that she has all kinds of expectations about both the genre and about the discourse embodying it. Both modernist and post-modernist writing are deeply preoccupied with this kind of concern. In terms of empowerment, however, a major difficulty with such highly literary writing is its élitism. It is totally inaccessible to the general reader (and here I mean a reader who has not been through higher education specializing in literary studies; a large category, globally speaking). Another way of offering empowerment through reading, one which is rather more accessible and for that reason perhaps more likely to succeed, is through the disruption of particular situation- and character-types within specific genres, such as Angela Carter's reworkings of traditional fairy tales. I will look at some examples using the genres of romance and horror in the next section. There is more to the subversion of conventional writing practices, however, than undermining their 'obviousness' by disrupting the generically established relationship between author and reader, or the illusion of language as a transparent medium for transmitting content. We also need to consider the matter of *who* gets to produce fiction and who gets to read it. At the end of this chapter I will give some attention to the difficulty of gaining access to the fiction-producing industries and consider some attempts to give access to non-dominant voices.

The extreme example of an inaccessible work of fiction must, I suppose, be James Joyce's *Finnegans wake* (1939). It is true that this book can be enjoyed to an extent without much understanding, but it can only be read with any degree of comprehension given access to an enormous range of resources. Joyce's writing is dependent on large numbers of specific prior texts, many but not all of them, literary. As James Atherton has observed:

> More than any other writer I know of he needed a basis of some other writer's work on which to compose his own. He seems to have considered it as a sort of literary runway necessary to gain momentum before creative work could begin, and he always seems to have needed this stimulus.
>
> (Atherton 1960: 72)

The 'runway' metaphor Atherton uses here is building on Joyce's own frustrated observation that 'Such an amount of reading seems to be necessary before my old flying machine grumbles up into the air' (ibid.). His reader in turn needs knowledge of texts as wide ranging as *The Book of the dead, Alice in Wonderland* and Giovanni Battista Vico's *Scienza nuova*. The ability to read a variety of languages is also a distinct advantage. Joyce undermines the illusion that language is a transparent medium for transmitting content to such an extent that his result is effectively meaningless for the majority of people.

The reading of fiction which is inaccessible to most people can be used as a form of 'cultural capital' (Bourdieu 1984). On the analogy of economic capital, there are other kinds of asset available to dominant social groups. Cultural assets include access to educational and other resources supplying the prestige language or variety, and a high level of literacy. To appreciate the way such resources can be used as cultural capital, consider the following poem prioritizing Cuban learning and cultural experience. It was written by the director of the National Association of Cuban Writers, Nicolás Guillén, and the addressee is a Cuban whose own national history and language is not valued. It is ironically titled 'Problemas del subdesarrollo' ('Problems of underdevelopment'):

Monsieur Dupont calls you uneducated
because you don't know which was

the favorite grandchild of Victor Hugo.

Herr Muller has started shouting
because you don't know the day
(the exact one) when Bismarck died.

Your friend Mr. Smith,
English or Yankee, I don't know,
becomes incensed when you write Shell.
(It seems that you hold back an "l"
and that besides you pronounce it chel.)

O.K. So what?
When it's your turn,
have them say cacarajícara,
and where is the Aconcagua
and who was Sucré,
and where on this planet
did Martí die.

And please:
make them always talk to you in Spanish.

(Guillén 1972 trans. Ellis 1983)

The Cuban implied reader constructed in this poem has knowledge of aspects of French and German culture, the languages of English and Spanish, as well as Cuban and South American history, language and culture. The implied reader also knows which can be used as cultural capital, which are considered worth knowing about in the unequal power relations of dominant colonial discourse; Cuban and South American history, language and culture are not valued. This poem asserts their importance over those of Europe and the United States (*Shell* presumably refers to the multinational corporation). The histories, languages and cultures of Europe and the United States are reduced to the trivial concerns of Monsieur Dupont, Herr Muller and Mr Smith: three irritable individuals. Such decentring of colonial-imperialist discourses is an act of empowerment for a reader who is, or has been, subjected by them. A European or United States reader, for whom the implied reader is distant, has the enlightening experience of being constructed as *ignorant*. Texts which do not position readers within familiar discourses are difficult to read.

DISRUPTING GENERIC CHARACTER AND SITUATION TYPES

Writing 'against the grain' can pose problems, as it can make fiction difficult to understand. Undermining the view of language as transparent and instrumental can produce fiction which is inaccessible to a wide audience. A way around this problem is to restrict the disruption to recognizable elements of specific genres.

One text which plays with elements within the horror genre is a short story by Suzy McKee Charnas (1990) called 'Boobs'. It appeared in a volume of horror fiction written by women and opens like this:

> The thing is, it's like your brain wants to go on thinking about the miserable history mid-term you have to take tomorrow, but your body takes over. And what a body!

> (Charnas 1989: 18)

The first sentence sets up a high-school setting and a contrast between 'brain' and 'body'. These, along with the exclamation that follows and the title itself, encourage the reader to draw in some kind of knowledge frame relating to teenage boys and their emergent sexuality. This sets up an expectation of a horror theme particularly common in films (see Chapter 5). The next sentence, however, is this:

> You can see in the dark and run like the wind and leap parked cars in a single bound.

> (ibid.)

What is the 'missing link' needed to read this third sentence as coherently connected with the previous two? We need to do inferential work, trying out other knowledge frames. The 'body' in question is clearly not – or not only – the location of desirable *sexual* characteristics, but apparently one with the attributes of some large and powerful animal. This story opens, then, with a kind of doubleness. It turns out to be about a young *female* teenager who, instead of menstruating, turns into a wolf. It also deals with the emotional and social aspects of emergent sexuality, but from a female perspective: the embarrassment of the bodily manifestations of sexual maturity, being bothered by boys.

Recalling the detailed discussion and analysis of Herbert's *Lair* in Chapter 5, there are some similarities and some interesting differences. There is a victim who, like so many victims in Herbert's horror fiction, deserves 'punishment' for a transgression which is sex related. But the nature of the transgression is very different; the victim is a teenager called Billy who bullies and sexually harasses the narrator-protagonist both in and out of school. His harassment of her begins at her sexual maturity. It is what triggers off her lycanthropic tendencies:

> Billy is the one that started it, sort of, because he always started everything, him with his big mouth. At the beginning of term, he came barrelling down on me hollering, 'Hey, look at Bornstein, something musta happened to her over the summer! What happened, Bornstein? Hey, everybody, look at Boobs Bornstein!
> He made a grab at my chest, and I socked him in the shoulder, and he punched me in the face, which made me dizzy and shocked and made me cry, too, in front of everybody.
>
> (ibid.: 18–19)

In contrast with Herbert's frequent shifts of focus, Charnas's narrative is closely focalized through first person narration throughout. *Lair* is narrated mainly from the perspective of the hero, with occasional shifts to the 'evil' killer rats, and focusing through the thoughts of victims just before their demise. In 'Boobs', events are narrated exclusively from the lycanthropic teenager's viewpoint; we are not drawn into the victim's thoughts at all. Other contrasts, evident in the following passage, are the powerlessness of the male character and his evident lack of control of the situation:

> wasn't so big and strong laying there on the ground with me straddling him all lean and wiry with wolf-muscle. And plus, he was in shock. . .
> I nosed in under what was left of Billy's jaw and I bit his throat out. Now let him go around telling lies about people.
>
> (ibid.: 34–5)

Like the victims in *Lair*, Billy's gruesome 'punishment' for his transgression is to be eaten alive. Not by rats of course but, with great appreciation, by the recipient of his unwanted attentions ('it was better than Thanksgiving dinner. Who would think that somebody as horrible as Billy Linden could taste so *good*?').

A similar revenge figure in some respects is the murderous Bella in *Dirty weekend* (Zahavi 1991). In terms of empowerment, 'Boobs' hijacks the horror genre to deal with – and denaturalize – kinds of experience which are probably only too familiar to all women as young teenagers. Puberty, which can be an uncomfortable enough stage to go through in any case, can become intolerable coupled with sexual harassment by boys of around the same age. The fictional resolutions of such real world problems in 'Boobs' are clearly not being offered as real solutions. Charnas is not *recommending* lycanthropy as a viable alternative to having periods, or suggesting cannibalism as an appropriate way of dealing with sexual harassment. With these preposterous, horror fiction 'solutions', she makes creative use of the generic practice of 'going too far', crossing taboo boundaries. In doing so, she draws attention to the genre and readers' expectations of it, exposing and undermining the more conventional character and situation types. The refusal of victim status by the former victim is deliberately overdone. She is empowered to the extent of turning the tables: reversal.

Some writers have appropriated types of character and situation from horror for critical purposes beyond the genre. Lynne Truss's *Possunt quia posse videntur* (1992) is a recent 'non-genre' short story making comic use of the transforming beast from horror fiction. Translated in a sub-title as 'they can because they seem to be able to', this story is a witty attack on the fur trade. The transforming beasts are not werewolves, simply fur coats taking over their wearers.

Other writers have used generic elements in order to interrogate the genre itself. I mentioned Helen Zahavi's *Dirty weekend* above, a novel narrated by a female serial killer whose victims are all men. Like 'Boobs', it undermines the subject positioning, frequently reproduced in horror fiction, of women as weak and vulnerable. It brings about a savage reversal. An example of fiction examining the subject positioning reproduced in romance – and very much gentler than the above – is Anita Brookner's *Hotel du Lac* (1985). In Brookner's novel, the protagonist is herself a romance writer, who seems to have a low opinion of her craft. The closely focalized third person narration (a characteristic of the romance) refers to her work as 'her daily task of fantasy and obfuscation' (Brookner 1985: 50).

The novel exposes the contradictions romantic fiction works so hard to conceal. It is worth bearing in mind Cranny-Francis's suggestion that:

> romances construct a representation not of patriarchal gender ideology, but of bourgeois, patriarchal ideology; . . . these are not love stories so much as economic stories displaced into love story terms.
>
> (Cranny-Francis 1990: 183)

Hotel du Lac exposes the tensions, smoothed over in romance fiction, between desire for love and economic security. Upward mobility, another aspiration of Mills & Boon heroines,[16] is not an issue in Brookner's novel. It is set in the dizzy social heights that Mills & Boon heroines aspire to: the company of the aristocracy and people with wealth through trade. The two desires, love and riches, are embodied in the characters. The heroine (called Edith Hope and longing for love) stands in contrast with the rest of the characters. A male character called Neville is established as the would-be hero. Marriage between Neville and Edith is the narrative resolution that romance conventions lead us to expect. However, Neville is established as quite obviously unsuitable. Brookner brings in various elements of romance in order to parody them. He is presented as a forceful, dominant character who is helping the heroine to learn about herself, as is required of romance heroes. However, in this case, he simply comes across as overbearing:

> He settled her at a table in the shade of a striped awning, picked up the menu which an attentive waiter had immediately placed before him, and said, 'I should have the duck if I were you.'
> Edith ignored him. . .
> '. . .You may not be fascinating, Edith, but you certainly know how to make a man feel uncomfortable.'
> Edith smiled demurely. 'Am I to take that as a compliment?' she asked.
> Mr Neville regarded her with a cold look. 'That is the sort of remark I associate with a lesser woman. You are unsettling. Simply leave it at that. You don't have to dimple and bridle, like an ingenue. Am I to take that as a compliment, indeed. I hope you are not going to turn into the kind of woman who leans across the table, props her chin in her hand, and says, "What are you thinking?"'
> 'All right, all right,' said Edith, with a sudden return of joviality. 'I am not here to pass tests, you know. I am supposed to be enjoying myself.'
> (Brookner 1985: 161–2)

The speaker rights Neville assumes in this exchange do not go down too well with the heroine. She doesn't care for the way he critically assesses her utterances and reprimands her. Later in the same scene, she is chilled by his cold, unromantic proposal:

> 'I think you should marry me, Edith,' he said.
> She stared at him, her eyes widening in disbelief.
> 'Let me explain,' he said, rather hurriedly, taking a firm grip on his composure. 'I am not a romantic youth. I am in fact extremely discriminating. I have a small estate and a very fine house, Regency Gothic, a

really beautiful example. And I have a rather well-known collection of *famille rose* dishes. I am sure you love beautiful things.'
'You are wrong,' she said, her voice cold. 'I do not love things at all.'
(ibid.: 164)

He makes no bones about the economic nature of the relationship he is offering. The capitalist discourse on property and antiques – appropriate for establishing the hero's suitability in 'proper' romance fiction – is comically *in*appropriate here. Apart from Edith, the only 'romantic' in the book, the characters in *Hotel du Lac* are an unpleasant bunch of people who seem to have dispensed with the desire for loving relationships altogether. The novel brings the economic motive to the surface. Interpersonally, it follows the generic convention of providing intensively focalized narration and matching protagonist and implied reader. But the focalizing character responds negatively to the character type of the romance hero represented by Neville, and finally rejects him. As a consequence, the reader will probably reject him too.

Some works of fiction are recognizable as hybrids of different genres. Genre-mixing is not necessarily subversive. *Macabre manor* (Grayson 1974), for example, is a formulaic romance of the Mills & Boon type with horror elements providing an exotic setting: voodoo practices on the hero's Caribbean island, with a few gothic elements thrown in for good measure. A novel which incorporates, reworks and subverts the Mills & Boon romance is *The tent peg*, by Aritha Van Herk (1981). It combines Mills & Boon with an adventure story of the kind targeted at male readers. In the romance tradition, heterosexual relationships are central; the differences between women and men are exaggerated and eroticized, male violence is transformed into passion. Van Herk's female protagonist is central, as in Mills & Boon, and not peripheral love interest, as in adventure stories. As Vicki Bertram observes:

> she manages to combine qualities of the conventional romance heroine with a wild spirit and daring. She wins success on the men's terms. They come to accept and admire her. Never having even held a gun before in her life, she hits the bull's eye on her second attempt. She flies the helicopter. She becomes the smartest prankster in the camp. When they find gold she goes out staking with the rest of them, hammering away all day. And on top of this, she cooks sumptuous delicately spiced meals, home made bread, and sews little sachets of tundra moss for the men to remember their summer.
>
> (Bertram 1993)

The protagonist, like the hero of the James Herbert horror novel examined in Chapter 5, displays heroic qualities (one notable similarity being her extraordinary facility with firearms). For Bertram, and myself, the combination of characteristics is highly comical. Van Herk combines the two contrasting generic character types in order to draw attention to and undermine both.

ACCESS

Fiction production is highly professionalized. There is little room for 'little' people. In the major fiction-producing industries, the type of fiction text produced for mass circulation is determined by creators' access to the key resources of financing and distribution. In the UK, the most severely constrained fiction-producing industry is the cinema. The industry, if it can be called that, is kept alive by funding from television companies, especially *Channel 4*. Other than that, it is dependent on experienced professional practitioners (not exactly 'little people') forming cooperatives for individual projects and securing financial backing where they can. A limited number of local Arts Council grants are available to contribute to production costs – these are available to natives or residents of particular regions (e.g. Northwest England). Screening of the finished product is of course another matter again.

For professional *writers* of fiction things are not *quite* so difficult, although publishers have been making severe cutbacks in recent years. Access for 'little people' is limited, however. Mills & Boon continues to thrive on a constant stream of unsolicited manuscripts, a few of which are published. For the publishers, there is a pool of material always available; very little commissioning is needed. This is one route, then, through which some marginal writers gain access. However, the price of access is extreme conservatism; the constraints on what they can write, and how they can write it, are rigid. Successful applicants are the ones whose manuscripts conform to the guidelines most closely. In such a situation, subversion of the generic conventions is unlikely, to say the least (Mills & Boon claim to be able to spot 'insincere' romance writing, for instance) and articulations of patriarchal and 'enterprise' discourses are morely likely to be well received, and end up in print, than contestations.

The most notable provision of access to minority voices in the UK, and an interesting contrast with Mills & Boon, is The Women's

Press. Unlike Mills & Boon, The Women's Press does not stifle those voices it permits access to. It started life in 1978, as a project run from a front room by Stephanie Dowrick (now Chair of Women's Press's Board of Directors). She founded it, with the financial backing of the publisher she was working for, as a publishing house exclusively for women. It was, and remains, explicitly feminist in political orientation and devoted in particular to publishing the work of marginal 'voices', including fiction: 'a feminist and political press dedicated to making the voices of women heard, and with a policy of particularly supporting the writing of black, lesbian and disabled women, amongst other groups' (Kathy Gale, personal communication). The Women's Press has opened up fiction production for a great many writers whose work would have been unlikely to find a publisher otherwise. Some work is commissioned, other books are acquired by direct submissions and submissions via agents and other publishers. They also reprint material already published elsewhere, most of which was not previously either widely known or readily available in the UK. Their feminist science fiction series, launched in 1985 by Sarah Lefanu, is notable in this respect. Where previously science fiction that had a feminist content cropped up occasionally, this series has provided a forum for it as a sub-genre. It has contributed substantially to the provision of a kind of authenticity or official status to feminist science fiction within the science fiction community. At science fiction conventions, for instance, The Women's Press generally has a stall, alongside those run by role-playing game shops, specialist bookshops, and so on.

In its own way, a community of convention-goers opens up the processes of production and interpretation. At conventions, the relationship between writers and readers is not only generic, as is more usually the case (see Chapter 2). Critics and fans meet, and influence, professional creators; creators in turn have the benefit of face-to-face interaction with some of their mass audience. Small presses run by enthusiasts are an outlet for previously unpublished writers; they provide a training ground for amateurs with creative aspirations. By far the biggest such community is made up of science fiction convention-goers. Compared with other marketing category genres, science fiction has a large and influential participatory readership. It is a readership which contributes to the decision-making processes that determine the genre. It resists and counteracts the monopolies of publishing and academia (Martin

Jordin 1987: 160). Particularly influential are the awards presented at conventions, such as the Hugo and Nebula Awards. A recent addition is the James Tiptree Junior Memorial Award, presented for a novel or short story exploring gender issues in science fiction and fantasy, as 'a validation, another brick knocked out of the wall' of a genre previously dominated by gender-blind writers (Gwyneth Jones, letter in *Interzone* August 1992: 4).

A rather special kind of access is provided by community publishing. A surviving example in the UK is Gatehouse Publishing, Manchester. Gatehouse is not a commercial publishing house, but depends on Manchester City Council and Arts Council funding, supplemented with the support of local businesses and individuals. It is an Adult Basic Education publisher, whose writers are going through the experience of adult basic education themselves. Most of Gatehouse's publications are written by adult learners who are in the process of acquiring literacy. As Gatehouse say: 'the best people to write for adult learners are those who have been through the same process themselves' (Annual report 1991/1992: 3). Manchester Adult Basic Education students can attend workshops where they can contribute to decision-making along with Gatehouse staff. Regular editorial workshop sessions share out the power and responsibility of selecting what writing to publish and how. A significant result is the empowerment of both writers and readers. The writers are encouraged by having their efforts taken seriously, validated to the extent of being printed and published. They may be involved in all stages of the production of their book, from initial planning right through to printing and distribution. Readers have the benefit of texts written specifically for them, instead of having to make do with books intended for young schoolchildren.

One of these locally produced books, Frances Holden's *Keep your hair on*, begins with a reproduction of the first handwritten draft. Readers can then see for themselves the progression from the first version, produced by the learner-writer herself, to the final printed version. The author's comments on the back cover are there to provide additional encouragement:

> When I look at my story, how do I do it? I go back in my memory for stories to write down. Sometimes I tape them and then I get so many words down myself, and I have somebody to help me with the rest. You could do the same. Perhaps you already do!
>
> (Holden 1983)

Keep your hair on is a generic mix of school primer and humorous anecdote. In layout it is very similar to a school primer. It is illustrated, in large print, and the text is line broken, so that phrases never span over more than one line. Here are two pages from it:

> So me and Kathleen went out for a drink.
> We went in the Crown
> and we enjoyed it.
>
> When we come out,
> on the way home
> we was talking and laughing.

(ibid.: 4–5)

Another characteristic textual property it shares with school primers is relatively simple internal organisation. For example, there are rarely more than two clauses to a sentence and cohesion is frequently cued explicitly from one clause to the next. In the above extract, the pronominal linkage with *we* is maintained clause by clause.

Elements of another genre, the anecdote, make the Gatehouse primer a very different kind of text from the primers that the adult learners probably encountered (and struggled unsuccessfully with) as school children. An interpersonal element it shares with other anecdotes is the use of vernacular forms, including the narrative present. Holden's story has been amended to conform with standard orthography, but she has not been forced to use unfamiliar syntactic forms. Features of her local Manchester variety of English have been preserved. Perhaps most noticeable is the use of *me* in the noun phrase compound 'me and Kathleen', a phrase which is functioning as the grammatical subject of a clause. This is a feature of northwest varieties of British English. Another is the use of *was* in the first person plural. Two other vernacular features later in the story are in the clause: 'she couldn't see hardly' (ibid.: 12), which contains both an adverbial in final placement which would not occur in 'Standard' and multiple negation. In this preservation of vernacular variants, *Keep your hair on* differs from the primers normally used in schools. It is speaking the same language as its readers.

Early readers published by Gatehouse include two collections of stories and recollections by Afro-Caribbeans settled in the Manchester area. As with *Keep your hair on*, the writers' 'non-standard' language has not been tampered with before publication. Instead it has been preserved, providing other West Indian Basic

Education students with reading materials containing 'voices' like their own.

TAKING IT FURTHER

Fiction specifically for children is often written to help them resist dominant values, with the objective of bringing about social change. This is an area I have not dealt with; it is discussed at length in Stephens (1992). Stephens also examines the way writing in varieties other than standard English creates new reading positions for users of those varieties, an aspect of fiction and empowerment I considered briefly above. For more on adult basic education, see David Barton and Roz Ivanic (eds) (1991). For extensive coverage of Third World political writing, try Barbara Harlow (1987). For a detailed study of Guillén, see Keith Ellis (1983).

The approach to critical reading I have presented in this book is of course only one of many. Fairclough (1989; 1992), Hodge and Kress (1988) deal extensively with the critical analysis of text and discourse. Other books concentrate on specific genres or types of publication; for example Fowler (1991) on newspapers. Fowler (1981) and Hodge (1990) deal specifically with the discourse of fiction.

SEVEN

Feminist Science Fiction

The science fiction genre has provided feminist writers and critics with a valuable framework for criticizing dominant patriarchal patterns of gender relations and for speculating about alternatives. In doing so, writers have had to be very selective within the genre. The character types of what is sometimes nostalgically referred to as 'Golden Age' science fiction, for instance, would be of little use to feminists, except perhaps for parodic purposes. 'Golden Age' science fiction, science-based fantasies for a male readership appearing in the US between the mid-1920s and the mid-1940s, had very little use for women characters, let alone women's issues. As Susan Wood (1980) reports, women tended to be restricted to three broad types. The more scientifically orientated stories contained 'interminable examples of woman-as-recipient-of-expository-lump', someone to whom scientific complexities could be explained in simple terms a lay reader would understand. In the stories devoted to adventure and heroism (the 'space operas'), there were two possibilities open to women: 'blonde Victims, shrieking "eek"', or 'dark, sultry Temptresses, eternally trying to seduce the hero away from his rescue mission'. 'The latter,' Wood observes, 'had rather more fun', but generally ended up dead (Wood 1980: 66).

Of course, science fiction also has a tradition of social criticism and has been used in exploring political issues. Some well-known science fiction novels with a clear monitory function are H G Wells' *The time machine* (1896), George Orwell's *Nineteen eighty-four* (1949) and more recently John Brunner's *Stand on Zanzibar* (1968). Science fiction is long-established as a genre suited to warning a society about possibilities to be avoided. Some of Wells' 'scientific romances' are clearly monitory, warning against the possible consequences of uncontrolled technological advancements (e.g. *The food of the gods*, 1923). It is this speculative aspect of the genre which has attracted writers interested in feminist concerns.

Many writers of feminist science fiction are actively involved in 'putting the margins into the centre'; that is, in dealing with usually more marginalized issues or people. So, for instance, in Jane Palmer's two lighthearted novels, *The planet dweller* (1985) and *Moving Moosevan* (1990), her main character is a woman going through menopause: hardly typical in science fiction (and moreover, she goes space travelling equipped with handbag and sensible shoes!). Other fiction dealing with margins is the wealth of short stories by Lisa Tuttle. One of these, 'The family monkey', deals with a human girl's close friendship with a marooned alien, who has befriended her, teaching her his language and ways, in order to pass the years before his rescue. Tuttle movingly presents a pet's-eye-view of abandonment by an owner. Another story, 'The other kind', is a subtle examination of 'otherness' which seems to deal with ethnicity, species and gender orientation simultaneously.

This final chapter concentrates on feminist science fiction, which I present as an example of fiction that has been used extensively as a forum for both social criticism and speculation. I continue with more detailed attention to fiction that works to estrange readers from familiar, everyday situations, identities, relationships. I then examine other, more 'positive' uses of science fiction as a contributor to social change: work which does not simply draw attention to some existing undesirable state of affairs, but makes suggestions about alternatives. Here I first discuss feminist science fiction as a testing ground for language reform, detailing fiction in which writers have tried out alternatives to the 'masculine generic', or identified and filled in lexical gaps. I follow this by closely examining a 'critical utopia', attending particularly to the way it foregrounds the possibility, and *desirability*, of social change. I also examine another perspective on social change within feminist science fiction, with a detailed example of a novel which speculates on the consequences of cutural takeover by aliens.

MAKING THE FAMILIAR STRANGE

An aspect of science fiction making it valuable for feminist creators of fiction is that it can be used to estrange readers from the familiar, from everyday situations, activities, people. Doris Lessing's *The marriages between Zones Three, Four and Five* (1981), the second novel in her *Canopus in Argus* series, contains some sensitive observations about face-to-face interaction between people from different cultural backgrounds, particularly between women and men.

Lessing devotes most of her attention to the consequences of differences in the power relations in a militaristic, hierarchical society (Zone Four) and in an egalitarian, non-military one (Zone Three). In the extract below, 'they' are a troop of soldiers from Zone Four. Their task is to collect Al-Ith, the 'queen' of Zone Three, who is to marry their king. Lessing´s observations draw the reader's attention to interpretations of pragmatic and paralinguistic cues. In the following, Al-Ith´s apology and accompanying sigh are intended to pragmatically and paralinguistically convey her polite regret at an imposition:

> 'My apologies.' She sighed, and they all heard it. They thought it weakness . . . She was quiet and patient but they heard subservience.
>
> (Lessing 1981: 20)

The soldiers from Zone Four interpret her apology and sigh as a sign of weakness (they evidently attended the John Wayne school of etiquette!). In the passage below, Al-Ith is returning to her own land, having escaped from Zone Four. She encounters one of her own countrymen, who speaks to her as an equal:

> 'Ah, I see who you are. And how is marriage in Zone Four?' This was the sort of friendly enquiry that she would normally have expected, but she gave him a quick suspicious glance, which she was categorizing as 'a Zone Four look'. But no, of course he meant nothing 'impertinent' – a Zone Four word! Oh, she had been very much changed by her day and a half in that low place.
>
> (ibid.: 71)

Al-Ith is suspicious of his enquiry, which as a native of Zone Three she knows is a friendly one, because she has been treated as 'queen' in the hierarchical society of Zone Four. Utterances can only be considered as 'impertinent' when the speaker is a subordinate. Her response to another utterance a little later prompts her to observe that Zone Four is 'a place of compulsion':

> 'Sit down, Al-Ith.' This command, which was as she heard it, brought her to sit down: and she sat thinking that he had not meant an order, a command, but it was the sort of suggestion a friend made, yet she had heard an order.
>
> (ibid.: 74)

Unfortunately, *Marriages* lapses into thinly disguised religious instruction. Al-Ith becomes a guru figure living in a hut in the shadow of the mountains of Zone Two, pining for contact with (to borrow a phrase from genre-parodist, Douglas Adams) 'intelligent shades of the colour blue'. The shortcomings of the *Canopus in Argus* series as feminist science fiction are succinctly expressed by Sarah LeFanu (1988):

> the stories unfold against a background of imperialist domination that is nowhere challenged while they treat with some of the more mystical aspects of the 'woman's viewpoint', extra-intuitive horses and perfect complementary marriages being just two examples.
>
> (LeFanu 1988: 92)

It is unfortunate that Lessing does not subject imperialism and mysticism to the kind of 'defamiliarizing' critical scrutiny that she devotes to face-to-face interaction.

The short story format is well suited to putting into critical focus specific aspects of dominant gender relations and subject positions. Tanith Lee's 'Love alters' (1985), for instance, is set in a society in which heterosexual relationships are abnormal and considered to be 'sick'. Another well-known example of fiction which sets out to make the familiar strange is a non-realist short story by Pamela Zoline called 'The heat death of the universe'. Zoline was one of the few women who were contributing to the New Wave science fiction writing in the United States and Britain in the late 1960s. The so-called New Wave was characterized by an avoidance of traditional science fiction settings, character-types and, above all, by minimal attention to plot. The most widely known writer of New Wave science fiction is probably J G Ballard. Zoline's short story first appeared in *New worlds* in 1967 (reprinted in Zoline [1967] 1988). Like a lot of New Wave writing, her story deals with entropy; uniquely, it also deals with *housework*. Its solitary protagonist is a housewife and mother. LeFanu (1988) praises 'Heat death' as one of her 'favourite of all science fiction stories, expressing as it does with such elegance and wit the vistas of emptiness hidden behind the slogan 'a woman's work is never done' (LeFanu 1988: 98). It consists of fifty-four paragraphs of varying lengths, all numbered, and opens like this:

1. ONTOLOGY: That branch of metaphysics which concerns itself with the problems of the nature of existence or being.
2. Imagine a pale blue morning sky, almost green, with clouds only at

the rims. The earth rolls and the sun appears to mount, mountains erode, fruits decay, the Foraminifera adds another chamber to its shell, babies' fingernails grow as does the hair of the dead in their graves, and in eggtimers the sands fall and the eggs cook on.

3. Sarah Boyle thinks of her nose as too large, though several men have cherished it. The nose is generous and performs a well-calculated geometric curve, at the arch of which the skin is drawn very tight and faint whiteness of bone can be seen showing through, it has much the same architectural tension and sense of mathematical calculation as the day-after-Thanksgiving breast-bone on the carcass of turkey; her maiden name was Sloss, mixed German, English and Irish descent; in grade school she was very bad at playing softball and, besides being chosen last for the team, was always made to play centre field, no one could ever hit to centre field; she loves music best of all the arts, and of music, Bach, J.S.; she lives in California, though she grew up in Boston and Toledo.

4. BREAKFAST TIME AT THE BOYLES' HOUSE ON LA FLORIDA STREET, ALAMEDA, CALIFORNIA, THE CHILDREN DEMAND SUGAR FROSTED FLAKES.

    With some reluctance Sarah Boyle dishes out Sugar Frosted Flakes to her children, already hearing the decay set in upon the little milk-white teeth, the bony whine of the dentist's drill. The dentist is a short, gentle man with a moustache who sometimes reminds Sarah of an uncle who lives in Ohio. One bowl per child.

5. If one can imagine it considered as an abstract object by members of a totally separate culture, one can see that the cereal box might seem a beautiful thing. The solid rectangle is neatly joined and classical in proportions, on it are squandered wealths of richest colours, virgin blues, crimsons, dense ochres, precious pigments once reserved for sacred paintings and as cosmetics for the blind faces of marble gods. Giant Size. Net Weight 16 ounces, 250 grams. 'They're tigeriffic!' says Tony the Tiger. The box blats promises: Energy, Nature's Own Goodness, an endless pubescence. On its back is a mask of William Shakespeare to be cut out, folded, worn by thousands of tiny Shakespeares in Kansas City, Detroit, Tucson, San Diego, Tamua.

(Zoline [1967] 1988: 50–1)

As we can see from this opening, 'Heat death' is fragmented, so much so that it is scarcely recognizable as a story at all. A look at the text population in its opening will be useful in examining the voices in these fragments. In Chapter 3, I provided a list of possible features, under three headings, for identifying voices in a text's population. Examining the Prior texts/characters means looking for antecedent texts, actual or supposed, including speech representation. For Interaction/interactants we can look for signs of interaction between the implied writer and reader, between characters. For Discourse types/subject positions we need to turn to discourses, genres and the identities they set up.

Starting with Interaction/interactants, there is a single example of direct address in paragraph 2 ('Imagine . . .'). A brief indication of implied writer and reader interaction, this is not synthetic personalization but distant and formal, the highly conventional pedagogic voice of an encyclopaedia. There is no dialogue at all. In paragraph 4, a demand from the children elicits a reluctant nonverbal response from their mother. Apart from this, the daily interaction between mother and children is not represented.

Turning to prior texts/characters, there is just one instance of explicitly cued speech representation: *'They're tigeriffic!'* This advertising slogan quoted from a cereal packet (and attributed to a cartoon tiger called Tony) is flanked by other words of the anonymous copy-writers. The capitalized heading to paragraph 4 reports, as if it were a news item, the children's demand for the sugary cereal. In the passage beneath it a cognitive process noun and two verbs report the protagonist's thoughts. 'Heat death' opens with an embedded fragment from a dictionary: a definition of 'ontology' (which establishes existence as a presupposed problem). Later in the story, in paragraph 15, we are told of Sarah Boyle's obsessive interest in dictionaries and encyclopaedias:

> She is passionately fond of children's dictionaries, encyclopaedias,
> ABCs and all reference books, transfixed and comforted at their simulacra of a complete listing and ordering.
>
> (ibid.: 54)

Listing and ordering are textual properties of dictionaries and encyclopaedias as generic text types.

Turning to discourse-types/subject positions, what discoursal and generic elements are there in the opening passage? As the beginning of a short story it is unusual; peculiar, even. The numbering of fragments reduces generic expectations of narrative structure. This textual organization contributes to the imitation of encyclopaedia-like genres; another contributor is the interpersonal aspect of distanced formality. I have already noted the report genre imitated in paragraph 4 and the advertising copy iterated in paragraph 5. A genre which is notably not incorporated into 'Heat death' is conversation. Still on the topic of genre, in terms of science fiction as a generic category, you might say 'Heat death' is science fiction because it claims to be; it does not share many characteristics with other texts in the marketing category. The only recognizable science fiction elements are the scientific discourses: fragments of geometry, astronomy, archaeology, such as one would find in an encyclopaedia. For example, in paragraph 2 scientific discourses are evident in the astronomical accuracy of *'earth rolls and the sun appears to mount'*, in the latinate terminology as used by marine biologists, and so on. (Foraminifera, incidentally, is a kind of plankton, which when it dies contributes to the chalk deposits forming the seabed.) The disparate, bizarrely juxtaposed elements of paragraph 2 together form a contextualization of the protagonist introduced in paragraph 3 in terms of physical, not social, sciences, in a natural, not social, universe the scale of which reduces her to insignificance.

The implied reader is knowledgeable, with some background in the sciences to draw upon, or at least access to reference books. In this respect, the implied reader is close to the protagonist. But there is no straightforward matching of implied reader and main character here, and certainly no intensive character focalization to encourage close identification with her. On the contrary, Sarah Boyle *herself* seems to be distanced from herself, as though perceiving herself from another's perspective (this is particularly evident in later paragraphs; for example *'"That way madness lies, says Sarah," says Sarah'*, ibid.: 56). The cognitive processes reported in paragraph 4 do indicate that the narration is focalized through the character's thoughts at that point, but this is not sustained. The paragraph preceding it could be construed as self-reflection in the third person, by someone seriously alienated and acutely bored. Most of the narration, as we have seen, is made up of fragments from diverse (diverting?) sources. Many of the fragments are notes she has written to herself, as in the following paragraph:

14. CLEANING UP THE HOUSE. TWO.
Washing the baby's diapers. Sarah Boyle writes notes to herself all over the house; a mazed wild script larded with arrows, diagrams, pictures; graffiti on every available surface in a desperate/heroic attempt to index, record, bluff, invoke, order and placate. On the fluted and flowered white plastic lid of the diaper bin she has written in Blushing Pink Nitetime lipstick a phrase to ward off fumy ammoniac despair. 'The nitrogen cycle is the vital round of organic and inorganic exchange on earth. The sweet breath of the Universe.' On the wall by the washing

machine are Yin and Yang signs, mandalas, and the words, 'Many young wives feel trapped. It is a contemporary sociological phenomenon which may be explained in part by a gap between changing living patterns and the accommodation of social services to these patterns.' Over the stove she has written 'Help, Help, Help, Help, Help.'

(ibid.: 53)

Sarah Boyle seems to be fragmented into other voices, other texts. She is in a state of crisis and is losing her sense of identity, snowed under with the repetitive menial tasks that are part of childcare in her society. 'Heat death' undermines the dominant values surrounding family life, the assumption that women have a central place in it and, in particular, that women are naturally inclined to devote themselves to children and find childcare fulfilling as a way of life. There is something not quite right about Sarah Boyle's reflection on children in the passage below. Notice also the reporting clause compound; even her active agency in the reflective process of 'musing' is put into question:

How fortunate for the species, Sarah muses or is mused, that children are as ingratiating as we know them. Otherwise they would soon be salted off for the leeches they are, and the race would extinguish itself in a fair sweet flowering, the last generation's massive achievement in the arts and pursuits of high civilisation.

(ibid.: 58)

As LeFanu observes, this is a story which 'at once centralises and deconstructs "woman"' (LeFanu 1988: 98). It centralizes women in that it claims their experiences are worth dealing with in science fiction; childcare and housework – and the frustrations of those whose lives are dominated by them – are established as issues worthy of attention. It deconstructs in that it undermines the naturalized patriarchal stereotype of the happy, home-centred woman; in 'Heat death', the little treasure at home is going out of her mind with boredom, engaged in 'a doomed struggle against the slipping of self into other' (ibid.: 97). The story offers no satisfactory imaginary solution to the real dilemma represented. All we are given by way of narrative resolution/closure are: i) the death of the family's pet turtle, as anticipated, ii) Sarah's tearful outburst of egg- and crockery-throwing, and iii) the surreal performance of 'a well-calculated geometrical curve' by the eggs in the last two sentences (an ironic link with paragraph 3):

The eggs arch slowly through the kitchen, like a baseball, hit high

against the spring sky, seen from far away. They go higher and higher
in the stillness, hesitate at the zenith, then begin to fall away slowly,
slowly, through the fine, clear air.

(Zoline [1967] 1988: 65)

Within the domain of journalism in which professional science
fiction writers, critics and fans interact, adverse critics of the New
Wave (e.g. Kingsley Amis) have frequently cited Zoline's 'The heat
death of the universe' as a prime example of what went wrong with
science fiction in the 1960s (Kaveney 1989: 85). Perhaps it was sin-
gled out because, among the fragmented and genre-disrupting
texts produced by the New Wave, it was the one that had an additional irritant: the oppositional discourse of feminism.

Some science fiction produced by feminists has interrogated its
generic situation and character types. Joanna Russ's *We who are
about to* . . . (1987), for example, challenges the post-apocalyptic,
survivalist type of situation, typified by Robert Heinlein's novel,
Farnham's freehold (1965). These stories deal with survival: either
after crash-landing on an uninhabited planet or in the outback,
newly enlarged by global warfare or other catastrophe to cover the
earth. The small number of dominant males take it upon themselves to preserve the race, by making sure all the surviving women
are pregnant. The implied reader of Russ's novel knows the field.
Her book comments on specific prior texts with which the reader is
assumed to be familiar, and refutes the patriarchal and heterosexist
assumptions underlying them. The female protagonist of *We who
are about to* . . . refuses to cooperate, arguing eloquently against
attempts to survive in the hostile environment into which she and
her fellow passengers have crash-landed. Death being the only real
future for them, she intends to die with dignity and is prepared to
murder for the privilege. Another example of Russ's 'guerrilla
tactics' within the genre of science fiction is 'Clichés from outer
space' (1985). This is a small collection of parodies, in which
she identifies a range of story types relating to particular areas of
women's experience (e.g. 'The-weird-ways-of-getting-pregnant-
story').

LANGUAGE REFORM

Language reform as part of the emancipatory preliminary to social
change needs some explanation, since politically correct (PC) lan-

guage has had a particularly bad press in recent years. There has been a good deal of resistance to PC incentives recommending non-discriminatory alternatives to existing language practices (for example, the National Union of Journalist's guidelines for non-sexist usage within the journalistic order of discourse, and codes of practice within educational institutions). Ironically, the recommendations themselves have frequently been labelled oppressive, mistakenly (or wilfully) perceived as unjustified coercion and infringement of freedom of speech, rather than attempts to create equity with precious little coercive power at all (for detailed discussion of some 'classic arguments' against intervention, see Maija Blaubergs 1980). There are various frequently used strategies for containing language reform: ridicule, marginalization and, most insidiously, appropriation. PC language has been appropriated and used to the advantage of precisely those groups whose discriminatory practices it was designed to challenge. As Henry Beard and Christopher Cerf observe in their lighthearted PC 'handbook':

> The term 'politically correct', co-opted by the white power elite as a tool for attacking multiculturalism, is no longer 'politically correct'.
>
> (Beard and Cerf 1992: 82)

With all this in mind, it is perhaps as well to recollect for a moment that the point of language reform is to engender and support social reforms. The first step towards social change is showing the need for it:

> To change language may not be to embark on drastic social changes directly, but it does involve consciousness-raising; that is, bringing awareness of a problem to the public's attention. The assumption underlying consciousness-raising is that before a behavior can be changed, there must be awareness that a situation exists warranting alteration.
>
> (Van Den Bergh 1987: 132)

Language change brings the need for social change out into the open. The strategies of containment (ridicule and so on) are best understood as conservative resistance to, and attempts to combat, consciousness-raising. Part of this consciousness-raising endeavour involves identifying 'lexical gaps' in the language – that which 'cannot be said', if you like – and then filling those gaps; that is, producing neologisms. The term 'sexism' is one example; 'parenting', a PC term now broadly taken up in childcare literature, is another. Cheris Kramarae and Paula Treichler's *A feminist dictionary* contains many other neologisms which have not gained such wide currency ('femicide', to name just one).

Science fiction is a particularly suitable genre for contributing to the identification and filling in of lexical gaps. It is after all a genre concerned with alternatives, possibilities; science fiction creators have dreamed up 'interrossiters', engines running on 'dialithium crystals', 'ftl' travel, 'learnsharing'.[17] Experiments in fiction can take up a position, along with codes of practice and alternative dictionaries, as contestation of sexism, racism and other discriminatory -*isms* in language.

The most concerted lexical gap-filling in feminist science fiction has to be in Suzette Haden Elgin's *Native tongue* (1985). In this novel, women linguists are creating a new language, Láadan. This is to be a 'women's language', specifically designed to make up for the inadequacies of other languages for representing events, people, actions from women's perspectives. Here are few items of Láadan vocabulary, with definitions, from the novel's appendix (a sampler from *A first dictionary and grammar of Láadan*):

lowithelaad: to feel, as if directly, another's pain/grief/surprise/
               joy/anger
raahedethi: to be unable to feel lowithelaad, above; to be empathically
               impaired
radama: to non-touch, to actively refrain from touching
radamalh: to non-touch with evil intent
radíidin: a non-holiday, a time allegedly a holiday but actually so
               much a burden because of work and preparations that it is
               a dreaded occasion; especially when there are too many
               guests and none of them help.

(Elgin 1985: 302)

Outside the novel, the value of the neologisms is in the glosses attached; they identify gaps in the English lexicon. The last one can probably not be expressed in a single word in any language, but how familiar the event is for women, whether the alleged 'holiday' is Diwali, Christmas, the first of Ramadan or some other festival! By articulating a woman's-eye-view of a festival, this neologism does more than simply lexicalize women's place. Naming from a woman's perspective is part of an active struggle for change. However, I have to say that, within Elgin's novel, lexicalization alone seems to bring about social changes, as though rewordings alone are sufficient to transform reality. As Jacob Mey remarks in his review of *Native tongue*:

> if we want to do something about the world (e.g. change it), then the indispensable condition (apart from having the right lexicalizations) is that we pool our resources and act together, as a group or a class. Clearly, for [Elgin], in the beginning is the word; action is a consequence of wording.
>
> (Mey 1989: 1041)

Some feminist writers of science fiction have scrutinized the androcentrism behind the masculine pseudo-generic (*Man, Mankind; he, him, his*). Generic nouns and pronouns in English and other European languages are supposed to have general as well as specific reference: that is, to be generic (referring to the whole species) as well as sex-specific (referring to the male half of the species, or to some male in particular). Is it a true generic, or are human beings assumed to be male? An early example of fiction addressing this question is Charlotte Perkins Gilman's *Herland* (1992). In this novel, three male explorers discover a 'lost world', a utopian land inhabited entirely by women. The narrator, Vandyck, is the only one of the three male visitors to Herland who really learns from the experience. He comes to recognize the androcentrism of his own society:

> When we say *men, man, manly, manhood*, and all the other masculine derivatives, we have in the background of our minds a huge vague crowded picture of the world and all its activities ... full of marching columns of men, of changing lines of men, of long processions of men; of men steering ships into new seas, exploring unknown mountains, breaking horses, herding cattle, ploughing and sowing and reaping, toiling at the forge and the furnace, digging in the mine, building roads and bridges and high cathedrals, managing great businesses, teaching in all the colleges, preaching in all the churches; of men everywhere, doing everything – 'the world'.
>
> And when we say *women*, we think female – the sex.
>
> But to these women, in the unbroken sweep of this two-thousand-year-old feminine civilization, the word woman called up all that big background ... and the word man meant to them only male – the sex.
>
> (Gilman [1915] 1992: 137)

By the end of his visit, Vandyck is capable of 'seeing women not as females but as people' (ibid.). Gilman's critical scrutiny of the pseudo-generic first appeared in 1915. Psycholinguistic research into the reception of the 'generic' has since endorsed Gilman's conclusion that it is androcentric. Wendy Martyna (1983) found that male and female college students in the United States interpreted candidate 'generic' elements differently. Only the women were interpreting them as generic:

> males appear to be using and understanding *he* in its specific more often than generic sense. Females both avoid the use of *he* and respond to its use with a more generic than specific interpretation. To do otherwise would be to encourage self-exclusion.
>
> (Martyna 1983: 31)

Some writers have experimented with alternatives to the pronouns *he* and *she*. The most extensive and, in my view, most successful and thought-provoking attempt is in Marge Piercy's *Woman on the edge of time*. Part of Piercy's novel is set in a utopian community in the future, a community in which neither sex dominates the other. The people in this community never specify sex in pronominal reference. The subject pronoun is *person*; elsewhere *per* is used. The effect is not to eliminate the sexual identity of the characters, simply to background it. Here are some examples of it in action:

> 'Sappho perself made that tale long ago.' Jackrabbit was watching the old woman with admiration. 'Many people now tell that story, but none better. At Icebreaking I taped per telling with the latest varia for the holifile'
>
> (Piercy [1976] 1979: 132)

> 'Magdalena? Ah, person is coming. Magdalena is unusual. Person does not switch jobs but is permanent head of this house of children. It is per calling. Sometimes a gift expresses itself so strongly . . . person must do what person has to do.'
>
> (ibid.: 136)

> 'Person's way of insinuating into other people's beds was not always productive,' a young person said, standing on one foot. 'Jackrabbit came to me once after a dance and then never again. I felt I was an apple person had taken a bite of and spat out.'
> 'Person was so curious, began far more friendships than could be maintained,' Bolivar said dryly, without raising his head.
>
> (ibid.: 312)

By continuing to use sex-specific pronouns and possessives in the narration, Piercy manages to have it both ways. As a result, the

reader can distinguish between women and men (unless the focalizing character is at a loss as to their sex, which is sometimes the
case: see next section) and can see the inhabitants make no distinction between them. In the utopian community, there are no gender
differences. In a discussion of science fiction as a 'laboratory' for
testing out new pronouns, Nancy Henley observes that:

> when a community does not have gender as a primary social criterion
> for allocation of its goods and status, it does not need, nor wish, to spec-
> ify sex in its pronouns . . . possible futures develop our intuition that
> sexist language is closely bound to sexist society
>
> (Henley 1987: 16)

There is one work of science fiction I've not yet mentioned which
presents such a world in detail: Ursula Le Guin's *The left hand of
darkness* ([1969] 1981). This remarkable book presents a world in
which people are neither male nor female, except when they are in
estrus, at which time they temporarily become either one or the
other. Le Guin represents her fascinating, androgynous human
beings with the male generic. Through her main narrator – an outsider, who is male – she justifies her choice as follows (the state of
'somer', referred to in the passage, is the stage of their sexual cycle
in which these people are dormant):

> you cannot think of a Gethenian as 'it'. They are not neuters. They are
> potentials, or integrals. Lacking the Karhidish 'human pronoun' used
> for persons in somer, I must say 'he', for the same reasons as we used
> the masculine pronoun in referring to a transcendent god: it is less
> defined, less specific, than the neuter or the feminine. But the very use
> of the pronoun in my thoughts leads me continually to forget that the
> Karhider I am with is not a man, but a manwoman.
>
> (Le Guin [1961] 1981: 85)

By this means, Le Guin draws the reader's attention to the absence
of a truly genderless 'human pronoun' in English. However, since
she uses the male pseudo-generic throughout, the reader is left
with the inescapable impression that all the characters are male.

UTOPIAN VISIONS

Perhaps the most concerted fictional engagement in denaturalizing
familiar social structures, social relations and the discourses

sustaining them is in feminist utopian fiction. Part of the utopian endeavour is to undermine a society's appearance of fixity and imperviousness. The fictional ideal worlds in utopian fiction do not provide blueprints for the future, or predictions. What they do is foreground the possibility, and desirability, of social change. Societies are exposed as not fixed and inevitable but products of historical processes.

Socialist-feminist politics in the United States was the historical base for Gilman's early feminist utopia, *Herland*. Political activism in the 1960s was at the base of Joanna Russ's vision of possibilities in *The female man* (1975). Russ's novel articulates the oppositional discourse of feminism in a text that consists of four fragmentary interweaving narratives (producing a text which appears dislocated, but not to the extent of the Zoline short story examined earlier). For several years *The female man* existed only in manuscript form, circulating among various writers of science fiction (Moylan 1986: 57). Its eventual publication in 1975 was in part a consequence of the pressure-group power of science fiction writers and readers as a community. The contribution of this community to the patrolling of the genre meant that, as Moylan says,

> *The female man* smuggled utopia into the dystopian world of the latter half of our century and initiated the revival and transformation of utopia in the 1970s.
>
> (ibid.)

Other feminist utopias first published in the 1970s in the US are Suzy McKee Charnas's *Motherlines* [1978] (1989), Sally Gearhart's *The wanderground* (1979), Marge Piercy's *Woman on the edge of time* (1976) and, in the 1980s, Joan Slonczewski's *A door into Ocean* (1987). These novels all present contrasting societies and give close attention to everyday life in the utopian world as experienced by the no-longer-oppressed, particularly women. It is perhaps not so surprising, therefore, that of the novels mentioned above, only one, Piercy's *Woman on the edge of time*, contains a utopian vision with both women and men in it. There is another novel which needs mentioning at this juncture that is not exactly a utopia, even though it employs science fiction's speculative capacity to represent a world in which women have never been oppressed. This is Esmé Dodderidge's *The new Gulliver* (1979), which presents a comic reversal of dominant patriarchal practices and the gender identities and relationships they bestow.

Piercy's protagonist and focalizing character in *Woman on the edge of time* is a marginalized figure: a poor, working-class Chicana who, at the time the novel begins, has already been committed once to a psychiatric institution. She is the eponymous woman on the edge of time, existing for much of the novel in a drugged stupor, in periodic contact with someone very much like herself from a utopian future and, once, with a dystopian version. The novel opens on to the tensions of utopian vision and present realities: her identity as a 'crazy' woman and the effects of male violence. The person Connie refers to as 'him' in sentence 2 is her utopian visitor, Luciente:

> Connie got up from her kitchen table and walked slowly to the door. Either I saw him or I didn't and I'm crazy for real this time, she thought.
> 'It's me – Dolly!' Her niece was screaming in the hall. 'Let me in! Hurry!'
> 'Momentito.' Connie fumbled with the bolt, the police lock, finally swinging the door wide. Dolly fell in past her, her face bloody. Connie clutched at Dolly, trying to see how badly she was hurt. 'Que pasa? Who did this?'
>
> (Piercy [1976] 1979: 9)

Dolly's attackers were her pimp-boyfriend and his henchmen, and they soon catch up with her. In the ensuing scene, Connie's defence of her niece leads to severe beatings and recommittal. Admitted semi-conscious by Dolly's pimp, who is wily enough to take her to the hospital that has records of her previous admission, she takes the blame for the injuries of both:

> He pretended she had attacked him and Dolly at Dolly's apartment on Rivington. He would take no chance that they might not accept her as a crazy woman. . . . How could Dolly sit there sniveling and nod when the doctor asked if Connie had done that to her face? . . . She had been screaming – okay! Did they think you had to be crazy to protest being locked up? Yes, they did. They said reluctance to be hospitalized was a sign of sickness
>
> (ibid.: 17)

As narrator, Connie provides an alert, critical commentary on events, showing the gulf between the perceptions of the hospital staff and her own. Her identity, constructed in the psychiatric discourse impinging on her, is defined by the white middle-class professionals wielding power over her. Connie is labelled as violently insane. Once 'hospitalized' – the staff's medical rewording of her 'locked up' – she ceases to exist as a full person. A characteristic of the medical discourse in which Connie is caught up is severely restricted speaker rights. Ignored by the doctor admitting her, as she will later be ignored by nurses, nothing she can say or do will remove the labels 'crazy' and 'violent' attached to her. In drawing discourses of medicine into the novel, Piercy sometimes reproduces the blurring of agent-process relations frequent in medical texts (noted in Chapter 1). Examples of such blurred representations of actions are some authentic sounding nominalizations of processes that are attached to Connie as her attributes, symptoms of her sickness (e.g. 'your hostile episodes . . . your illness behavior' (ibid.: 374)).

There are severe restrictions on her speaker rights in the other scrutinizing discourse which impinges upon her. One person who does speak to her, in an official capacity, shortly after her readmission is a social worker. In questioning Connie, the social worker distances herself from Connie's viewpoint, dissociating herself from her repetitions of Connie's utterances and from Connie's vocabulary choices: '*The Porto Rican man you describe as your niece's "pimp" – is that the same man as her fiance?'; 'Who are the "they" you believe knocked you down?*'; and even, '*Where do you believe you feel pain?*' (ibid.: 27). The social worker is making clear the limits to the common ground she is prepared to share with Connie. Connie's views are scrutinized, they are looked at as objects for examination by the expert. But they lack authority, even on the matter of whether or not she is in pain. If the social worker had asked 'where do you feel pain?', she would have been sharing Connie's presupposed idea. The cognitive verb *believe* clearly restricts the presupposed idea to Connie's unauthoritative opinion. There is a strikingly similar passage in Sylvia Plath's autobiography: '"Suppose you try and tell me what you think was wrong" . . . What did I *think* was wrong. That made it sound as if nothing *really* wrong, I only thought it was wrong' (1963: 137). Crazy people, like sinners in the confessional, are called upon to make divulgences and then await the expert's judgement. Unfortunately for Connie, she is not granted absolution.

By the end of the first chapter of *Woman on the edge of time* the protagonist has been signed in to another mental institution by her brother, Dolly's father: 'Some truce', as Connie reflects on her way there, 'negotiated between the two men over the bodies of their women' (Piercy 1979: 31). Things go from bad to worse as she is taken to another hospital and, along with her fellow 'patients', becomes an experimental subject in electrode implantation. By

inserting into the realist narrative of Connie's incarceration a utopian vision – a future in which such patterns of domination no longer
exist – Piercy lifts what would otherwise be very depressing reading. From chapter 3 onwards, Connie makes frequent visits to the
utopian world. Because of her contact with that world (by a kind of
telepathic linkage) she learns that people can live differently, that
social change *for the better* is possible.

Her utopian visitor, Luciente, turns out to be a woman, her coun-
terpart in the utopian future community of Mattapoisett. Connie
has been interpreting her posture and manner according to her own
cultural expectations, only recognizing her femaleness on a visit to
Mattapoisett, and then with difficulty:

> Luciente spoke, she moved with that air of brisk unselfconscious
> authority Connie associated with men. Luciente sat down, taking up
> more space than women ever did. She squatted, she sprawled, she
> strolled, never thinking about how her body was displayed.
>
> (ibid.: 67)

In Mattapoisett, 2137, gender differences have been abolished.
Mental illness is not only respected, but admired. Piercy's utopia is
populated with enlightened and unoppressed peasants, men and
women, with access to advanced scientific knowledge. They are
non-racist, feminist, and communist environmentalists. The content
of Piercy's utopian vision is not my primary concern here, however
(for such detail, see Rosinsky 1982; Moylan 1986; Cranny-Francis
1990). What I want to look at is Piercy's presentation of it to
empower the reader.

The frequent direct contrasts between the two societies reflect
badly on the twentieth-century world. The contrasts repeatedly
point out the iniquities in our institutions. But Piercy is not presenting a perfect society from the élite position of an expert, above
criticism. The implied reader constructed is critically distant from
the utopian world. Perceiving it from Connie's perspective, the
reader may share her doubts, incredulity, even revulsion. One feature of the utopian society Connie responds to with anger and
distaste is the 'baby brooder'. In Mattapoisett, the link between sexual relations and reproduction has been severed: women no longer
produce babies. The use of technology to liberate women from their
'biological destiny' is directly inspired by Shulamith Firestone's *The
dialectic of sex*. Piercy presents it as a possibility, not as the solution.
In an earlier work of science fiction, Aldous Huxley's dystopian

Brave new world (1932), babies growing in a central brooder are presented as horrific. Connie's initial negative response may well be shared by many readers, whether or not they have read Huxley's novel. Connie's strong reaction is rooted in her own loss and guilt (her only child has been taken from her). A brief switch to first person narration draws the implied reader close to her bitterness and resentment:

> How could anyone know what being a mother means who has never carried a child nine months heavy under her heart, who has never borne a baby in blood and pain, who has never suckled a child. Who got that child out of a machine the way that couple, white and rich, got my flesh and blood. What do they know of motherhood?
> . . . She hated them, the bland bottleborn monsters of the future, born without pain, multicolored like a litter of puppies without the stigmata of race and sex.
>
> (Piercy 1979: 106)

Piercy presents a revealing view of the dignity of motherhood here. Motherhood is Connie's only real source of pride and achievement. In her bitterness, she has slipped into a Christian discourse, glorifying suffering itself, hating the prospect of babies born without 'stigmata': noble signs of victimhood.

Woman on the edge of time does not simply contrast the present with an ideal utopian future. It foregrounds the possibility of change, drawing attention to historical processes and the place in them of individual and collective action. As the inhabitants of the utopia explain to Connie, their world is only one of many possibilities and can only become a certainty if people in her, and our, time work together to make it happen: 'We must fight to come to exist, to remain in existence, to be the future that happens. That's why we reached you' (ibid.: 197–8). Connie and people like her must reject their identity as victim and learn resistance, how to fight back, otherwise the utopian future will never exist. As the implant operations begin, Connie engineers an escape from the hospital, fleeing from her turn to be operated on. Her eventual recapture and operation, and a fellow patient's suicide, make a low point at which she can no longer contact the utopian future. Events are making it too improbable. Instead she contacts the dystopian future that the experimental electrode implants are working towards. In this grim version of the future everyone has implants; they are an economical way of controlling populations. Cybernetic 'improvements' are highly valued; poor people, referred to as 'duds', are walking organ banks for the rich. Technology is in the service of 'the Multis'.[18]

Connie's frequent 'blackouts', as she visits the future, alarm the doctors for whom she is an unwilling experimental subject. Frightened of an embarrassing failure leading to the discontinuance of their research grant, they remove the implant. Connie has won a battle; she is beginning to think of her plight in military terms:

> The war raged outside her body now, outside her skull, but the enemy would press on and violate her frontiers again as soon as they chose their next advance. She was at war.
>
> (ibid.: 337)

She is no longer a passive, helpless victim. Having seen two possible futures, she has something to fight for and something to resist. Her counter-attack, with which her narrative ends, is the poisoning of the doctors experimenting on the mental patients:

> Connie fights the institutionalized violence of the welfare and asylum systems with a crude physical violence which is a demystification of her own treatment by her society.
>
> (Cranny-Francis 1990: 131)

As Cranny-Francis stresses, Piercy is not making a case for violent revolutionary overthrow of social and political institutions in the United States. Connie's act of poisoning is not being put forward as a recommendation, 'a blueprint for political activism' (ibid.). What Piercy *is* doing is denaturalizing and contesting dominant oppressive discourses and practices. Cranny-Francis continues:

> Connie's story reveals the violence endemic to the ideologies of gender, race and class dominant in her society; those ideologies must be revealed, analysed, and eradicated so that their violence is also removed.
>
> (ibid.)

The novel concludes with five pages of extracts from Connie's hospital records. In addition to technical details of her 'psychotic' condition, these records include the admission notes made at her re-entry in the first chapter, notes on her escape from the ward and on her brother, Luis, who signed various release forms enabling the psychiatrists to use her as an experimental subject:

> This evening this 37-year-old obese Puerto Rican woman allegedly attacked a relative and a relative's fiance with a bottle. Upon examination she was found lying on the floor, groaning incoherently, and

proved disoriented as to time and place. She was hostile, uncooperative, and threatening. She was abusive to relative and relative's fiance. Admit. Thorazine 1000mg by injection. Restraint.
. . .this patient wandered out of the hospital and was lost in the woods for two whole nights and days. She was recovered in a bus station in Fairview very confused and uncertain where she was trying to go.
Mr. Camacho is a well-dressed man (gray business suit) who appears to be in his 40's. He operates a wholesale-retail nursery and has a confident, expansive manner. I would consider him to be a reliable informant who expresses genuine concern for his sister.

(Piercy 1979: 379–81)

We have already had Connie's version of the events recorded here, and her views on the depth of her brother's 'concern'. As Rosinsky (1982) observes, the inclusion of the 'official' hospital records at the end of Piercy's novel 'directs the reader beyond the text itself' (1982: 95). It provides 'a narrative bridge' (ibid.) leading the reader towards both the utopian and dystopian possible futures. The direction depends on the *reader's* choice, which hangs on rejection or acceptance of the records' validity. Connie's story has constructed an oppositional position for reading these official records against the grain.

Piercy's utopian vision provides a fictional solution to real contemporary problems, working out in some detail what a more benign social system might actually be like. She emphasizes the processes of history and the necessity of individual and collective action in bringing about positive social changes. One consequence is that her 'critical utopia' (to use Moylan's term) counters the profound pessimism of twentieth-century dystopian fiction. *Brave new world* and *Nineteen eighty-four* are two of the best known dystopias; both present social change as profoundly disturbing and dangerous, and may well produce in a reader a sense of relief and retreat back into their own society. Viewed in this way, the monitory function of dystopias appears in a negative light. Dystopian fiction also functions as containment of criticism of current social systems, and indeed containment of utopian thinking altogether. Moylan sums up Piercy's appropriation of the utopia:

> She establishes a dialectical connection between consciousness raising and the historical situation that carries out the dynamic of power relations and social change within the literary operations of the utopian text. In both content and form, Piercy asserts the power of desire as a mechanism of the collective human subject.

(Moylan 1986: 155)

There is one final point to make on the subject of utopias. Writing and reading them is no substitute for action, but an emancipatory preliminary, along with other forms of consciousness-raising. As Connie says in *Woman on the edge of time*, 'we can imagine all we like. But we got to do something real' (Piercy 1979: 343). If we simply read utopian fiction without being open to working for social change, we are just fooling ourselves, consuming utopia like any other 'escapist' fiction. The most pessimistic expression of this view I have ever come across is Lennard Davis (1987), in which he argues that novel consumption is necessarily anti-emancipatory. To me, this is unnecessarily extreme, but it is certainly well worth examining.

EMBRACING OTHERNESS

A discussion of science fiction would be incomplete without aliens. Of all the character types found in science fiction, the alien is probably the most widespread. Stories of close encounters with alien life-forms, flying saucer sightings and abductions find their way into the ostensibly non-fictional reportage of newspapers. One of the lengthiest and most elaborate, known as 'The kidnappers from outer space', caused a flurry of alien-related news reportage in the media. It appeared as a serialized interview in *The Sunday Mirror*, a British tabloid, in the 1960s: 'The most fantastic flying saucer story of all time has only just been brought to light – a story that baffles even the scientists. It involves an ordinary American couple WHO SAY THEY WERE KIDNAPPED BY CREATURES FROM OUTER SPACE' (25 September 1966). The 'ordinary' American couple's sensational story no doubt appeared in United States newspapers too.

As well as infiltrating newspapers, the alien has also proliferated in the products of the fiction-producing industries. Films containing aliens are often generic hybrids of science fiction and horror (e.g. *The thing* (1982), *Alien* (1979)). In these genre hybrids, the aliens are malevolent, serving the same story function as the manifestations of evil we have seen in James Herbert's horror fiction: the absolute 'otherness' to be vanquished by the hero. Notable exceptions to the science fiction/horror cross in cinema are *The day the earth stood still* (1951) and *2001: A space odyssey* (1968), in which the aliens are godlike benefactors, and *2010* (1984), in which a once-human divine being saves humanity from self-destruction. Other 'friendly alien' films are *Close encounters of the third kind* (1977), *ET* (1982) and *Alien nation* (1988) (a 'buddy movie' with a top-dressing of science fiction). The earliest evil aliens in print were the Martians in Wells' *The war of the worlds* (1898).

A recent novel interrogating the alien invasion storyline is Gwyneth Jones' *White Queen* (1991). Jones uses this genre cliché to conduct a subtle examination of the collision of cultures and its consequences. In this respect its closest literary antecedent outside the science fiction genre is perhaps Chinua Achebe's *African trilogy*; like Achebe, she considers the devastating consequences of one culture's domination of another. She is, however, writing for a predominantly white, middle-class and monolingual English audience. Perhaps for this reason, Jones' novel refuses prolonged identification with any of the characters, in contrast with Achebe's work (particularly *Things fall apart*, 1958 and *No longer at ease*, 1960). *White Queen* offers no unitary reading position and no simple focal character. There are frequent shifts, often not overtly signalled, between a wide range of human and alien characters. These frequent shifts contribute to making it complex and intriguing, particularly when the narrative is focalized through an alien. They can also be very confusing, which is entirely appropriate given the amount of cross-cultural miscommunication.

The central cliché of alien invasion is, however, delightfully familiar. Two media people – a presenter called Braemar and an 'ee-jay' (electronic journalist) called Johnny – are the human protagonists, in search of the alien scoop-of-a-lifetime. In a secret rendezvous, they record an interview with an alien. But they do not scoop the earth-shattering news that 'the aliens have landed'. This is leaked by the 'Aleutians' themselves. The extra-terrestrials are not just the alien 'other'; they are people. The novel focuses on the alien invasion cliché to humorous effect. The aliens, being outsiders, are ignorant of the robust stereotype they exemplify. 'What I can't understand', says one, 'is how they came to be expecting us'. To which his friend replies, 'It wasn't us they were expecting. It was some other, important people' (Jones 1991: 90–1).

It is a science fiction truism that any extra-terrestrial visitors to Earth are bound to be technologically superior. 'Or else we'd be visiting them', as the ee-jay reflects (ibid.: 69). The native inhabitants of Earth simply assume, wrongly, that the Aleutians arrived by means of faster-than-light (ftl) travel. The Aleutians themselves, as a race, are indeed 'superior' technologically. But they are in many ways just ordinary people. Most importantly, they believe they mean no harm. The landing parties are sightseers and bargain hunters, on the look-out for potential 'trading partners'. They are mundanely selfish, but not by any means malevolent. They do not, cannot, perceive themselves or their presence as in any way harmful to the indigenous population of the planet they have descended upon. They have taken the name 'Aleutian' from a collection of islands in the North Pacific whose Indian inhabitants they imagine an affinity with. Like Achebe's Igbo people, they speak in proverbs and aphorisms. They have simple tastes and no interest whatsoever in the highly sophisticated media-technology of twentyfirst-century earth. In fact, they see film, video and TV as religious paraphenalia: faintly boring manifestations of the 'spirit world', the 'land of the dead'. They think the 'locals' on Earth are all religious fanatics, and refer to media people as 'priests'.

To earth people, the aliens fit the character-type of the benign godlike variety of extra-terrestrial visitor. With an instinct for bargaining power, the aliens allow the native inhabitants of Earth to think they have ftl travel (in fact, they have a multi-generation ship parked surreptitiously behind the moon). They themselves believe they are telepathic, since the collective 'Brood-Self' they are part of is one organism (this invention enables Jones to make some delightful speculations on pronominal reference: 'In Aleutia . . . did "we" dig holes in the road? Did "we" increase the gas bills, and predict the weather? Undoubtedly, yes' ibid.: 207). They are, in a sense, genuinely immortal. The 'Brood-Self' produces reincarnations of each individual from one generation to another. Individuals learn who they are, their 'narrative', as a matter of religious devotion (hence the misrecognition of the mass media on earth). The Earth media, with only partial understanding, report ftl ability, telepathy and immortality. They are after a good story, so they keep quiet about other, less impressive details that would spoil their image:

> The aliens were devout animists. They talked to furniture, treated their gadgets like pet animals. Reincarnation, animism, their strange response to certain technology . . . SETI considered it quite likely that the Aleutians were not in charge: that the real superrace, source of the ftl, had yet to reveal itself. This wasn't an idea the alien-watchers wanted to share with the global audience.

(ibid.: 110)

The global audience is awestricken. The visitors simply take advantage of the positive impression they make on the gullible locals. Like good poker players, they know how to use other people's weaknesses to their own advantage. The mass media unwittingly help them to dominate the natives.

The novel is set in the none too distant future. The human race is contending with overpopulation, exhausted resources, global warming, the aftermath of an earthquake which swallowed up Japan, and other comparatively speaking minor problems, such as the encroachment of 'livespace' on people's privacy. The apparently godlike aliens are received as saviours, or delivering archangels. But what will the impact of alien value systems be?

> The Aleutians wouldn't change. Humans had to find ways around the obstacles. Wasn't it always so, in the dialogue between native culture and their far-come conquerors?
>
> (ibid.: 305)

Similarly, in *Arrow of God*, an Igbo man observes: 'As daylight chases away darkness so will the white man drive away all our customs' (Achebe 1988: 365) (this character's choice of metaphor has no doubt been determined by his conversion to Christianity). The Aleutians are unaware of many of the differences between themselves and earth's native people. One aspect of being human the aliens do not understand is dual sexuality; they are androgynous. The aliens misrecognize men and women as two distinct warring 'broods'. This is because the only arena left for labour disputes is gender politics; the 'Eve-riots' are everywhere. A feminist reader is left in no doubt that the effect of their misrecognition of human affairs will be devastating. Braemar is no feminist, but she is troubled by what she learns about their attitude towards childbearers:

> The birthing body is a mere pod. . . What would the Aleutians think of earth's women when they understood human physiology? They'd think nothing of the question: no interest, so what? But those earthlings who had always hankered after Aristotle would soon be busy, with the supposed blessing of the master-race.
>
> (Jones 1991: 258)

Not all the native inhabitants are completely infatuated with the godlike aliens. Some individuals air their misgivings, in what little remaining privacy there is, and there is a small terrorist movement, known as White Queen. Braemar, who is a member of it, tries to enlist Johnny, impressing upon him that the 'reaction to the Aleutians is dangerous. It's mass hysteria. It is madness for us to treat them like gods' (ibid.: 176). White Queen is a 'preemptive resistance movement' (ibid.: 171). It is named after the character in Lewis Carroll's *Through the looking glass* who screams before she is hurt, 'to save time'. Johnny, a white American man, has mixed feelings about the movement, even after he has consented to join; he sees that it is made up of cranks and misfits. Braemar, an Asian-African woman who 'passes for white', has a keener sense of what is at stake and mocks him:

> When the wonderful white folk come along, the decent people are thrilled. It's only the mean, twisted witch doctor who plots against them, along with maybe good chief Mbongo's treacherous discarded wife. The proverbial minority of troublemakers.
>
> (Jones 1991: 222)

The discourse of this complex novel is such that the reader is offered a wide range of perspectives. It is composed almost entirely of character focalization and dialogue; 'omniscient' authorial comment is rare. The characters are not split into 'good guys' and 'bad guys'. The following extract illustrates the way Jones presents the perspectives of characters with conflicting views (both human in this case), without passing judgement herself. She does not try to impose one perception of the rights and wrongs of the matter, but leaves it to the reader. The setting is a press conference of sorts with the visitors. Notice the frequent shifts in focalization:

> 'What do you make of the alien attitude to gender politics?'
> Ellen was furious. The 360 cam that ogled her like a second little head beside Braemar's face had a vision field, a 'light shell', that included most of this room. There was no way she could escape with dignity. For a moment she was recklessly inclined to rely on censorship: but that too could be a gift to the media monster.
> 'We humans tend to perceive gender in them, but the Aleutians don't respond to that line of questioning. We have no idea how they reproduce, you know.' She smiled, putting the sex-mad media person in her place.
> Kershaw, old-maid socialist, saw brotherly love and no nasty sex. Even Poonsuk Masdit, a person you had to respect, spoke reservedly about 'medical possibilities'. She was dreaming of a cure for her mysterious wasting disease. Braemar was suddenly angry. They were blinded by privilege, all of them here. There was no way of warning them.

Nothing could make them see a new race of superiors through the eyes of the powerless.

'No gender. I see. But they have a rigid caste system. Isn't it true that most of those here are slaves of the dominant few, with no existence outside their hereditary tasks? Isn't that right?'

To the corrupt everything is corrupt. Ellen was morally certain that Aleutians didn't think like that, but Wilson could smear anything

(ibid.: 106)

Focalization is not always cued with mental process verbs or nouns. Sometimes expressive elements identify a particular character's viewpoint quite distinctly. The shift from Ellen in the second paragraph to Braemar in the third is signalled by their strong negative evaluations of each other: the pejorative terms of reference, 'sex-mad media person . . . old-maid socialist'.

The newcomers themselves are not portrayed as malevolent oppressors. On the contrary, when Clavel first arrives, he has no sense of 'them' and 'us'; he thinks of his people as 'human', and the native inhabitants are simply 'the locals'. However, this is because he is unaware of the gulf of cultural differences. He thinks he is still at home. His attitude, as a reviewer in the science fiction journal *Foundation* aptly puts it, is 'that of the smug hick who thinks everywhere is like Kansas' (Coldsmith 1992: 127). The division on race grounds comes later, when the Aleutians have realized their powerful position and are beginning to take advantage of it deliberately. Clavel is a poet; as such he considers himself as the conscience of his people. Even so, he does nothing to stop his people's invasion of Earth:

'the 'humans' are credulous fools. . . . As a nation, we were alarmed when we first found this planet, distrustful of success after so long without it. But planetfall and plunder was supposed to be the object of the exercise. Everyone's had time to remember that. There are plenty of takers now, eager for a piece of the action.'

Wrong, thought Clavel. We outgrew the false quest. We became the Aleutians: wanderers, islanders, surviving cleverly on the bounty of a cold and ungenerous ocean. It dawned on us that there can't be a world for people without a people who fill it.

Nobody paid attention to the poet, least of all himself. He had not the heart to exert his influence, to unfurl that secret banner and employ the backwards-pulling power. He told himself it was too late. He told himself that the notion of lasting harm is a childish fear.

(Jones 1991: 213–14)

A reader with any knowledge of, for example, the devastation caused by the Spanish in South America or by the British in West Africa will have some intimation of the 'lasting harm' in store for Earth's native people. Even without such knowledge of history, the piratical intentions of 'planetfall and plunder' are clear. And the colloquial formulaic expression, 'a piece of the action', is worthy of modern-day pirates: speculators, hucksters, petty capitalists.[19]

With reference to the White Queen who screams before she is hurt, Coldsmith observes that 'this book is screaming now' (Coldsmith 1992: 128). The novel's 'warning' is not of course to beware of aliens. The alien-invasion story provides a framework for a dystopian vision of the near future, based very much on current trends:

> Screaming now is one of the more important functions that sf can per-
> form – but Jones recognizes the difference between screaming to alert
> someone and screaming because it's already hopeless. 'Fail again. Fail
> better,' Braemar advises. Jones gives us a depressing vision of the future
> but there's no sign of what has been called the 'anticipatory shell shock'
> of post-modernism.

> (ibid.)

White Queen does not provide satisfying fictional resolutions to the global problems represented in it. What it does is point out the regressiveness of some fictional solutions, offered for mass consumption, that science fiction has provided for them: the fantasy of benign, godlike beings bailing us out at the last moment, like patient and selfless parents. Given the belief in divine intervention this entails, perhaps the Aleutians' perception of Earth people as religious fanatics is not so far off the mark after all.

As I said earlier, *White Queen* is a complex novel. In it, Jones is also examining sexuality and patterns of gender relations, and speculating about alternatives. This most recent of her novels was co-winner of the James Tiptree Junior Memorial Award in 1992 for its detailed attention to gender. (James Tiptree Junior was the pseudonym of Alice Sheldon, a writer of science fiction whose contribution to the realm of gender/sexual relations in the genre was enormous.) In inventing her 'Aleutians', Jones is examining human beings. She presents the Aleutians as 'looking glass' versions of human beings (the intertextual connection is made explicit). Sexual partnerships are cross-generational. Their loving relationships and romantic ideals are tied up with their belief in reincarnation: 'It's their big romantic quest, to find another edition of your self: your "true" parent or your "true" child' (Jones 1991: 201). One only has to consider common English terms of endearment to see the similarity with human love ties. Jones points to another kind of similarity. Towards the end of the novel, Johnny, who has been pining for the company of his young daughter, recollects dancing with her:

> He looked down at the two-year-old face, so lost in bliss. You won't remember a moment of these years, he thought. . . . But one day you will be dancing in someone's arms: and you won't know it but this is what you'll be looking for. It takes love to make love, sweet baby. He decided there was not much to choose between the Aleutian and earthly view, after all.
>
> (ibid.: 299)

The aliens are androgynous, but they do have a distinction between psychological types on a continuum they identify as similar to the human 'masculine' and 'feminine', although they think the 'local obsession' with it is 'a huge joke' (ibid.: 117). It seems to be a distinction of little real importance to them, about on a par with astrological birth-signs. When the narrative is focalized through one of them, all the active participating characters are referred to as *he*, including Braemar and other human females. Gender reference shifts according to focalizing character, with a curious destabilizing effect. Clavel, a 'feminine' Aleutian character, is referred to by the humans as *she* throughout, but by his/her fellow Aleutians as *he*. (On the subject of pronominal reference and gender, in a brief passage focalized through a transsexual, Jones uses Timothy Leary's genderless generic inventions: *SHe, hir*, ibid.: 222–3.)

More literal embracing of otherness can be found in another recent examination of contact between human and alien: Octavia Butler's *Xenogenesis* trilogy (1988). In Tanith Lee's *The silver metal lover* (1981) the alien 'other' is of another kind: the robot. The link between men and machines, so common in twentieth-century science fiction, has been broken in this novel (and in Trina Robbins' reworking of it in the comic book medium, 1985). The monster-robot character type is also subverted, in the name of romance: the eponymous robot is a beautiful male, and a perfect love machine!

CONCLUSION

The universe is made of stories,
not of atoms.

(Muriel Rukeyser 1968 [20])

Or at least, not just of atoms. Our world comes to us as stories; through them we understand the world around us. I have suggested that reading and watching fiction may 'solve' problems for us that we feel powerless to address in the real political-economic world. These fictional resolutions may develop into narrative formulae, repetitions of which provide a satisfying (and indeed necessary) 'escape'. We saw an early example of this in Chapter 1. *Pamela* provided its contemporary readers with the fantasy 'solution' of upward mobility through marriage for real, unresolvable social problems of the time. Modern romantic fictions seem to offer readers temporary substitutes for real nurturant relationships. Modern horror is another enormously popular genre. It addresses not desires but fears, and provides some kind of 'solution' for those fears by confronting and overcoming them. In some horror fiction, as we saw in Chapter 5, this is a matter of calling in the army to sort things out.

But, of course, fiction writing can do no more than offer fictional solutions for real-world problems and sometimes, I have argued, they can serve to perpetuate deeply conservative ideas and values. Nuptial solutions are not always appropriate, either in fiction or in life; nor indeed are military ones. In Chapter 6, I looked at a novel which drew attention to the narrative expectations of the romance genre in order to contest the 'nuptial solution'. I also presented a horror story playing with the generic practice of 'going too far', in which a former victim turns aggressor, with a vengeance.

Science fiction is a genre rich in possibilities for engagement in social criticism and a common element of a lot of feminist work in the genre is awareness of fictions at work. Science fiction provides a framework for explorations of fictional genres and the false solutions they offer for real-world problems, whether these problems are on the scale of impending global catastrophe or of individuals' needs for love and companionship. It also provides an ideal framework for the denaturalization of contemporary social identities and relationships, and for imagining alternatives.

TAKING IT FURTHER

A theme in feminist science fiction which I have not had space to examine is the presentation of men as the alien other. An outstanding example is James Tiptree Jr's 'The women men don't see' (1975); there is an excellent analysis of this story in Cranny-Francis (1990). For details on the pseudonymous James Tiptree Jr, see the chapter devoted to her in LeFanu (1988) (LeFanu's book title, *The chinks in the world machine*, is taken from Tiptree's story mentioned above). Annette Kuhn ed. (1990) is an interesting collection of essays on science fiction films, including a study of messianic aliens by Hugh Ruppersberg, an exploration of feminist elements in the film *Alien* by James Kavanagh and a speculative essay by Cranny-Francis on a non-existent sub-genre: the feminist science fiction film.

Notes

1. This kind of 'reminder' to the reader through altered spelling is sometimes known as *eye-dialect* (Traugott & Pratt 1980: 339)
2. An exception is the almost unreadable *eye-dialect* of Charles Dickens' character, Sleary, in *Hard Times*. In the represented speech of this lisping, permanently half-drunk circus-owner, every *s* is replaced by *th*. This *eye-dialect* seems to be functioning in exactly the same way as authentic dialect representation; that is, to mark off an exotic, marginal character from the 'normal' language community of standard users.
3. The functional grammar notion of projection structure introduces a dialogic element into grammatical description. It is useful in pinpointing voices which might otherwise escape notice, bringing together quotation ('direct speech'), reportage ('indirect speech') and more syntactically embedded presentations of people's words and ideas, such as *it was too late* in 'his reminder that it was too late was completely ignored'. (For details, see Halliday 1985: 227–51.)
4. In fact I have done elsewhere. A fuller treatment, in 'lay' language, of the two-page article of which this extract was a part is in Talbot (1992). I subject it to exhaustive analysis in Talbot (1990).
5. This is not some witty and disparaging feminist reference to Darwin's proposed link between us and our simian relatives, but use of a very prosaic term from discourse analysis to account for a particular type of background information needed for coherent interpretation. In order to combine these two sentences:

   She has bought a bicycle.
   The frame is too large.

   we need to bring in a third, namely

   The bicycle has a frame.

6. For example

   A man's mind – what there is of it – has always the advantage of being masculine – as the smallest birch-tree is of a higher kind than

the most soaring palm – and even his ignorance is of a sounder quality. Sir James might not have originated this estimate; but a kind
Providence furnishes the limpest personality with a little gum or
starch in the form of tradition (1979: 44).

7. 'Eliot herself'? 'George Eliot' was Mary Ann Evans, a woman whose
writing has always been and still is caught up in patriarchal social
practices. Her subject positions as woman and author contradict one
another. Her entries in older reference books provide illuminating
examples of the tenuousness of a woman's relation to her name. For
example, *The Oxford Companion to English Literature* (1934) begins with
the heading: ELIOT, GEORGE (MARY ANN CROSS, born EVANS). I
was rather surprised at this entry, never having heard of her as Mary
Ann Cross. She was legally Cross for the last six or seven months of
her life, which is apparently enough for us to bear it for her lifetime (no
apologies for the pun.)
   Incidentally, while on the topic of naming practices appearing in
commentaries: Fowler, presumably unconsciously, reproduces patriarchal naming conventions (referring to the characters differently:
Dorothea gets her first name; Will gets his surname, Ladislaw, which
does not appear in the extract).

8. 'Head cant' is one of the postures signalling subordinate status named
by Erving Goffman in *Gender advertisements* (1976). Others that he notes
are commonly seen performed by women in advertising are the 'bash-
ful knee bend' and nuzzling inanimate objects!

9. In fact, Collins, a Brit living in Los Angeles, uses the term 'dragon lady'
inappropriately. The original dragon lady was not a *battleaxe* (which is
the stereotype we have to supply to understand the exchange in the
extract) but a *femme fatale*, a dangerous woman who is both powerful
and glamorous. She was a force to be reckoned with in Milton Caniff's
Terry and the pirates, a long-running American newspaper comic strip
which started in the early 1930s.

10. Some of the fiction I refer to here came out as a novel before it was
reworked, and given a wider audience, as a film. In such cases, I pro-
vide the details here, for interest's sake and to avoid the distracting
piling up of references (I do not include novelizations of films):
   Harris T 1989 Silence of the lambs. Heinemann
   Silence of the lambs 1991 (Director: J Demme)
   King S 1987 Misery. Hodder
   Misery 1990 (Director: R Reiner)
   Blatty W P 1971 The exorcist. Blond & Briggs
   The exorcist 1973 (Director: W Friedkin)
   Levin I 1967 Rosemary's baby. Joseph
   Rosemary's baby 1968 (Director: R Polanski)

11. The reference is to *Beyond freedom and dignity*, written by the behaviourist B F Skinner.

12. There is one idiomatic expression I have excluded altogether because it is problematic in terms of both transitivity and process-type; namely, 'to take his eyes off the broken pane' in (14). It is probably best seen as containing a phrasal verb (hence transitive) that is being used in a grammatical metaphor for a mental/behavioural process. If included in Table. 5.1, it brings Luke's quota of transitive verbs up to fifteen.

13. There is a wonderful irony in this, since Burgess's novel on which the film was closely based was conservative in intent. It was written as a critique of behaviourist psychology from a Catholic perspective and presents the grim possibilities of a socialist future.

14. Coherence construction and the constitution of subjectivity is examined in Gough and Talbot (1993). The text sample in the article is a problem page letter and its reply.

15. This passage, and indeed the novel as a whole, recalls for me the wisdom of the following judgement: 'the Cavaliers (Wrong but Wromantic) and the Roundheads (Right but Repulsive)' (from Sellar and Yeatman's *1066 and all that*: a post-First World War 'history' book parodying the history taught in British schools).

16. Interestingly, the romance text we examined in Chapter 4 disrupted this convention of class interaction. The heroine initially *thinks* she wants to marry 'above her', but eventually marries one of her own kind – suitably bourgeoisified, of course. We can perhaps interpret this as a response to contemporary 'democratizing' tendencies in Britain.

17. The 'interrossiter' is a time travel machine, donated by suspiciously generous scientists from the future, in the film, *This island earth*. 'Dialithium crystals' fuel the interstellar craft of *Star trek*. Ftl (faster-than-light) travel is common currency in the SF genre. The society in which all education is egalitarian 'learnsharing', with no hierarchical teacher–pupil relationships is on Shora, the utopian ocean world in *A door into Ocean*.

18. In Piercy's recent science fiction novel, *Body of glass* (1992), she demonstrates that even in a world like that, people resist, fight against the apparently inevitable.

19. Another work of feminist science fiction, *The Judas rose* (Elgin's sequel to *Native tongue*), presents the devastating consequences of bungling alien interference in 'Terran' affairs, even with the most benign concern on the part of the superior beings.

20. cited in Rosinsky 1982: 105.

Bibliography

FICTION

A clockwork orange 1971 (Director: S Kubrick)
Achebe C 1958 *Things fall apart* Heinemann
Achebe C 1960 *No longer at ease* Heinemann
Achebe C 1964 *Arrow of God* Heinemann
Achebe C 1988 *The African trilogy* Picador
Alien 1979 (Director: R Scott)
Alien nation 1988 (Director: G Baker)
Amis K 1978 *The alteration* Triad
Atwood M 1987 *The handmaid's tale* Virago
Austen J [1818] 1894 *Pride and prejudice* George Allen

Banks I 1984 *The wasp factory* Futura
Banks I 1992 *The crow road* Scribners
Blatty W P 1971 *The exorcist* Blond & Briggs
Brontë E [1847] 1963 *Wuthering Heights* Heinemann
Brookner A 1985 *Hotel du lac* Triad Grafton
Burgess A [1961] 1970 *A clockwork orange* Heinemann
Butler O 1988 *Dawn. Xenogenesis: 1* Gollancz
Butler O 1989 *Adulthood Rites. Xenogenesis: 2* Gollancz
Butler O 1990 *Imago. Xenogenesis: 3* Gollancz

Campbell R 1988 *The influence* Century Hutchinson
Campbell R 1989 *Ancient images* Century Hutchinson
Campbell R 1991 *Midnight sun* Tor Books, New York
Charnas S McKee 1989 *Motherlines* The Women's Press
Charnas S McKee 1990 Boobs. In Tuttle L (ed.) *Skin of the soul* The
    Women's Press pp. 18–38
Close encounters of the third kind 1977 (Director: S Spielberg)
Collins J 1990 *Lady boss* Heinemann
Conrad J [1902] 1989 *Heart of darkness* Penguin

Day-Lewis C [1935] 1954 Two songs. In *Collected poems 1929–1936* Jonathan Cape pp. 139–40
Defoe D [1722] 1989 *Moll Flanders* Penguin
Dodderidge E [1979] 1988 *The new Gulliver or the adventures of Lemuel Gulliver Jr in Capovolta* The Women's Press
Donne J [1633] 1993 The bait. In *The Norton anthology of English literature* 6th edn. vol 1 New York p1092
Du Maurier G 1894 *Trilby* Osgood McIlvaine

E.T. 1982 (Director: S Spielberg)
Eliot G [1871–2] 1979 *Middlemarch* Penguin
Eliot G [1876] 1986 *Daniel Deronda* Penguin
Elgin S H 1985 *Native tongue* The Women's Press

Frankenstein 1931 (Director: J Whale)
Frenzy 1972 (Director: A Hitchcock)

Gallagher S 1989 *Down river* New English Library
Gallagher S 1991 *The boat house* New English Library
Gearhart S [1979] 1985 *The wanderground* The Women's Press
Gilman C Perkins [1915] 1992 *Herland* The Women's Press
Go S 1985 *Requiem* The Women's Press
Grayson E 1974 *Macabre Manor* Manor Books, New York
Green J, LeFanu S (eds.) 1985 *Despatches from the frontiers of the female mind* The Women's Press
Greene G [1938] 1970 *Brighton rock* Heinemann
Greenwood W [1933] 1970 *Love on the dole* Jonathan Cape
Guillén N 1972 *La rueda dentada* UNEAC, Havana

Halloween 1978 (Director: J Carpenter)
Harris T 1989 *Silence of the lambs* Heinemann
Herbert J 1974 *The rats* New English Library
Herbert J 1975 *The fog* New English Library
Herbert J 1976 *The survivor* New English Library
Herbert J 1979 *Lair* New English Library
Herbert J 1980 *The dark* New English Library
Herbert J 1981 *The Jonah* NewEnglish Library
Herbert J 1985 *Moon* New English Library
Hoban R 1980 *Riddley Walker* Picador
Holden F 1983 *Keep your hair on* Gatehouse
Huxley A 1932 *Brave new world* Chatto & Windus

I married a monster from outer space 1958 (Director: G Fowler)
Invasion of the body snatchers 1956 (Director: D Siegel)

James H [1886] 1986 *The Bostonians* Penguin
Jones G 1985 *Divine Endurance* Unwin
Jones G 1991 *White Queen* Gollancz
Joyce J [1916] 1968 *A portrait of the artist as a young man* Viking, New York

King S 1987 *Misery* Hodder
Kumalo A N C 1972 Red our colour. In Feinberg B (ed.) *Poets to the people: South African freedom poems* Allen & Unwin pp. 41–42

Lawnmower Man 1992 (Director: B Leonard)
Le Guin U [1969] 1981 *The left hand of darkness* Macdonald Futura
Lee T 1985 Love alters. In Green J, LeFanu S (eds.) pp. 60–73
Lee T 1982 *The silver metal lover* Daw, New York
Lessing D 1981 *The marriages between Zones Three, Four and Five* Granada
Levin I 1967 *Rosemary's baby* Joseph

Marlowe C [1599] 1993 The passionate shepherd to his love. In *The Norton anthology of English literature* 6th edn. vol 1 New York p. 767
Misery 1990 (Director: R Reiner)
Morrison T [1970] 1990 *The bluest eye* Picador
Morrison T 1993 *Jazz* Picador

Nightmare on Elm Street 1985 (Director: W Craven)

Orwell G 1949 *Nineteen eighty-four* Gollancz

Palmer J 1985 *The planet dweller* The Women's Press
Palmer J 1990 *Moving Moosevan* The Women's Press
Piercy M [1976] 1979 *Woman on the edge of time* The Women's Press
Piercy M 1992 *Body of glass* Penguin
Plath S 1963 *The bell jar* Faber
Psycho 1960 (Director: A Hitchcock)

Rabelais [1534] 1934 *Gargantua* (trans. W F Smith) Cambridge University Press
Ralegh W [c. 1600] 1993 The nymph's reply to the shepherd. In *The Norton anthology of English literature* 6th edn. vol 1 New York p. 1022
Richardson S [1740] 1985 *Pamela* Penguin
Robbins, T 1985 *The silver metal lover* Harmony, New York
Rosemary's baby 1968 (Director: R Polanski)
Russ J [1975] 1985 *The female man* The Women's Press
Russ J 1985 Clichés from outer space. In Green J, LeFanu S (eds.) pp. 27–34
Russ J 1987 *We who are about to. . .* The Women's Press

Seltzer D 1976 *The omen* Futura
Shelley M 1818 *Frankenstein*
Silence of the lambs 1991 (Director: J Demme)
Slonczewski J 1987 *A door into Ocean* The Women's Press
Storey D 1984 *Saville* Penguin

The day the earth stood still 1951 (Director: R Wise)
The exorcist 1973 (Director: W Friedkin)
The godfather 1971 (Director: F F Coppola)
The omen 1976 (Director: R Donner)
The thing 1982 (Director: J Carpenter)
The war game 1967 (Director: P Watkins)
This island earth 1955 (Director: J Newman)
Thomas A 1981 *Two in the bush and other stories* McClelland & Stewart, Toronto
Threads 1984 (Director: M Jackson)
Tiptree Jr J 1975 The women men don't see. In *Warm worlds and otherwise* Ballantine, New York pp. 131–64
Truss L 1992 'Possunt quia posse videntur' They can because they seem to be able to. In Smith J (ed.) *Femmes de siècle* Chatto & Windus pp. 45–56
Tuttle L 1987 The family monkey. In *A spaceship built of stone* The Women's Press pp. 35–75
Tuttle L 1987 The other kind. In *A spaceship built of stone* The Women's Press pp. 165–82
Tuttle L (ed.) 1990 *Skin of the soul* The Women's Press
2001: a space odyssey 1968 (Director: S Kubrick)
2010 1984 (Director: P Hyams)

Van Herk A 1981 *The tent peg* Virago

Walker K 1992 *No gentleman* Mills & Boon
West N 1981 *Lucifer's brand* Mills & Boon
Willard 1971 (Director: D Mann)
Woolf V [1929] 1977 *A room of one's own* Granada
Wyatt J 1976 *The shining levels* Penguin

Zahavi H 1991 *Dirty weekend* Flamingo
Zoline P [1967] 1988 The heat death of the universe. In *Busy about the tree of life* The Women's Press pp. 50–65

SECONDARY SOURCES

Atherton J S 1960 *The books at the wake. A study of literary allusions in James Joyce's Finnegans Wake.* Viking, New York

Bakhtin M M [1927] 1984 *Problems in Dostoevsky's Poetics.* (trans. C Emerson) Manchester University Press
Barker M 1984 *A haunt of fears. The strange history of the British horror comics campaign* Pluto
Barker M 1989 *Comics: ideology, power and the critics.* Manchester University Press
Barthes R 1970 *S/Z* Seuil, Paris
Barthes R (1972) Textual analysis of Poe's 'Valdemar'. In Young R 1981 *Untying the text.* Routledge & Kegan Paul pp. 133–61
Barton D, Ivanic R (eds) 1991 *Writing in the community.* Sage
Beard H, Cerf C 1992 *The official politically correct dictionary and handbook.* Grafton
de Beaugrande R, Dressler W 1980 *Introduction to text linguistics.*Longman
Belsey C 1980 *Critical practice.* Methuen
Bertram V 1993 From nubile naivety to necrophiliac nymph: breaking the rules of romance. Paper presented at the Romance Revisited conference, Lancaster University
Birch D, O'Toole M (eds) 1988 *Functions of style.* Pinter
Blaubergs M 1980 An analysis of classic arguments against changing sexist language. In *Women's studies quarterly* **3:** 135–47
Bourdieu P 1984 *Distinction: a social critique of the judgement of taste* (trans. R Nice). Routledge & Kegan Paul
Brown G, Yule G 1983 *Discourse analysis.* Cambridge University Press

Campbell R 1988 Foreword. In Newman K, Jones S (eds) *Horror: 100 best books.* Xanadu
Carr H (ed) 1989 *From my guy to sci-fi: genre and women's writing in the post-modern world.* Pandora
Clark R, Fairclough N L, Ivanic R, Martin-Jones M 1987 *Critical language awareness.* CLSL Working Paper Series 1, Lancaster University
Clover C 1992 *Women, men and chainsaws.* British Film Institute
Coldsmith S 1992 Review of Jones' *White Queen.* In *Foundation.* **55:** 124–8
Cook J 1988 Fictional fathers. In Radstone S (ed.) pp. 141–74
Cranny-Francis A 1988 Sexual politics and political repression in Bram Stoker's *Dracula.* In Bloom C, Docherty B, Gibb J, Shand K (eds) *Nineteenth-century suspense: from Poe to Conan Doyle.* Macmillan, pp. 64–79
Cranny-Francis A 1990 *Feminist fiction. Feminist uses of generic fiction.* Blackwell

Cranny-Francis A 1990 De-fanging the vampire: S M Charnas's *The vampire tapestry* as subversive horror fiction. In Docherty B (ed.) *American horror fiction: from Brockden Brown to Stephen King*. Macmillan, pp. 155–75

Culler J 1981 *The pursuit of signs: semiotics, literature, deconstruction* Routledge & Kegan Paul

Dalby R 1990 Introduction. In Dalby R (ed.) *The Virago book of ghost stories* Virago pp. ix–xvi

Davis L 1987 *Resisting novels: ideology and fiction* Methuen

Department of Education and Science (DES) 1988 *Report of the committee of inquiry into the teaching of English language (Kingman Report)*. HMSO

Dyer R 1988 Children of the night: vampirism as homosexuality, homosexuality as vampirism. In Radstone S (ed), pp. 47–72

Eagleton M (ed.) 1986 *Feminist literary theory: a reader*. Blackwell

Ellis K 1983 *Cuba's Nicolas Guillén: poetry and ideology*. University of Toronto Press, Toronto

Ellman M 1979 *Thinking about women*. Virago

Fairclough N L 1988 Michel Foucault and the analysis of discourse. CLSL Research Papers 10, Lancaster University

Fairclough N L 1989 *Language and power*. Longman

Fairclough N L 1992 *Discourse and social change*. Polity

Fairclough N L(ed.) 1992 *Critical language awareness*. Longman

Fairclough N L (forthcoming) *Media and language*. Arnold

Firestone S (1970) 1979 *The dialectic of sex: the case for feminist revolution*. The Women's Press

Foucault M 1974 *The archaeology of knowledge* (trans. A Sheridan). Tavistock

Fowler R 1981 *Literature as social discourse: the practice of linguistic criticism*. Batsford

Fowler R 1991 *Language in the news. Discourse and ideology in the press*. Routledge

Gamman L, Marshment M (eds) 1988 *The female gaze: women as viewers of popular culture*. The Women's Press

Gatehouse Basic Education Publishers' Annual Report 1991/1992

Goffman E 1976 *Gender advertisements*. Macmillan

Gough V, Talbot MM 1993 'Guilt over games boys play': coherence as a focus for examining the constitution of heterosexual subjectivity on a problem page. In *Liverpool studies in language and discourse* 1: 3–20

Graver S 1984 *George Eliot and community: a study in social theory and fictional form*. University of California Press, Berkeley

Greenland C 1992 *Michael Moorcock: death is no obstacle*. Savoy

Grixti J 1989 *Terrors of uncertainty. The cultural contexts of horror fiction*. Routledge

Hall S 1980 Encoding/decoding. In Hall S et al. (eds) *Culture, media, language*. Hutchinson pp. 128–38

Halliday M A K 1985 *An introduction to functional grammar*. Arnold

Halliday M A K, Hasan R 1985 *Language, context, and text*. Deakin University Press, Victoria

Harlow B 1987 *Resistance literature*. Methuen

Hawkins H 1990 *Classics and trash. Traditions and taboos in high literature and popular modern genres*. Harvester

Hodge R 1990 *Literature as discourse. Textual strategies in English and history*. Polity

Hodge R, Kress G 1988 *Social semiotics*. Polity

Hogan D 1986 *Dark romance: sex and death in the horror film*. Equation

Hollings J 1985 The portrayal of women in romance comic strips 1964–84. Unpublished BA dissertation: University of Reading

Ivanic R 1988 Critical language awareness in action. In *Language issues* **2**(2): 2–7

Jameson F 1981 *The political unconscious. Narrative as a socially symbolic act*. Methuen

Jordin M 1987 Science fiction, genre and a new battle of the books. In Cashdan A, Jordin M (eds) *Studies in communication*. Blackwell pp. 151–65

Kaveney R 1989 The science fictiveness of women's science fiction. In Carr H (ed.), pp. 78–97

King S 1982 *Danse macabre*. Futura

Kramarae C, Treichler P 1985 *A feminist dictionary*. Pandora

Kress G 1985 *Linguistic processes in sociocultural practice*. Deakin University Press, Victoria

Kress G 1988 Textual matters: the social effectiveness of style. In Birch D, O'Toole M (eds) pp. 126–41

Kress G, Threadgold T 1988 Towards a social theory of genre. In *Southern review* **21**: 216–43

Kristeva J 1980 *Desire in language*. Blackwell

Kristeva J 1982 *Powers of horror. An essay on abjection* (trans. L S Roudiez). Columbia University Press

Kuhn A (ed.) 1990 *Alien zone. Cultural theory and contemporary science fiction cinema*. Verso

LeFanu S 1988 *In the chinks of the world machine; feminism and science fiction*. The Women's Press

LeFanu S 1989 Popular writing and feminist intervention in science fiction. In Longhurst D (ed.) *Gender, genre and narrative pleasure*. Unwin Hyman, pp. 177–91

Leitch V B 1983 *Deconstructive criticism. An advanced introduction.* Hutchinson

Lovecraft H P 1969 Supernatural Horror in Literature. In *Dagon and other macabre tales.* Panther, pp. 141–70

Mace R 1987 Dialekt, Dialektsprecher und Dialektgemeinschaft in David Storeys *Saville.* In **Goetsch P, Raible W, Roemer H** (eds) *Dialekte und Fremdsprachen in der Literatur.* (ScriptOralia 2) Gunter Narr Verlag, Tubingen pp. 27–42

McCloud S 1993 *Understanding comics.* Kitchen Sink Press, Northampton, Mass.

McRobbie A 1978 *Jackie: an ideology of adolescent femininity.* CCCS Occasional paper, University of Birmingham

McRobbie A 1991 *Feminism and youth culture: from Jackie to Just Seventeen.* Macmillan

Mann P 1969 *The romantic novel: a survey of reading habits.* Mills & Boon

Mann P 1974 *A new survey: the facts about romantic fiction.* Mills & Boon

Martin J 1989 *Factual writing: exploring and challenging social reality.* Oxford University Press

Martyna W 1983 Beyond the he/man approach: the case for nonsexist language. In Thorne B, Kramarae C, Henley N (eds) *Language, gender and society* Newbury House, Rowley, Mass., pp. 25–37

Medvedev P N, Bakhtin M M [1928] 1978 *The formal method in literary scholarship: a critical introduction to sociological poetics* (trans. A J Wehrle) Johns Hopkins University Press

Mey J L 1985 *Whose language? A study in linguistic pragmatics.* Benjamins, Amsterdam

Mey J L 1989 Not by the word only. Review of Elgin's *Native tongue.* In *Journal of pragmatics* **13**: 1035–45

Mills & Boon (cassette) 1986 *And then he kissed her . . . a Mills & Boon guide to writing romantic fiction.* Mills & Boon

Modleski T 1982 *Loving with a vengeance.* Methuen

Moi T 1982 Feminist literary criticism. In Jefferson A, Robey D (eds) *Modern literary theory.* Batsford, pp. 204–21

Moi T 1988 *Sexual/textual politics. Feminist literary theory.* Routledge

Montgomery M 1988 D-J talk. In Coupland, N *Styles of discourse.* Croom Helm pp. 85–104

Moylan T 1986 *Demand the impossible. Science fiction and the utopian imagination.* Methuen

Murray D 1987 Dialogics. In Tallack D *Literary theory at work: three texts.* Batsford, pp. 115–34

Nash W 1990 *Language in popular fiction.* Routledge

Ngugi wa Thiong'o 1981 *Writers in politics.* Heinemann

Owen M 1990 Women's reading of popular romantic fiction: a case study in the mass media. A key to the ideology of women. Unpublished PhD thesis, University of Liverpool

Palmer 1991 *Potboilers*. Routledge
Parrinder P 1980 *Science fiction: its criticism and teaching*. Methuen
Pearson G 1984 Falling standards: a short, sharp history of moral decline. In Barker M (ed.) *The video nasties*. Pluto, pp. 88–103
Pêcheux M 1982 *Language, semantics and ideology: stating the obvious* (trans. H Nagpal). Macmillan

Radstone S (ed.) 1988 *Sweet dreams: sexuality, gender and popular fiction* Lawrence & Wishart Radway J 1987 *Reading the romance: women, patriarchy and popular literature* Verso
Richards I A 1924 *Principles of literary criticism*. Kegan Paul
Rosinsky N 1982 *Feminist futures: contemporary women's speculative fiction*. UMI Research Press, Ann Arbor, Michigan
Russ J 1984 *How to suppress women's writing*. The Women's Press

Sabin R 1993 *Adult comics: an introduction*. Routledge
Said E 1985 Orientalism reconsidered. *Cultural critique* 1: 89–107
Saussure F de 1916 *Cours de linguistique générale*. Payot, Paris
Schmied J 1991 *English in Africa*. Longman
Sellar W C, Yeatman R [1930] 1991 *1066 and all that*. Mandarin
Showalter E 1977 *A literature of their own. British women novelists from Bronte to Lessing*. Princeton University Press
Showalter E 1979 Towards a feminist poetics. In Jacobus M (ed.) *Women writing and writing about women*. Croom Helm, pp. 22–41
Spencer J 1986 *The rise of the woman novelist. From Aphra Behn to Jane Austen*. Blackwell
Spender D 1986 *Mothers of the novel. 100 good women writers before Jane Austen*. Pandora
Steedman C 1986 *Landscape for a good woman: a story of two lives*. Virago
Stephens J 1992 *Language and ideology in children's fiction*. Longman
Stubbs M 1983 *Discourse analysis: the sociolinguistic analysis of natural language*. Blackwell
Suvin D 1979 *Metamorphoses in science fiction*. Yale University Press, New Haven

Talbot M M 1990 Language, intertextuality and subjectivity: voices in the construction of consumer femininity. Unpublished PhD thesis, Lancaster University
Talbot M M 1992 The construction of gender in a teenage magazine. In Fairclough N L (ed.) pp. 174–99

Taylor H 1989 Romantic readers. In Carr H (ed.), pp. 58–77
Threadgold T 1988 Stories of race and gender: an unbounded discourse.
In Birch D, O'Toole M (eds) pp. 169–204
Traugott L, Pratt M 1980 *Linguistics for students of literature* . Harcourt Brace
Jovanovich
Treacher A 1988 What is life without my love?: desire and romantic fiction.
In Radstone S (ed.), pp. 73–94
Twitchell J 1985 *Dreadful pleasures. An anatomy of modern horror.* Oxford
University Press

Van den Bergh N 1987 Renaming: vehicle for empowerment. In Penfield J
(ed.) *Women and language in transition.* State University of New York,
pp. 130–6
Vestergaard T, Schrøder K 1985 *The language of advertising.* Blackwell

Watt I 1972 *The rise of the novel.* Pelican
Widdowson H 1979 *Explorations in applied linguistics.* Open University
Press
Woods S 1980 Women and science fiction. In Williamson J (ed.) *Teaching
science fiction: education for tomorrow.* Owlswick, Philadelphia pp. 65–72

Index